ICSA Study Text

Diploma in Offshore Finance and
Administration
Financial Reporting and Governance

ICSA Study Text

Diploma in Offshore Finance
and Administration

Financial Reporting and Governance

Bruce Horwood

icsa.
Publishing

First published 2012
Published by ICSA Information & Training Ltd
16 Park Crescent
London W1B 1AH
©ICSA Information & Training Ltd, 2012

Typeset by Paul Barrett Book Production, Cambridge
Printed by Hobbs the Printers Ltd, Totton, Hampshire

British Cataloguing in Publication Data
A catalogue record for this book is available from the British Library

ISBN: 978 186072 535 7

Contents

How to use this study text

ICSA study texts developed to support ICSA's Certificate in Offshore Finance and Administration (COFA) follow a standard format and include a range of navigational, self-testing and illustrative features to help you get the most out of the support materials.

Each text is divided into three main sections:

- introductory material
- the text itself
- additional reference information

The sections below show you how to find your way around the text and make the most of its features.

Introductory material

The introductory section of each text includes a full contents list and the module syllabus which re-iterates the module aims, learning outcomes and syllabus content for the module in question. Where relevant, the introductory section will also include a list of acronyms and abbreviations or a list of legal cases for reference.

The text itself

Each **part** opens with a list of the chapters to follow, an overview of what will be covered and learning outcomes for the part.

Every **chapter** opens with a list of the topics covered and an introduction specific to that chapter. Chapters are structured to allow students to break the content down into manageable sections for study. Each chapter ends with a summary of key content to reinforce understanding.

Features

The text is enhanced by a range of illustrative and self-testing features to assist understanding and to help you prepare for the examination. Each feature is presented in a standard format, so that you will become familiar with how to use them in your study.

These features are identified by a series of icons.

The texts also include tables, figures and other illustrations as relevant.

Reference material

The text ends with a range of additional guidance and reference material, including a glossary of key terms, a directory of web resources and a comprehensive index.

Stop and think

Test yourself

Worked examples

Making it work

Case law

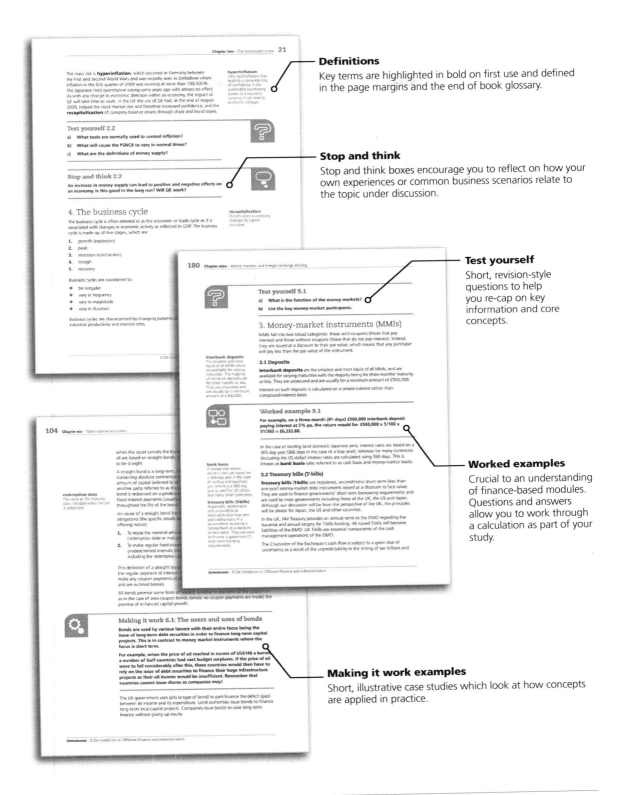

Definitions

Key terms are highlighted in bold on first use and defined in the page margins and the end of book glossary.

Stop and think

Stop and think boxes encourage you to reflect on how your own experiences or common business scenarios relate to the topic under discussion.

Test yourself

Short, revision-style questions to help you re-cap on key information and core concepts.

Worked examples

Crucial to an understanding of finance-based modules. Questions and answers allow you to work through a calculation as part of your study.

Making it work examples

Short, illustrative case studies which look at how concepts are applied in practice.

Financial Governance and Reporting syllabus

Aims

The module is aimed specifically for those employed as administrators in junior supervisory roles, whose present or future position requires a broad knowledge and understanding of the perspective of the industry, whilst demanding a high degree of operational knowledge covering legal, regulatory and financial frameworks.

The module aims to enable students to understand the importance of the two significant and highly relevant aspects of offshore finance, "financial reporting and interpretation" and "governance" and to develop knowledge, understanding and key skills within these legal, regulatory and financial frameworks.

Learning outcomes

On successful completion of this module candidates will be able to:

◆ Demonstrate a sound knowledge and understanding of corporations, their legal position and financing, returns to financial stakeholders and the importance of sound corporate governance and social responsibility.

◆ Justify and discuss the key components of a sound regulatory framework for financial accounting and reporting, including the relevance and implementation of Generally Accepted Accounting Practice (GAAP) including key International Financial Reporting Standards.

◆ Understand and interpret, with reference to GAAP, key aspects of financial sector regulation.

◆ Demonstrate comprehension of the corporate and private use and misuse of offshore vehicles.

◆ Explain the main principles underpinning the recognition of revenue, assets and liabilities, the impact on corporate reporting and demonstrate sound understanding of the importance of "substance over legal form" including references to 'fair value'.

◆ Select and apply appropriate tools and techniques to calculate and interpret measures of financial performance.

◆ Prepare and interpret cash flow statements.

◆ Prepare and interpret non-complex trust accounts.

Syllabus

1 The financial reporting environment
Generally Accepted Accounting Practice (GAAP)
International Financial Reporting Standards (IFRSs)
UK Companies Acts

2 Accounting concepts
Conceptual framework
Qualitative characteristics
Revenue recognition and measurement

3 Reporting financial performance
Accounting policies
Presentation of financial statements
Reporting the substance of transactions
Financial instruments
The impact of foreign currency exchange rate changes

4 Events after the reporting period
Events after the reporting date: Terminology and accounting treatment

5 Provisions, Contingent Liabilities and Contingent Assets
Provisions
Contingent liabilities
Contingent assets

6 Financial Ratio Analysis
Profitability ratios
Liquidity ratios
Efficiency ratios
Gearing ratios
Earnings per share and other key investor ratios

7 Cash flow statements
Preparation of cash flow statements
Interpretation of cash flow statements

8 Trust accounting
Trusts: Income and capital
Trusts: Preparation and interpretation non-complex financial statements

9 Reporting requirements of companies, trusts and other offshore vehicles
Public and private limited companies
Share and loan capital
Implications of gearing and taxation
Corporate and private offshore vehicles
Accounting methods
Legitimate uses, misuses and private uses of offshore jurisdiction
Tax jurisdictions
Partnerships

10   Financial sector regulation
Banking
Banking licenses
The role of central banks

11   Frameworks and governance
Agency theory
Corporate governance – codes and reports
Corporate social responsibility
The Walker Review
Basel II and III
Sarbanes–Oxley Act (2002)
Dodd–Frank Act

Acronyms and abbreviations

AFS	Available-for-sale financial assets
AIC	Association of Investment Companies
ASB	Accounting Standards Board
CDO	Collateralised debt obligations
CEO	Chief Executive Officer
CFO	Chief Financial Officer
CFPB	Consumer Financial Protection Bureau
CSR	Corporate social responsibility
DGS	Deposit guarantee schemes
EPS	Earnings per share
ESD	European Savings Directive
ESMA	European Securities and Markets Authority
FASB	Financial Accounting Standards Board
FRC	Financial Reporting Council
FRED	Financial Reporting Exposure Drafts
FRS	Financial Reporting Standards
FRSSE	Financial Reporting Standard for Smaller Entities
FSOC	Financial Stability Oversight Council
GAAP	Generally accepted accounting principles
GP	General partners
IAS	International Accounting Standards
IASB	International Accounting Standards Board
IASC	International Accounting Standards Committee
ICC	Incorporated cell companies
IFRS	International Financial Reporting Standards
ILP	Incorporated Limited Partnerships
IMF	International Monetary Fund
JIT	Just in time procurement
LDF	Liechtenstein Disclosure Facility
LLP	Limited liability partnerships
LP	Limited partnership
LPA	Limited partnership agreement
NED	Non-executive directors
OECD	Organisation for Economic Co-operation and Development
OFR	Office of Financial Research
PBIT	Profit before interest and taxation

PCAOB	Public Company Accounting Oversight Board
PCC	Protected cell companies
ROA	Return on assets
ROCE	Return on capital employed
ROE	Return on equity
ROI	Return on investment
SEC	Securities and Exchange Commission
SLP	Separate Limited Partnerships
SSAP	Statements of Standard Accounting Practice
STRGL	Statement of Total Recognised Gains and Losses
UITF	Urgent Issues Task Force

Acknowledgements

This study text was funded by the ICSA Education and Research Foundation.

Part One

In this part, students will learn about Generally Accepted Accounting Principles (GAAP), International Financial Reporting Standards (IFRS) and the UK Companies Act 2006, all of which set out requirements for a company's financial reporting.

Students will gain an insight into the reporting framework, the development of accounting standards, the benefit of accounting standards and the implementation of GAAP and IFRS in the UK and US. Students will also learn about the future of UK GAAP and the global convergence of GAAP with IFRS.

Part One of this study text also discusses some of the key requirements of the UK Companies Act 2006 and a number of landmark cases that highlight the duties of directors.

Learning outcomes

At the end of this part, students should be able to:

◆ explain what is meant by GAAP and IFRS;

◆ summarise the UK financial reporting framework and standard setting process;

◆ discuss some of the benefits of accounting standards;

- explain the proposals for the future of UK GAAP;
- understand what is meant by the term convergence in relation to global accounting standards;
- state a few of the benefits and drawbacks of IFRS;
- list the principal Acts of Parliament relating to companies in the UK;
- state some of the aims of the Companies Act 2006;
- discuss the key features of the Companies Act 2006;
- explain the duties of directors;
- discuss the common law case known as *Re City Equitable Fire Insurance Co* [1925];
- discuss the common law case *Re D'Jan of London Ltd* [1994];
- summarise the *Weavering* judgments of 2011 in the Cayman Islands and the 2012 in the UK;
- explain some of the differences between private and public companies in terms of statutory requirements; and
- discuss the changes introduced by the Companies Act 2006 in respect of a company's share capital and reserves.

Chapter one
The financial reporting environment

List of topics

1 GAAP
2 IFRSs
3 UK Companies Acts

Introduction

In this chapter, students will learn about Generally Accepted Accounting Principles (GAAP), and the Accounting Standards Board in the UK. Students will also have a brief introduction to types of accounting standards issued, the development of accounting standards and how pressing accounting issues are addressed by the Urgent Issues Task Force.

The chapter also discusses International Financial Reporting Standards (IFRS) and the convergence of US GAAP with IFRS as part of the move towards a single set of global accounting standards.

Finally, students will be introduced to some of the provisions of the UK Companies Act 2006 such as the statutory duties of directors, financial reporting requirements and some of the key features of the Companies Act in relation to share capital and reserves. Significant common law cases are discussed in relation to director duties and an outline is given of the recent *Weavering* case in Cayman and in the UK.

1. GAAP

GAAP (or Generally Accepted Accounting Principles/Practice) are a common set of principles-based accounting standards used for the preparation and presentation of an entity's financial statements. The standards are country specific and vary from one jurisdiction to another. Examples are US GAAP, which are the main accounting standards in the US, and UK GAAP which is adopted by many UK companies for financial reporting purposes. UK companies are, however, increasingly adopting IFRS. It is now a requirement for UK listed

GAAP (or Generally Accepted Accounting Principles/Practice) are a common set of principles-based accounting standards used for the preparation and presentation of an entity's financial statements.

companies to prepare their financial statements using international accounting standards and non-listed UK companies are being encouraged to move from UK GAAP to IFRS for Small and Medium-sized Entities.

GAAP covers the accounting treatment of the statement of financial position and profit and loss items such as revenue recognition, assets and liabilities. The application of GAAP should help to ensure that financial information is reported consistently and objectively to enable investors, analysts, regulators and other stakeholders to make decisions based on comparable and reliable information. US GAAP and UK GAAP are still commonly applied by offshore companies, although there is increasing use of IFRS.

The **Accounting Standards Board (ASB)**, which forms part of the **Financial Reporting Council (FRC)** is the standard-setting body in the UK responsible for issuing Financial Reporting Standards (FRS). UK GAAP also comprises Statements of Standard Accounting Practice (SSAPs), which are accounting standards, issued by the ASB's predecessor, the Accounting Standards Committee. Many SSAPs have been superseded by FRS but there are still a few SSAPs in force.

The UK GAAP standard setting process also includes Discussion Papers and Financial Reporting Exposure Drafts (FREDs) which are issued by the ASB as a form of consultation on newly proposed concepts and standards. Once the consultation period in respect of a FRED is over, the issues raised by respondents need to be resolved before the draft standard is finalised and issued as an FRS.

Accounting issues that need to be addressed as a matter of urgency are dealt with by the **Urgent Issues Task Force (UITF)**, a body made up of senior industry representatives and accountants. The UITF issues Abstracts which take immediate effect.

UK GAAP, like International Financial Reporting Standards, is a principles-based approach to financial reporting. In some countries, the standards are based very much on rules, although as countries are gradually working on convergence of accounting standards (towards a global set of accounting standards), the principles-based approach of IFRS is becoming more widely adopted.

In the US, it is the Financial Accounting Standards Board (FASB) that is the chief standard setter for US GAAP. Whilst US GAAP is gradually being converged with IFRS, the US, along with Japan and India, has still made no firm commitment regarding the adoption and implementation of IFRS.

The main benefits of accounting standards may be summarised as follows:

◆ reduced disparity and variations in accounting treatment from one reporting entity to another, and from one reporting period to another, enabling greater comparability;

◆ standardised approach;

◆ less scope for interpretations and subjectivity;

◆ less scope for disguising liabilities and holding them off the statement of financial position;

Accounting Standards Board (ASB)
forms part of the Financial Reporting Council (FRC) and is the standard-setting body in the UK responsible for issuing Financial Reporting Standards (FRS).

Financial Reporting Council (FRC)
is the UK's independent regulator responsible for promoting high quality corporate governance and reporting to foster investment.

Urgent Issues Task Force (UITF)
is a body made up of senior industry representatives and accountants which handles pressing accounting issues that require urgent attention. The UITF issues Abstracts to address such issues and these abstracts take immediate effect.

- ◆ less scope for manipulating asset valuations;
- ◆ provide the framework for financial statements to show a "true and fair" view (as required by the Companies Act 2006); and
- ◆ users of accounts, such as analysts, investors and regulators, can place greater reliance on the financial statements knowing that recognised accounting standards have been applied.

Company Secretaries should not consider GAAP in isolation. They should also ensure their companies adhere to relevant stock exchange listing requirements and any statutory requirements such as the UK Companies Act 2006.

1.1 The Future of UK GAAP

The ASB issued three new FREDs in January 2012 setting out revised proposals for the future of financial reporting in the UK and the Republic of Ireland. An overhaul of the current FRSs has been proposed to:

- ◆ provide greater cohesion and unifying principles and address the perceived mismatch of accounting standards (SSAPs, FRSs and IFRS-based standards issued as part of the convergence with international standards);
- ◆ address the reporting requirements for financial instruments to ensure certain transactions no longer go unrecognised if they are relevant to the assessment of the entity's financial position; and
- ◆ reduce costs of training accountants in two accounting frameworks, IFRS and UK GAAP.

The proposals are set out in the following FREDs:

- ◆ FRED 46 – Application of Financial Reporting Requirements (Draft FRS 100);
- ◆ FRED 47 – Reduced Disclosure Framework (Draft FRS 101); and
- ◆ FRED 48 – The Financial Reporting Standard applicable in the UK and Republic of Ireland (draft FRS 102).

The proposals include:

- ◆ replacing all existing FRSs, SSAPs and UITF Abstracts with a single FRS;
- ◆ introducing a reduced disclosure framework for the financial reporting of certain qualifying entities on the basis that the disclosure requirements under EU-adopted IFRS or equivalent give rise to reporting costs that may not be commensurate with the benefits to users of the accounts; and
- ◆ retaining the **FRSSE**

FRSSE
is the Financial Reporting Standard for Smaller Entities which enables smaller entities to apply accounting standards which have reduced reporting and disclosure requirements compared with UK GAAP. Where the FRSSE does not cover a particular issue, the entity can fall back on UK GAAP and apply the relevant principles to ensure appropriate accounting treatment.

In order to determine which entities should apply a reduced disclosure framework under FRED 47, the ASB says that the following principles should be applied:

- ◆ relevance (i.e. capable of making a difference to the decisions of users of financial statements);

◆ cost constraint on useful financial reporting (i.e. the costs to the reporting entity should not outweigh the benefits to the users of the financial statements); and

◆ avoidance of gold plating (i.e. no need to disclose if this overrides an existing statutory exemption).

The ASB's overall objective which it hopes to achieve from the proposals is:

"To enable users of accounts to receive high-quality, understandable financial reporting proportionate to the size and complexity of the entity and users' information needs."

Test yourself 1.1

List some of the merits of accounting standards.

Summarise the proposals set out in FREDs 46, 47 and 48?

2. IFRS

International Financial Reporting Standards (IFRS) are principles-based accounting standards and interpretations issued by the International Accounting Standards Board (IASB). The standards comprise:

◆ International Financial Reporting Standards;

◆ International Accounting Standards (IAS) issued by the IASB's predecessor, the International Accounting Standards Committee (IASC); and

◆ **Interpretations**.

interpretations are statements issued by standard setters (e.g. IASB) to clarify how standards should be applied. Interpretations are typically published to address issues arising that were not foreseen when the standards were first set.

The standards apply to all companies listed on an EU-regulated stock exchange and the UK's Alternative Investment Market. Whilst most companies that are not listed on a stock exchange or secondary market are still able to choose the accounting standards they apply, many offshore regulators will expect accounts to be prepared under UK GAAP, US GAAP or IFRS.

IFRS offers a single set of globally accepted accounting standards and has been adopted by the large majority of countries around the world, with the notable exception of the US, Japan and India. Until these important global economies adopt IFRS, there will be reporting variations and disparity arising between those entities reporting under IFRS and those reporting under their national GAAP.

2.1 The US and IFRS

The US is still to make any formal recommendations on the adoption of IFRS in place of US GAAP, despite the fact that the FASB in the US and the International Accounting Standards Board (IASB) have been working jointly towards the convergence of accounting standards since 2002 with the common goal of achieving a single set of high-quality global accounting standards. The US is considering a phased transition to IFRS through a gradual continuation of convergence measures and the US Securities and Exchange Commission (SEC) is expected to make a decision on the adoption of IFRS by the end of 2012.

The SEC staff work plan published in May 2011 on the implementation of IFRS into the US financial reporting system addresses six fundamental areas:

1 Sufficient development and application of IFRS for the US domestic reporting system.

2 The independence of standard setting for the benefit of investors.

3 Investor understanding and education regarding IFRS.

4 Examination of the US regulatory environment that would be affected by a change in accounting standards.

5 The impact on issuers, both large and small, including changes to accounting systems, changes to contractual arrangements, corporate governance considerations, and litigation contingencies.

6 Human capital readiness.

The IASB and the FASB have made good progress on convergence since they signed a Memorandum of Understanding in 2006. For example, in 2007 the SEC withdrew the requirement for non-US companies registered in the US, and reporting under IFRS, to reconcile their financial statements with US GAAP. The IASB and FASB still have differences of opinion on certain issues, such as with the financial instruments project; despite recent progress in this area, as reported by the IASB and FASB in April 2012, any disagreement could affect the US decision on whether to adopt IFRS.

2.2 The UK and IFRS

In the UK, companies which are not listed have the option to report either under IFRSs or under UK GAAP. UK GAAP is, however, becoming increasingly more aligned with IFRS and, to facilitate the international convergence of accounting standards, recently issued FRSs are, broadly speaking, in line with their corresponding IFRSs.

The main benefits of having one set of global financial reporting standards are summarised as follows:

◆ Improve the standard of financial reporting worldwide.

◆ Improve comparability of financial statements.

◆ Elimination of IFRS/GAAP reconciliations.

◆ Easier access to capital markets and enhanced globalisation of business and investment.

◆ Common global accounting framework.

◆ Flexible principles-based approach.

◆ Reduce costs for multinational companies as only one global reporting standard and staff will no longer need to learn the various requirements for reporting in multiple jurisdictions.

Arguments against convergence:

◆ One size does not fit all, leading to countries opting out if they disagree with a particular rule and resulting in varying levels of disclosure and application of the standards depending on a reporting entity's jurisdictional requirements.

◆ The cost of initial implementation can be high and the benefit is neither immediate nor easily measureable.

◆ Initial training requirement for accountants to understand the requirements and standards.

◆ There is still scope to deviate from IFRS but only where the financial statements would otherwise be misleading to users.

◆ Standards are more rigid in certain areas, for example with construction contracts, IFRS does not permit the completed contract method of accounting, which means revenues and expenses must be recognised in the period in which they are incurred and, consequently, tax liabilities cannot be deferred to future periods.

◆ The effects of convergence are not just accounting related, for example the SEC in the US is concerned that the adoption of IFRS will mean an overhaul of their current regulatory package.

Test yourself 1.2

What are the merits of having one set of global accounting standards?

3. UK Companies Acts

The principal Acts of Parliament relating to companies in the UK are:

◆ Companies Act 1985

◆ Companies Act 1989

◆ Companies (Audit, Investigations and Community Enterprise) Act 2004

◆ Companies Act 2006

3.1 The Companies Act 2006

secondary legislation is subordinate legislation which supplements primary law. It is enacted by a person or body, other than the legislature, who has been granted the relevant authority. This enables secondary legislation to be enacted in a more timely manner. For example, in Jersey, primary legislation must be put before the UK's Privy Council whilst secondary legislation, such as an Order, may be approved locally by the relevant Minister (e.g. The Minister for Economic Development for financial services secondary legislation).

The Companies Act 2006 received Royal Assent on 8 November 2006. It consolidates and supersedes many of the provisions of the Companies Acts of 1985 and 1989 and comprises some 1,300 sections supplemented by **secondary legislation**.

As the 1985 and 1989 Acts are no longer relevant, the focus of this chapter is on the 2006 Act which was introduced with the aim of reforming company law and:

◆ improving shareholder communication and engagement;

◆ enhancing a long term investment culture;

◆ strengthening regulation;

◆ protecting the interests of consumers by increasing a company's disclosure requirements;

- making it simpler to incorporate and run a company; and
- affording flexibility for the future.

The Act was implemented over a two-year period, commencing October 2007, to enable companies to have sufficient time to adapt to the changes introduced to the 1985 Act and it sets out the statutory requirements of UK companies. As well as replacing the Companies Acts of 1985 and 1989 by consolidating them, the 2006 Act introduced new provisions for both private and public companies and implemented the EU's Takeover Directive and the Transparency Obligations Directives. The 2006 Act also incorporated the duties of directors and other matters based on common law principles.

The general duties of directors are set out as follows:

- Section 171: Duty to act within powers;
- Section 172: Duty to promote the success of the company;
- Section 173: Duty to exercise independent judgement;
- Section 174: Duty to exercise reasonable care, skill and judgment;
- Section 175: Duty to avoid conflicts of interest;
- Section 176: Duty not to accept benefits from third parties; and
- Section 177: Duty to declare interest in proposed transaction or arrangement.

3.2 Directors' duties

The common law duties of care and skill are demonstrated by a number of company law cases dating back to 1925. More recently, section 174 of Companies Act 2006 introduced a more objective test for directors who, in carrying out their functions, have a duty to exercise reasonable care, skill and judgement.

Case Law 1.1 Re City Equitable Fire Insurance Co [1925]

In *Re City Equitable Fire Insurance Co* [1925] the company lost over £1m due to underperforming investments and fraud perpetrated by a certain Mr Bevan, the company chairman. The liquidator sued Mr Bevan's fellow directors and, whilst it was found that some directors had breached their duty of care, they were held not liable by the Court of Appeal because their lack of care did not amount to gross negligence. They had acted honestly and the court held that in the performance of his duties, a director need not display a greater degree of skill than may reasonably be expected from a person of his knowledge and experience.

Case Law 1.2 Re D'Jan of London Ltd [1994]

A more recent landmark case, *Re D'Jan of London Ltd* [1994], which influenced s.174 of the Companies Act 2006, demonstrates the tests used to determine if directors have acted with due skill, care and judgement. The case establishes that directors owe an objective standard of care based on what should reasonably be expected from a person in their position. The case concerns a director, Mr D'Jan, who signed an incorrectly completed insurance policy document without checking it. This led to the insurance company refusing to pay up when the company made a claim for fire damage. The company lost most of its stock and went into liquidation. The liquidators subsequently sued Mr D'Jan for negligence in order to recover payables' funds. It was found that the common law duty of care owed by a director is the conduct of a reasonably diligent person having both:

- the general knowledge, skill and experience that may reasonably be expected of a person carrying out the same functions as are carried out by that director in relation to the company; and

- the general knowledge, skill and experience that the director has.

It was held that Mr D'Jan did not demonstrate reasonable diligence when he signed the insurance policy and was therefore in breach of his duty of care. The fact that it did not amount to a gross breach of duty (on the basis that Mr D'Jan was found to be honest and reasonable) mitigated his damages and he was only held liable for an amount not exceeding any unpaid dividends to which he would otherwise be entitled as an unsecured creditor.

Case Law 1.3 Re Weavering Capital (UK) Limited [2012]

As with the cases of *Re City Equitable Fire Insurance Co* [1925] and *Re D'Jan of London Ltd* [1994] in *Re Weavering Capital (UK) Limited* [2012] (covered in more detail in Chapter 9), Weavering Capital (UK) Limited and its liquidators also sought relief under the Insolvency Act 1986. The judgment of the *Weavering* case of 30 May 2012 refers to proceedings against two directors of a Cayman Islands hedge fund, the Weavering Macro Fixed Income Fund (the "Macro Fund"), which was managed by Weavering Capital (UK) Limited.

The 2011 Cayman judgment on Weavering found the two directors, one of whom was in his 80s, guilty of wilful neglect or default of their duties as directors of the Macro fund. The Cayman judgment found they had failed to detect that Mr Magnus Peterson of

Weavering Capital (UK) Limited had "dishonestly manipulated the Macro Fund's statement of financial position and defrauded its investors". The financial implications of the judgment against them amounted to US$111m each.

In the UK, on 30 May 2012, the High Court of Justice awarded payables of Weavering Capital (UK) Limited more than $450m in civil damages. The judgment states that: "Mr Peterson admittedly owed Weavering Capital (UK) Limited fiduciary duties as a director. For example, to act at all times in good faith and in Weavering Capital (UK) Limited's best interests, not to put himself in a position where his interests and duties conflicted, to act in accordance with Weavering Capital (UK) Limited's constitution, statutory duties under ss.171–177 of the 2006 Act and duties to exercise reasonable care, skill and diligence in performing his duties as a director."

3.3 Key features of the Companies Act 2006

As well as setting out the statutory duties of directors, other key features of the Companies Act 2006, which apply to both private and public companies, include:

◆ ability for companies to make greater use of electronic means of communications when corresponding with shareholders;

◆ three ways to incorporate a company (electronic software filing, web incorporation service, paper filing);

◆ a shorter **Memorandum of Association** because all the constitutional rules of the company are contained in the Articles of Association;

◆ ability for directors to use a service address, in place of their home address, for public record requirements, for example a director's service address may be stated to be "the company's registered office";

◆ 14 days' notice requirement for shareholder meetings;

◆ removal of requirement for companies to specify their objects on incorporation meaning companies have unlimited capacity and greater flexibility to choose how they operate, unless otherwise restricted in the articles;

◆ all companies are required to have at least one natural person appointed as a director, although corporate directors are still permitted;

◆ no maximum age restriction for directors other than a minimum age requirement of 16 for all directors who are natural persons;

◆ directors' service contracts are to be made available for inspection at the registered office of the company, the principal place of business, or at the location where the register of members and other records are kept (s.228 and s.1136);

◆ requirement for the directors of every company to prepare accounts for the company for each of its financial years in the prescribed format or in accordance with international accounting standards (s.395), to sign the

memorandum of association
is a document evidencing the subscribers' intention to incorporate a company and become members of that company on incorporation. For a company that is to be limited by shares, the memorandum also confirms the agreement of the members to take at least one share each in the company. Once the company has been incorporated, the Memorandum cannot be amended;

statement of financial position and to ensure that the financial statements give a true and fair view of the assets, liabilities, financial position and profit or loss of the company (s.396);

◆ failure to maintain accounting records under s.386 of the Act could be a criminal offence for every officer of the company who is in default (s.387);

◆ the requirement for directors' to prepare a directors' report for each financial year of the company (s.415) and for the report to be approved by the board of directors and signed on behalf of the board by a director or the company secretary (s.419);

◆ auditors should be fit and proper, independent and conduct their work with integrity; and

◆ a lifting of the ban on company loans to directors, as long as approval of shareholders has been obtained.

3.4 Private companies

Key features of the 2006 Act specific to private companies include:

◆ straightforward model **Articles of Association** (students should refer to the **Model Articles** at the back of this chapter/study text);

◆ special code of accounting and reporting requirements for small private companies;

◆ no requirement to appoint a company secretary;

◆ if a company secretary is appointed and made responsible for meeting the company's various disclosure and filing requirements, it is still the board that is primarily accountable should there be any material filing omissions or misstatements;

◆ 14 days' notice required for general meetings unless otherwise stated in the company's articles;

◆ ability to convene meetings at short notice where 90% shareholder consent is given (providing the shares are eligible and carry the necessary voting rights);

◆ removal of the requirement of the 1985 Act for unanimity in shareholders' written resolutions with a simple majority of the eligible shares being required for ordinary resolutions and 75% for special resolutions;

◆ no requirement to hold an AGM unless the holding of an AGM is self-imposed. 10% of shareholders can demand a meeting (5% in certain circumstances);

◆ private company financial statements must be filed with Companies House (thereby making them available to the general public) within nine months of the year end (as opposed to 10 months under the 1985 Act) [Note that where the financial period end date is a month end, the filing deadline is the last day of the relevant month, e.g. a private company with a 31 May year end must file it accounts by 28 February the following year and a private company with a 28 February year end must deliver its accounts by 30 November in the same year. If the accounting reference date is not a

articles of association form the main constitutional document of a company and lay out the rules for the running of the company, for example directors powers and responsibilities, decision making of directors, the appointment of directors, the allotment of shares, the payment of dividends, capitalisation of profits, the rules governing meetings, voting powers, the production of financial statements and various administrative functions.

model articles Many companies rely on model articles which are set out in Schedules 1–3 of The Companies (Model Articles) Regulations 2008. Although the members of the company can determine their own Articles, the Model Articles provide a good standard set of rules often used by members as a guide or framework around which they develop their own specific Articles. For example, where a company only has two directors, the directors may decide to remove the Chairman's casting vote clause which is provided for in the Model Articles.

month end, e.g. 5 April, the company has until 5 January (not 31 January) of the following year to file the accounts; and

◆ auditors may have limited liability for breach of duty, breach of trust or negligence claims provided the limitation is agreed with shareholders up front and the limitation is "fair and reasonable".

3.5 Public companies

Key features of the 2006 Act specific to public companies include:

◆ a company secretary is a mandatory requirement and irrespective of the company secretaries' duties, the board maintains a statutory responsibility for meeting filing and disclosure requirements (s.386);

◆ public company financial statements must be filed with Companies House within six months of the year end (as opposed to seven months under the 1985 Act);

◆ requirement for public companies to hold AGM within six months of the end of the reporting period;

◆ 21 days' notice required for general meetings, although 14 days' notice is permitted if (i) the general meeting is not the AGM; (ii) the members are given an electronic voting facility; and (iii) the company has passed a special resolution to permit a 14-day notice period;

◆ requirement to publish the annual report and accounts on the company's website and to disclose the results of polled votes;

◆ less onerous provisions relating to shareholder approval for political donations (s.364) and political expenditure (s.365) than was previously the case under the Companies Act;

◆ strengthening of non-financial disclosure of companies listed on the London Stock Exchange to include information in the financial statements about such matters as **corporate social responsibility** (see Chapter 11);

◆ implementation of the EU's Takeover Directive and the Transparency Obligations Directives; and

◆ enabling powers regarding voting disclosure by institutions and paperless share transfers.

corporate social responsibility (CSR) is a term used to describe the processes an organisation uses to produce a positive impact on society through its activities. It is about the ongoing commitment of businesses to behave ethically and responsibly towards its employees, its customers, the environment and the community at large. It is about doing business in a responsible and sustainable manner.

3.6 Share capital and reserves

With regards to a company's share capital and reserves, the 2006 Act introduced the following changes to the 1985 Act for private and public companies:

◆ private companies do not require shareholder consent to allot shares where there is only one class of share capital as long as the Articles of Association carry no restrictions;

◆ the 2006 Act permits companies to issue an unlimited number of shares, effectively removing the requirement for authorised share capital, unless required by the Articles;

- ◆ simpler procedures for amending class rights;
- ◆ restrictions on public companies allotting shares where offers are not fully subscribed;
- ◆ less onerous requirements for limited companies wishing to purchase their own shares and for the issuance of redeemable shares; and
- ◆ new procedures for private companies seeking to reduce their share capital which enables them to reduce the level of capital without having to seek a court order.

Upon joining the board of an offshore company, directors with a UK background should, as part of their induction, familiarise themselves with legal and regulatory requirements in that jurisdiction, e.g. Companies (Jersey) Law 1991; The Companies (Guernsey) Law, 2008; BVI Business Companies Act, 2004; The Companies Law 1961, as amended (Cayman); The Companies Act 2006 (IOM). The company secretary, fellow directors and/or compliance officers should be able to assist in this respect. It is not sufficient to assume that the principles and requirements of the Companies Act 2006 will apply elsewhere.

Stop and think 1.1

Why is there an increasing focus on the collective responsibility of directors rather than just individual responsibility?

Test yourself 1.3

What are the filing requirements for public company financial statements under the Companies Act 2006?

Briefly explain the provisions of section 174 of the Companies Act 2006.

Chapter summary

- ◆ GAAP (or Generally Accepted Accounting Principles) are a common set of principles-based accounting standards used for the preparation and presentation of an entity's financial statements.

- ◆ The application of GAAP should help ensure financial information is reported consistently and objectively to enable stakeholders to make decisions based on comparable and reliable information.

- ◆ The Accounting Standards Board (ASB) forms part of the Financial Reporting Council (FRC) and is the standard-setting body in the UK responsible for issuing Financial Reporting Standards (FRS).

- ◆ UK GAAP, like International Financial Reporting Standards, is a principles-based approach to financial reporting.

◆ In the US, it is the Financial Accounting Standards Board (FASB) that is the chief standard setter for US GAAP. Whilst US GAAP is gradually being converged with IFRS, the US, along with Japan and India, has still made no firm commitment regarding the adoption and implementation of IFRS.

◆ Proposals in the UK concerning the future of UK GAAP include replacing all existing FRSs, SSAPs and UITF Abstracts with a single FRS, a reduced disclosure framework and retaining the FRSSE.

◆ The objective of the ASB's proposals is "to enable users of accounts to receive high-quality, understandable financial reporting proportionate to the size and complexity of the entity and users' information needs".

◆ IFRS offers a single set of globally accepted accounting standards and has been adopted by the large majority of countries around the world.

◆ The US is considering a phased transition to IFRS through a gradual continuation of convergence measures and the US Securities and Exchange Commission (SEC) is expected to make an decision on the adoption of IFRS by the end of 2012.

◆ In the UK, companies which are not listed have the option to report either under IFRSs or under UK GAAP.

◆ UK GAAP is becoming increasingly more aligned with IFRS and, to facilitate international convergence of accounting standards, recently issued FRSs tend to be in line with their corresponding IFRSs.

◆ The Companies Act 2006 was introduced to reform company law and improve shareholder communications, strengthen regulation, improve disclosure requirements as a consumer protection measure, make company formation a simpler process and allow greater flexibility in the running of a company.

◆ The Companies Act 2006 sets out the general duties of directors which are set out in s. 171–177 of the Companies Act.

◆ The duty of directors to exercise due skill, care and judgment is highlighted by a number of common law cases, notably *Re City Equitable Fire Insurance Co* [1925] and *Re D'Jan of London Ltd* [1994]. The judgment in respect of *Weavering Capital (UK) Limited* [2012] refers to the statutory duties of directors as set out in ss.171–177 of the Companies Act 2006.

◆ The articles of Association form the main constitutional document of a company and lay out the rules for the running of the company, for example directors' powers and responsibilities, decision making of directors, the appointment of directors, the allotment of shares, the payment of dividends, capitalisation of profits, the rules governing meetings, voting powers, the production of financial statements and various administrative functions.

Part
Two

In this part, students will learn about the conceptual framework, qualitative characteristics of financial statements as well as revenue recognition and measurement. Students will also learn about accounting policies and the reporting of financial performance. Important accounting issues are explained, such as reporting the substance of transactions, financial instruments and the impact of foreign exchange rate changes.

Finally, Part Two of this study text discusses material events occurring after the reporting period and the accounting treatment for provisions, contingent liabilities and contingent assets.

Learning outcomes

At the end of this part, students should be able to:

◆ discuss the fundamental accounting concepts of going concern and accruals;

◆ discuss the accounting concepts of prudence and consistency;

- list some of the advantages of the conceptual framework and briefly discuss the common conceptual framework being worked upon by the IASB and FASB;

- explain the qualitative characteristics of financial statements;

- explain the pertinent points in respect of IAS 18 "Revenue" including being able to define "revenue", being able to discuss the measurement of revenue and explain what is meant by "fair value";

- outline the objectives of FRS 18 "Accounting Policies" and define what accounting policies are, and explain the difference between accounting policies and estimation techniques;

- state the disclosure requirements in respect of FRS 18 and be able to explain what is meant by "true and fair override";

- discuss the difference between UK GAAP and IFRS in the determination of accounting policies;

- understand the basic components and layout of the statement of financial position, the statement of comprehensive income, the statement of changes in equity, the statement of cash flows, notes to the accounts;

- discuss the basic requirements for the presentation of financial statements;

- explain what is meant by substance over form (FRS 5) and be able to discuss this in the context of consignment inventory, sale and repurchase agreements, debt factoring, securitisation, loan transfers and the private finance initiative;

- explain the differences between various types of financial instruments and be able to account for options;

- appreciate the significance of foreign currency translation and understand how monetary and non-monetary items should be translated at the income statement date;

- explain the difference between functional currency and presentation currency;

- understand when it might be appropriate to account for events after the reporting period;

- define what is meant by constructive obligation in the context of financial provisions;
- explain how provisions can be used to smooth profits and how IAS37 has restricted the use of provisions to prevent irresponsible use and profit smoothing; and
- understand the concept of contingent assets and contingent liabilities.

Chapter two
Accounting concepts

List of topics

1 Conceptual framework
2 Qualitative characteristics
3 Revenue recognition and measurement

Introduction

This chapter deals with the four fundamental accounting concepts which underpinned the UK accounting framework for three decades and which, today, still play an important role in the conceptual framework. Students will learn about the concepts – going concern, consistency, prudence and accruals – and will see how the development of accounting standards has led to the fundamental concepts of consistency and prudence being downgraded to desirable concepts which serve to enhance the two remaining fundamental accounting concepts – going concern and accruals. Students will also gain an understanding of what is meant by a common conceptual framework and will learn some of the advantages of a conceptual framework.

The qualitative characteristics of financial statements are also described in this chapter and students will learn what is meant by qualitative characteristics and how there were previously considered to be four main characteristics whilst today, there are generally considered to be two fundamental attributes supported by four other important characteristics which, together, help make financial statements more useful and meaningful for users.

Finally, the chapter discusses revenue recognition. The difference between revenue and income is explained. Students will learn about the objective of the principal international accounting standard governing revenue recognition, how to measure the fair value of revenue, how revenue derived from goods sold on credit should be treated in the accounts, the criteria that apply for revenue recognition in respect of the sale of goods and the provision of services and other receivables such as interest, royalties and dividends.

1. Conceptual framework

Accounting practice in the UK has traditionally been underpinned by four fundamental accounting concepts as described in the accounting standard known as Statement of Standard Accounting Practice (SSAP) 2 "Disclosure of Accounting Policies":

1 **Going concern**

2 **Consistency**

3 **Prudence**

4 **Accruals**

After 29 years in force, SSAP 2 was superseded by FRS 18 "Accounting Policies" in December 2000 in order for there to be greater consistency between financial reporting standards and with the **Accounting Standards Boards Statement of Principles for Financial Reporting**.

FRS 18 views the SSAP 2 concepts of consistency and prudence as merely desirable; the two remaining concepts, going concern and accruals, continue to feature as fundamental concepts in financial statements and accounting policies.

1.1 Fundamental concepts

Going concern

The UK accounting standard, FRS 18 states that an entity should prepare its financial statements on a going concern basis, unless:

◆ the entity is being liquidated or has ceased trading, or

◆ the directors have no realistic alternative but to liquidate the entity or to cease trading,

in which circumstances the entity may, if appropriate, prepare its financial statements on a basis other than that of a going concern.

If trading is to cease and the entity is no longer a going concern, then the financial statements should be prepared on a break-up basis and a note should be made in the financial statements to state that the entity is no longer a going concern. Accounting on a break-up basis provides shareholders with a more realistic snapshot of what their investment will be worth once the company is liquidated. This basis is, however, not relevant to stakeholders wishing to assess the income-generating ability and financial adaptability of the company and, therefore, should only be used when the company is not a going concern and will be broken up within 12 months of the financial reporting date.

FRS 18 states that when preparing financial statements, directors should assess whether there are significant doubts about an entity's ability to continue as a going concern. When making their assessment (using all available information concerning the foreseeable future), any material uncertainties regarding the going concern of the company should be disclosed in the financial statements.

going concern
refers to an entity that has the ability to continue to operate in the foreseeable future.

consistency
is the concept that reporting entities should be consistent with their accounting policies and methods, from one reporting period to the next.

prudence
an accounting concept which aims to ensure that income and assets are not overstated and that expenses and liabilities are not understated.

accruals
a concept that transactions should be accounted for in the reporting period to which they relate, rather than the period when payment is made.

Accounting Standards Boards Statement of Principles for Financial Reporting
is the conceptual framework underpinning the accounting standards set by the ASB.

Where the financial statements are not prepared on a going concern basis, the reasons why the company is no longer considered a going concern should be stated.

Accruals

FRS 18 states that an entity should prepare its financial statements, except for cash flow information (see Chapter 7), on the accruals basis of accounting. This means that non-cash transactions should be accounted for in the financial statements in the reporting period to which they relate, rather than in the period when cash changes hands.

For example, an offshore financial services provider with a 31 December year end accounts for invoices up to the end of December in the financial statements.

asset
is the right or other access to future economic benefits controlled by an entity as a result of past transactions or events.

liability
is the obligation of an entity to transfer economic benefits as a result of past transactions or events.

To be consistent with the ASB's Statement of Principles, the accruals basis should reflect only those items that meet the definition of an **asset** or **liability**. The Statement of Principles defines an asset as "rights or other access to future economic benefits controlled by an entity as a result of past transactions or events". Ideally, all assets and liabilities should be recognised when they arise but, as companies operate in an uncertain business environment, it is not always appropriate to accrue for assets and liabilities (e.g. where there is material uncertainty that the transfer of economic benefit will actually occur) and there are, therefore, criteria and rules governing when assets and liabilities should be recognised. If the recognition criteria are not met, then the asset or liability should not be recognised in the statement of financial position.

In the above example, the raising of invoices creates sufficient evidence that the assets exist at the year end and may be reliably measured in monetary terms. They should therefore be recognised in the accounts as occurring in the reporting period to which they relate, rather than when the invoices are paid.

The accounting entries for the invoices raised in December and paid in January would be as follows:

December: DR Receivables
            CR Sales
January: DR Bank
            CR Receivables

The receivables accrued at the December year end is reversed out in January when the debt is paid. By accruing for the unpaid invoices at the year end, the amount due is treated as an asset in the statement of financial position and the income statement reflects the income in the period to which it relates. Under UK GAAP, this accounting treatment is consistent with FRS 5 "Reporting the Substance of Transactions", which defines an asset and determines items to be recognised in the statement of financial position.

1.2 Consistency

The concept of consistency is that a company should be consistent with its reporting from one period to the next by sticking to the same policies, principles and accounting treatment which the company has adopted and by treating transactions which are similar in nature in the same way. A company should only change its accounting treatment if it has reasonable grounds to do so; any changes will result in additional disclosures to explain the shift in policy. A change in policy will also mean the company has to restate the prior period figures in order to give a representative prior period comparative. This enables stakeholders to quickly and easily compare the entity's financial position and performance over time. Students should note that a change of accounting estimate only requires a disclosure note and prior year figures do not need to be restated. For example, a company has a straight line depreciation policy and depreciates an asset over 10 years. In 2012, after five years, the asset has a carrying value of £20,000 and the company concludes that the asset still has a further eight years of useful life. The company therefore depreciates the carrying value of the asset over the new estimated useful life and discloses the change in accounting estimate.

In 2012, based on the original accounting estimates, five years of useful economic life remained. Carrying value £20,000/5 years = £4,000 annual depreciation.

However, in 2012, the remaining useful life was re-estimated as eight years. Carrying value £20,000/8 years = £2,500 annual depreciation.

The change in the annual depreciation amount reflects a change in the application of the accounting policy rather than a change of accounting policy. Prior year figures should, therefore, not be restated, but the change in estimate should be disclosed.

1.3 Prudence

The prudence concept, as its name suggests, is an accounting concept which aims to ensure that income (in the income statement) and assets (in the statement of financial position) are not overstated and that expenses (in the income statement) and liabilities (in the statement of financial position) are not understated.

1.4 Common conceptual framework

The International Accounting Standards Board (IASB) has been working on a revised and updated conceptual framework in conjunction with the US Financial Accounting Standards Board (FASB) and has completed the first phase of this new improved framework for IFRSs and GAAP with the objective of creating "a sound foundation for future accounting standards that are principles-based, internally consistent and internationally converged". The common framework aims to reflect changes in business practices, markets and the economic environment that have occurred since the conceptual framework was first introduced. A common framework will also facilitate the convergence of accounting standards globally.

Advantages of a conceptual framework
◆ Principles-based approach means an overall reduction in the number of standards required.

◆ Sets out the objectives of financial reporting.

◆ Describes the qualitative characteristics of meaningful information.

◆ Leads to greater alignment of accounting standards and aids international convergence.

◆ Helps users and preparers of accounts determine how items such as assets and revenue should be recognised.

◆ Deals with concepts of capital and capital maintenance.

Test yourself 2.1

Under FRS 18, prudence and consistency are now defined as desirable qualities of financial information, rather than as fundamental concepts. What are the fundamental concepts?

2. Qualitative characteristics of financial statements

Financial statements should contain certain characteristics to ensure they are useful and meaningful for users. There are four main **qualitative characteristics** which help make financial statements meaningful and these four characteristics should always form part of any set of financial statements. They are:

qualitative characteristics
are the attributes that make the information in financial statements useful and meaningful for users.

1 Understandability
2 Relevance
3 Reliability
4 Comparability

2.1 Understandability

Financial statements are sometimes unduly complex such that users who do not have a good basic knowledge of accounts may struggle to understand the underlying information if not clearly presented. Users should be able to gain a good understanding of an entity's financial performance and financial position from a brief review of its financial statements. Notwithstanding the requirement for accounts to be readily understood, some financial transactions are inherently complex and difficult to understand but to omit such information would not give a fair representation of the financial statements. To advocate understandability, it is, therefore, important that the format and layout of the financial statements, the accounting policies applied, the terminology used and other statements made within the financial statements are clear and concise. All material information should be complete and presented in such a way as to ensure users readily comprehend the state of affairs of the entity.

2.2 Relevance

Stakeholders require financial statements to be relevant to the decisions they have to make. In determining what is relevant to users, preparers of accounts should consider **materiality** and the extent to which reliable information may be omitted. Information may be relevant simply because of its magnitude or because its omission from the financial statements could affect decision making. In this respect, the directors should consider the nature and completeness of information that is included in the directors' report and elsewhere in financial statements because users of accounts rely on this key information resource when making investment and other economic decisions. It should be remembered that relevant and reliable information may lose its relevance if not reported in a timely manner. The older the information, the less likely it is to influence decision making.

materiality
describes the effect of an item (or event) on the financial statements of an entity, such that its inclusion or omission (occurrence or non-occurrence) would significantly alter the position.

stakeholder
describes a person or organisation that holds a stake in a business, be it a financial stake or because the person or organisation is affected by the decisions and actions of the business.

2.3 Reliability

In terms of accounting, reliability means free from bias and material misstatement. Reliable information should reflect the true substance of transactions. Estimates and assumptions, which could have a material impact on the financial statements if they transpire to be incorrect, should be fully disclosed. This might include assumptions used for estimating goodwill. The financial statement should be consistently and fairly presented and should install user confidence. This is most effectively achieved by having them verified by an auditor because an unmodified (i.e. clean) audit opinion provides users of accounts with an independent third-party confirmation that the accounts are both reliable and relevant and present a "true and fair view" of the financial position and performance of the organisation.

2.4 Comparability

Financial statements should be comparable with prior year financial statements and with financial statements of similar entities in the same industry sector to enable users of financial statements to make informed decisions. If financial statements lack this attribute, analysts will be less equipped to assess trends and financial ratios. Not all financial statements will be easily comparable but the basic accounting concepts and policies employed should be the industry standard where possible to enable users to discern and evaluate differences within any one reporting period or over several reporting periods whether comparing its own figures over time or benchmarking against similar businesses in the same industry sector. If a reporting entity changes its accounting policies from one year to the next then it should ensure that the prior year's figures are restated to enable users to have a like for like prior year comparative when assessing performance and changes in the financial position.

2.5 2010 Framework

The common framework developed jointly by the IASB and the FASB in the US identifies two fundamental qualitative characteristics of financial information, namely:

◆   Relevance
◆   **Faithful representation**

faithful representation
means complete, free from bias and error.

The 2010 Framework uses the terminology faithful representation rather than reliability because the term reliability has not always been understood to mean faithful representation as was intended by the old framework.

The new framework considers that the following four qualitative characteristics are not fundamental characteristics themselves but are characteristics which serve to enhance the two fundamental characteristics of financial statements, namely relevance and faithful representation:

◆   Comparability – financial statements are more useful if comparable with financial statements of similar companies and if comparable with the company's own prior year financial statements.

◆   Verifiability – financial information is verifiable when it allows different knowledgeable and independent observers to reach a consensus that a depiction of an event is faithfully represented.

◆   Timeliness – information is timely and more relevant if made available to users in such time that it can influence their decisions.

◆   Understandability – financial statements that are clear and concise are more readily understandable.

In summary, the IASB aims to enhance the relevance and faithful representation of financial statements, so that they are more meaningful to users, whilst trying to keep the costs of producing financial statements to a minimum.

3. Revenue recognition and measurement

The revenue recognition principle is closely related to the accruals concept of accounting. Under the accruals concept, **revenue** and expenditure are recognised in the reporting period to which they relate rather than in the period when cash changes hands. In cash accounting, revenue is recognised when physical payment takes place irrespective of when the sale was made.

revenue
is the gross inflow of economic benefits such as cash and other receivables during the period arising from ordinary operating activities of an entity when those inflows result in increases in equity, other than increases relating to contributions from equity participants.

Revenue recognition is fundamental to the reporting of financial performance because revenue is used for a number of key ratios, such as EPS, (see Chapter 6 – Financial Ratio Analysis) and directly affects the operating profit of business. There are strict accounting principles setting out whether revenue should be recognised in a reporting period or not and the rules seek to minimise creative accounting practices whereby accounting transactions are manipulated to present the financial position and performance in a more favourable light. In the UK, revenue recognition principles are prescribed under Financial Reporting Standard (FRS) 5 "Reporting the Substance of Transactions" (which requires entities to report the commercial substance of a transaction even if this differs from the exact legal form of the transaction) and International Accounting Standard (IAS) 18 "Revenue" (which is summarised below).

The objective of IAS 18 is to provide guidance for the accounting treatment of revenue from the sale of goods, provision of services and revenue in the form of interest, royalties and dividends. Recognition criteria can vary depending on the circumstances and type of transaction. For example, the criteria for recognising proceeds from the sale of goods, differ from the criteria that need to be met for the recognition of revenue derived from the provision of a service.

Revenue is defined under IAS 18 as "the gross inflow of economic benefits during the period arising in the course of the ordinary operating activities of an entity when those inflows result in increases in equity, other than increases relating to contributions from equity participants". [IAS 18.7]. Any amounts received on behalf of third parties including goods and services tax or value added tax, are not treated as revenue.

Whilst revenue is commonly referred to by other terms such as sales, fees, income, commissions, interest, dividends and royalties, it is important to note that the definition of revenue pursuant to IAS 18 is specific and differs to the definition of income per International Accounting Standard Board's "Framework for the Preparation and Presentation of Financial Statements". Whilst revenue and income both exclude subscriptions for equity shares and increase in equity arising from capital contributions, income includes economic benefits arising from both operating and non-operating activities, whereas revenue only includes income arising from the ordinary activities of a business.

The difficulty is establishing when it is appropriate to recognise revenue in the financial statements and when it is not appropriate. Revenue should be recognised when the flow of future economic benefits is probable and can be reliably measured. IAS 18 provides guidelines for the application of the revenue recognition criteria to help businesses establish whether revenue should indeed be recognised. The standard applies to revenue arising from the following transactions and events:

◆ the sale of goods;

◆ the provision of services; and

◆ the use by others of assets resulting in income being generated in the form of interest, royalties and dividends.

Services contracts relating to construction, including project management and contracts undertaken by architects, are not covered by IAS 18. The revenue arising from construction contracts is, instead, covered by IAS 11 "Construction contracts". Revenue arising from various other specific circumstances and events such as revenue arising from leasing, insurance contracts, investments in associates, financial instruments, agriculture and the extraction of mineral deposits are all covered under separate accounting standards.

3.1 Measurement of revenue

Under IAS 18, revenue is measured at **fair value** of the consideration received or receivable. IAS defines fair value as "the amount for which an asset could be exchanged or a liability settled, between a buyer and a seller interested

fair value
is the amount for which an asset could be exchanged or a liability settled, between a buyer and a seller in a free transaction.

and informed, in a free transaction". This means that any discounts or rebates should be taken into account.

As most transactions are settled by cash or cash equivalents, the measurement of revenue is the amount of cash and cash equivalents receivable.

For example, if a company makes £3,000 of sales on credit, the basic accounting entries are:

DR accounts receivable £3,000
CR sales £3,000

When payment is received, the book keeping entries are:

DR cash £3,000
CR accounts receivable £3,000

The net effect is:

DR cash £3,000
CR sales £3,000

However, as IAS 18 requires revenue to be measured at the fair value of the consideration receivable, the cash flows should be discounted to reflect the fact that the inflow of cash or cash equivalent is deferred. Effectively this means that revenue is measured as the present value of future cash flows. If goods are provided on interest-free credit or if a client is granted a loan below prevailing rates the fair value of the consideration is less than the nominal amount of the receivables. To calculate the fair value, the discount factor should be based on the appropriate market rates. There is no need to discount if the time value of money is immaterial, for example, if the credit period is over just a few months rather than years.

3.2 Example of sales using discounting

Credit Sales Limited which has a financial year end of 31 December sells goods to a customer on credit on 1 July 2012 for a total value of £3,000. The terms of the sale are three years' interest free credit which is favourable for the customer who would otherwise have to borrow funds from the bank at 5% per annum. Credit Sales Limited must calculate the fair value of revenue by discounting the cash flows receivable.

The present value of cash flows as at the transaction date is as follows:

1 year discount: £3,000/1.05 = £2,857
2 year discount: £2,857/1.05 = £2,721
3 year discount: £2,721/1.05 = £2,591

£3,000 of revenue is recognised on the transaction date of 1 July 2012 and £409 (3,000–£2,591) of interest is expensed.

Six months later, at the statement of financial position date of 31 December 2012, the fair value should be recalculated to reflect the present value of the receivable which falls due in 2.5 years time:

1 year discount: £3,000/1.05 = £2,857
2 year discount: £2,857/1.05 = £2,721
2.5 year discount: £2721/1.025 = £2,655 [5% per annum × £6 months /
                     12 months = 2.5%].

3.3 Sale of goods

Pursuant to IAS 18, revenue arising from the sale of inventory should be recognised only when each of the following five conditions has been met:

1 the company has transferred the risks and rewards of ownership to the buyer;

2 the company ceases to act in any managerial capacity in respect of the assets sold and retains no control over them;

3 the amount of revenue can be reliably measured;

4 the costs associated with the transaction can be reliably measured; and

5 it is probable that the seller will receive the economic benefits of the transaction.

3.4 Provision of services

Provided each and every one of the following criteria are met, revenue should be recognised considering the degree of completion of the transaction for provision of services as at the statement of financial position date:

1 the amount of revenue can be reliably measured;

2 the degree of completion of the transaction can be reliably measured at the date of the statement of financial position;

3 the costs associated with the transaction can be reliably measured; and

4 it is probable that the service provider will receive the economic benefits of the transaction.

If the above conditions are unable to be met, revenue arising from the provision of services should be recognised only to the extent by which the expenses recognised are deemed recoverable.

This means that revenues are recognised when earned and when the contractual obligations have been met. Typically royalties are earned on a continuing basis and recognised in the financial statements at the reporting period date.

An example of revenue recognition based on the degree of completion of a service is set out below:

A college charges £7,500 per student for a year's accountancy course payable in equal instalments at the start of each trimester. The college's 31 December financial year end coincides with the end of the first trimester at which point in time only one third of the course has been completed. Accordingly, at the year-end, only one third of the revenue, i.e. £2,500 per student, should be recognised. If cash has been received in advance for the second or third trimesters, it is treated as deferred income and shown as a liability in the statement of financial position to reflect the fact that an obligation exists to deliver the tuition that has been paid for.

The transactions are accounted for as follows at the year end:

Where only the first trimester has been paid for

Dr Cash   £2,500
Cr Sales   £2,500

Where the second trimester has been paid for and the second trimester has been paid for in advance:

Dr Cash   £5,000
Cr Sales   £2,500
Cr Deferred income   £2,500

3.5 Interest, royalties and dividends

The following criteria must be met for revenue to be recognised in connection with interest, royalties and dividends:

1   the amount of revenue can be reliably measured; and

2   it is probable that economic benefits associated with the transaction will flow to the company.

Interest:

◆   The effective interest method should be used as per IAS 39 'Financial Instruments: Recognition and Measurement'.

Royalties:

◆   Royalties should be recognised on the accruals basis. This means that revenues are recognised when earned and when the contractual obligations have been met. Typically royalties are earned on a continuing basis and recognised in the financial statements at the reporting period date.

Dividends:

◆   Dividends should be recognised only when the shareholder's right to receive the dividend payment is established. This means that if a dividend is declared and approved by shareholders prior to the year-end, and if there are distributable reserves from which it may be paid, it should be recognised. A dividend that is declared after the year end should only be provided for in the financial statements where an obligation exists at the year end to pay the dividend. This, in effect, means that it must have had shareholder approval to be included in year-end provisions.

3.6 Disclosure of information

Entities are required to disclose the following information in their financial statements:

◆   the accounting policies adopted for revenue recognition;

◆ methods used to measure the degree of completion of a service contract;

◆ the amount of each of the following categories of revenue:

(i) sale of goods;
(ii) provision of services;
(iii) interest;
(iv) royalties;
(v) dividends.

◆ the amount of revenue derived from the exchange of goods or services broken down by category.

3.7 Current proposals

The International Accounting Standards Board (IASB) is currently working on a joint project with the Financial Accounting Standards Board of the United States (FASB) to develop a new accounting standard for revenue recognition to replace both IAS 11 "Construction contracts" and IAS 18 "Revenue". The standard is intended to improve comparability and understandability of the financial statements but is not without its complexities as it requires the calculation of probability-weighted amounts based on, inter alia, collectability, the time value of money and fair value in respect of the consideration for goods and services. With regards to collectability, for example, existing standards do not currently address whether the credit risk of a customer should be taken into account when measuring revenue. Under the proposals customer credit risk should be excluded from the measurement. Providing greater clarity and guidance on such issues should lead to greater consistency and comparability of financial statements.

Test yourself 2.2

XYZ Limited has a financial year end of 31 December. The company sells goods to a customer on credit on 1 January 2012 for a total value of £5,000. The terms of the sale are two years' credit at an interest rate of 2% which is favourable for the customer who would otherwise have to borrow funds from the bank at 6% per annum. Calculate the fair value of revenue at the transaction date and at the statement of financial position date of 31 December 2012.

Test yourself 2.3

Under the common framework of the IASB and the FASB, what are the two fundamental qualitative characteristics of financial statements?

Stop and think 2.1

Why is it important for accounts to show prior year comparatives?

Chapter summary

◆ FRS 18 recognises two fundamental accounting concepts – going concern and accruals.

◆ Consistency and prudence were recognised as fundamental accounting concepts under SSAP 2 but are no longer considered as fundamental under FRS 18.

◆ FRS 18 states that an entity should prepare its financial statements on a going concern basis, unless (i) the entity is being liquidated or has ceased trading, or (ii) the directors have no realistic alternative but to liquidate the entity or to cease trading, in which circumstances the entity may, if appropriate, prepare its financial statements on a basis other than that of a going concern.

◆ If trading is to cease and the entity is no longer a going concern, then the financial statements should be prepared on a break-up basis and a note should be made in the financial statements to state that the entity is no longer a going concern.

◆ Where the financial statements are not prepared on a going concern basis, the reasons why the company is no longer considered a going concern should be stated.

◆ FRS 18 states that an entity should prepare its financial statements, except for cash flow information, on the accruals basis of accounting. This means that non-cash transactions should be accounted for in the financial statements in the reporting period to which they relate rather than in the period when cash changes hands.

◆ The IASB has been working on a revised and updated common conceptual framework in conjunction with the FASB in order to provide a sound foundation for future accounting standards that are principles-based and consistent. The new framework should also facilitate the convergence of accounting standards globally.

◆ The advantages of a good principles-based common conceptual framework are that fewer accounting standards are likely to be required, accounting standards globally are more likely to be more aligned, it helps determine when revenue and other accounting items should be recognised, it deals with concepts of capital and maintaining capital requirements and it describes the qualitative characteristics of financial statements.

◆ Traditionally, four main qualitative characteristics of financial statements have been said to be key attributes in the provision of useful information. These are understandability, relevance, reliability and comparability.

◆ Today, the IASB and the FASB indentify just two fundamental qualitative characteristics of financial statements. These are relevance and faithful representation.

◆ Other characteristics serve to enhance the fundamental characteristics and these include comparability, verifiability, timeliness and understandability.

◆ Revenue is the gross inflow of economic benefits such as cash and other receivables during the period arising from ordinary operating activities of an entity when those inflows result in increases in equity, other than increases relating to contributions from equity participants.

◆ Revenue recognition is fundamental to the reporting of financial performance because revenue is used for a number of key ratios, such as EPS, and directly affects the operating profit of business.

◆ The recognition criteria seek to minimise creative accounting practices whereby accounting transactions are manipulated to present the financial position and performance in a more favourable light.

◆ The objective of IAS 18 is to provide guidance for the accounting treatment of revenue from the sale of goods, provision of services and revenue in the form of interest, royalties and dividends. The standard provides guidelines for the application of the revenue recognition criteria to help businesses establish whether revenue should indeed be recognised.

◆ Services contracts relating to construction, including project management and contracts undertaken by architects, are covered by IAS 11 "Construction contracts".

◆ Receivables in respect of goods provided on interest-free or low-interest credit should be discounted to reflect the time value of money over the credit period. The discount factor should take account of the difference between the interest charged and the amount of interest that the purchaser would ordinarily have to pay on the open market.

◆ The exchange of goods or services for similar goods or services does not give rise to revenue under IAS 18.

◆ Companies should make disclosures concerning revenue recognition in their financial statements. The disclosures should state the accounting policies adopted for revenue recognition, methods employed to measure the degree of completion of a service contract, the amount of revenue by category and the amount of revenue derived from the exchange of goods or services broken down by category.

◆ A new accounting standard is being developed by the IASB and FASB to replace IAS 11 and IAS 18. It aims to improve the comparability and understandability of financial statements.

Chapter three
Reporting Financial Performance

List of topics

1 Accounting policies
2 Presentation of financial statements
3 Reporting the substance of transactions
4 Financial instruments
5 The impact of foreign exchange rate changes

Introduction

In this chapter, students will learn about the importance of an entity adopting appropriate accounting policies in order to present a true and fair view of its state of affairs and financial performance. Students will also learn the objectives under which an entity should judge the appropriateness of accounting policies, the distinction between accounting policies and estimation techniques and the disclosure requirements of FRS 18 "Accounting Policies".

The key requirements governing the presentation of financial statements are also explained so that students will gain an understanding of the statements required to make up a complete set of financial statements under IAS 1, an understanding of the components of each of the statements, an appreciation for the requirement to restate prior year figures when there is a change in accounting policy, reclassification of assets or prior period error to be rectified.

Students will also learn what is meant by reporting the substance of a transaction, commercial effect and risks and rewards of ownership. FRS 5 is explained and students will gain an appreciation for the need to have accounting rules to prevent certain transactions being kept off the statement of financial position. Various examples are provided to show how certain types of transaction should be treated and whether or not they should be recognised in the statement of financial position, including transactions that feature consignment inventory, sale and repurchase agreements, debt factoring, securitisation, loan transfers, private finance initiatives and similar contracts.

This chapter also discusses financial instruments as well as the recognition, derecognition and measurement of financial assets and financial liabilities. Various types of derivative instruments are explained including hedging instruments such as interest rate swaps, currency swaps, futures contracts, forward contracts, options, caps, floors and collars. Students will gain a basic understanding of how to account for a call option. Hedge accounting under IAS 39 is also briefly explained.

Finally, the chapter discusses FRS 23 and IAS 21 and the impact of foreign currency exchange rate changes. Students will learn what is meant by functional currency and presentational currency. The chapter explains the rules that govern foreign currency translation and how foreign exchange differences are accounted for in the financial statements.

1. Accounting policies

1.1 UK GAAP: FRS 18 "Accounting Policies"

The accounting standard FRS 18 was issued by the Accounting Standards Board (ASB) in December 2000 and sets out requirements for the selection, application and disclosure of accounting policies. The standard applies to all financial statements that are intended to give a true and fair view of an entity's financial position and performance. The only exemption is for entities applying the Financial Reporting Standard for Smaller Entities (FRSSE).

1.1.1 Objective of FRS 18

The stated objectives of the standard are to ensure that:

◆ an entity adopts appropriate accounting policies for its particular circumstances which will give a true and fair view;

◆ accounting policies are regularly reviewed and changed when appropriate; and

◆ sufficient disclosures are made in the financial statements to enable users to understand the policies adopted and how they have been applied.

FRS 18 defines **accounting policies** as:

> "Those principles, bases, conventions, rules and practices applied by an entity that specify how the effects of transactions and other events are to be reflected in its financial statements through:
>
> ◆ recognising,
>
> ◆ selecting measurement bases for, and
>
> ◆ presenting
>
> assets, liabilities, gains, losses and changes to shareholders' funds."

accounting policies
are principles, bases, conventions, rules and practices for recognising, selecting measurement bases for, and presenting assets, liabilities, gains, losses and changes to shareholders' funds.

1.2 Distinction between accounting policies and estimation techniques

Per FRS 18, accounting policies do not include estimation techniques. The standard clarifies that policies are intended to set out the basis on which an item is to be measured whereas an **estimation technique** is used when there is uncertainty over the amount arising under the policy. This distinction is important because any change in accounting policy will result in prior year figures having to be restated, whereas a change in estimation techniques only applies to the current reporting period.

The key point to note with accounting policy is that, in accordance with its definition under FRS 18, it involves any or all of the following:

◆ recognition criteria;

◆ the selection of measurement bases; and

◆ presentation.

Examples:

1 An example of an accounting policy might be for an entity only to record trade debts that are likely to be recovered within X number of days in accordance with the relevant financial reporting standard(s), whereas an estimation technique might be the method used by the entity to work out the proportion of all trade debts that is likely to be recovered, particularly where the method considers a population as a whole rather than just individual debt balances.

2 Another example of an estimation technique is how an entity might measure the disposal value of an asset. It might estimate the value based on similar disposals made by itself or other companies or by reference to quoted prices.

3 With regard to depreciation of a non-current asset, if an entity changes its depreciation method for motor vehicles from, say, a reducing balance method at 40% per year to a straight line method over five years, then there would, under normal circumstances, be no change in the way the assets are recognised or presented. There would also be no change in the measurement basis as this would remain at historical cost basis (less accumulated depreciation). The only change would be in the estimation technique used for depreciation.

As various estimation techniques are all likely to arrive at a similar reasonable figure (e.g. Example 3 above), a change in estimation technique is not considered a change in accounting policy. This means that prior year comparatives do not need to be restated in the financial statements. A prior period adjustment should only be made where a change in estimation technique corrects a **fundamental error** or where another standard, legal requirement (i.e. companies legislation) or regulation (e.g. **UITF Abstract**) requires an adjustment to be made.

estimation techniques are the methods used by an entity to implement accounting policies and arrive at estimated values, corresponding to the measurement bases selected for assets, liabilities, gains, losses and changes to shareholders' funds, e.g. measuring depreciation of non-current assets, measuring obsolescence of inventory, measuring work-in-progress, measuring the fair value of financial assets and liabilities.

fundamental error is a significant material error which jeopardises the true and fair view statement in the accounts.

UTIF abstract is an immediately binding abstract, reflecting a consensus arrived at by the Urgent Issues Task Force, which sets out the accounting treatment that should be adopted where unsatisfactory or conflicting interpretations have developed in respect of accounting standards or the Companies Act.

Estimation techniques are used when it is not possible or simple to assign a value to a specific attribute. They are an important part of the preparation of financial statements and, provided the techniques selected are appropriate for the specific set of circumstances and will enable the financial statements to present a true and fair view, their reliability is unlikely to be successfully challenged.

1.3 Accounting policy – selection criteria

With regard to accounting policy, the selection criteria depend on suitability and appropriateness to an entity's specific set of circumstances. FRS 18 names the following four qualitative characteristics of financial statements as the objectives under which an entity should judge the appropriateness of accounting policies:

1   Relevance
2   Reliability
3   Comparability
4   Understandability

(see Chapter 2).

1.4 Accounting policy – change of policy

An entity might adopt new accounting practices to make its financial information more relevant and reliable. In order for it to establish whether the changes it has made, in making the accounts more relevant and reliable, amount to a change of accounting policy per FRS 18, it should establish if there has been a change to any of the following:

◆   recognition criteria;
◆   measurement bases; or
◆   presentation.

Changes in the way items are recognised and presented as well as changes pertaining to the selection and application of **measurement bases** are matters of accounting policy. For example, if an entity previously recorded assets on a historic cost basis and now applies current market value, there has been a change in accounting policy. A change that does not affect recognition, presentation or the measurement basis is a change of estimation technique.

measurement bases are defined in FRS 18 as the monetary attributes of the elements of financial statements – including assets, liabilities, gains, losses and changes to shareholders' funds – that are reflected in the financial statements. The attributes are the different qualities of an item which may have a value attributed to it. For example, one attribute may be an asset's historic cost and another might be its current market value.

Test yourself 3.1

With regard to FRS 18 "Accounting Policies", what is the difference between a change of accounting policy and a change of estimation technique?

FRS 18 requires an entity to regularly review its accounting policies and to ensure that the policies are changed when it is appropriate to do so. Comparability of financial information should be taken into account when considering a change in policy, but it should not dictate policy and should not prevent the introduction of improved accounting practices which may add value to users of financial statements. For the purposes of giving a true and fair view, an entity should select the most relevant policy which may be reliably measured.

Stop and think 3.1

An entity has previously shown certain overheads within cost of sales. It now proposes to show these overheads within administrative expenses. Why is this a change of accounting policy?

1.5 FRS 18 Disclosure requirements

The following disclosures should be made under FRS 18:

◆ specific disclosures in respect of the accounting policies adopted where this is material in the context of the financial statements;

◆ specific disclosures in respect of accounting policy changes setting out the particulars of the changes and the effect of the prior period adjustment on the results of the preceding period;

◆ description of estimation techniques used in applying the policies where these techniques, or changes to these techniques, are material (e.g. depreciation methods used);

◆ details of any information relevant to the assessment of an entity's status as a going concern, if it is known that the entity has going concern issues; and

◆ particulars of any true and fair view override (see below).

1.5.1 *The true and fair view override*

In exceptional circumstances, where compliance with standards may conflict with the requirement for the financial statements to give a true and fair view of the state of affairs and profit and loss of the entity, departure from the requirements of those standards is permitted to the extent necessary to give a true and fair view. The particulars of such departures should be disclosed in a note to the financial statements.

1.6 Comparison between UK GAAP and international requirements

Broadly speaking, the practice for determining accounting policies is the same under both UK GAAP and IFRS. FRS 18, however, gives more guidance than IAS 8 "Accounting Policies, Changes in Accounting Estimates and Errors" on the objectives against which the appropriateness of accounting policies should be judged, the objectives being relevance, reliability, comparability and understandability.

However, unlike IAS 8, FRS 18 does not give guidance where the restatement of prior year comparatives is impractical. For example, it may not viable to collect data relating to the previous period(s) to enable reliable retrospective application of new accounting policies. Where there is no standard or guidance note that expressly applies to a transaction, event or circumstance, IAS 8 permits entities to take into account the assertions of other standard setters provided they give rise to relevant and reliable information (i.e. the information is prudent, free from bias and reflects the substance of the transaction, event or circumstance). FRS 18 states that the concepts of going concern and accruals are fundamental in the selection of accounting policies. IAS 8 does not directly associate accounting concepts with accounting policies.

IAS 8 uses the terminology "accounting estimates" whereas FRS 18 refers to "estimation techniques". Appendix I of FRS 18 gives various examples of changes in accounting policy and changes in estimation techniques to make it easier to distinguish between accounting policy and estimation techniques. IAS 8 simply states that where it is difficult to establish whether a change is a matter of policy or not, it should be treated as an accounting estimate. The requirements under FRS 3 and FRS 18 are that prior year comparatives should only be restated where:

◆ there is a change in accounting policy; or

◆ where a change in estimation technique corrects a fundamental error; or

◆ where another accounting standard, companies legislation or UITF Abstract requires an adjustment to be made.

Where there is a change in accounting policy, the requirements of IAS 8 are similar. However, with errors, the requirements are more stringent under international standards and all material errors (not just fundamental errors) should be corrected by restating prior year comparative information in the financial statements.

The disclosure requirements of IAS 8 are broadly the same as the relevant disclosure requirements of FRS 3 "Reporting Financial Performance" and FRS 18. Under IAS 8, however, any expected and imminent changes in accounting policy need to be disclosed.

2. Presentation of financial statements (IAS 1)

2.1 The purpose of financial statements

Financial statements are a structured representation of the financial position and performance of an entity. The purpose of financial statements is to provide owners and other stakeholders with information on the financial position, financial performance and cash flows of the entity in which they have an interest. As the information reported is used by a number of stakeholders, whose investment decisions it influences, it is important that the financial statements are structured and presented in such a manner that they are understandable and comparable.

Financial statements also reflect the stewardship of the management team who run the business and have control of its underlying assets.

To improve the usefulness of financial information and help users in their decision making, financial statements categorise the information presented into the following elements:

◆   assets;

◆   liabilities;

◆   equity;

◆   income and expenses (including gains and losses);

◆   other changes in equity (contributions by and distributions to owners); and

◆   cash flows.

2.2 Objective of International Accounting Standard 1 (IAS 1)

IAS 1 lays out the foundations for the presentation of financial statements for general information purposes to ensure that an entity's financial statements are comparable with the financial statements of other like companies and with their own prior period financial statements. The standard prescribes the overall requirements for the presentation of financial statements, guidelines for determining their structure and minimum requirements for their content.

2.3 Scope of IAS 1

IAS 1 applies to all general purpose financial statements prepared and presented in accordance with IFRS.

2.4 Presentation of financial statements under IAS 1

Per IAS 1, an entity must present a complete set of financial statements (including prior period comparative information) on, at least, an annual basis. A complete set of financial statements, presented under the standard, should include the following components which should be given equal prominence within the annual report:

◆   statement of financial position (i.e. statement of financial position) as at the reporting date;

◆   statement of comprehensive income for the period or an income statement plus a statement showing other comprehensive income;

◆   statement of changes in equity for the period;

◆   statement of cash flows; and

◆   notes (comprising a summary of significant accounting policies and other explanatory notes).

The financial statements should be clearly identified and separated out from other information within the "annual report and accounts" documentation.

It is important to note that under IAS 1, when an entity applies an accounting policy retrospectively and makes an adjustment to the prior period figures in its financial statements, or when it reclassifies items in its financial statements, it must also present a statement of financial position as at the start of the earliest comparative period.

Test yourself 3.2

List the components of a complete set of financial statements as per IAS 1.

2.5 Fair presentation and compliance with IFRS

IAS 1 states that financial statements should present the financial position, financial performance and cash flows of an entity fairly and accurately. This is presumed to be achieved by following the relevant IFRS and ensuring transactions are fairly represented in accordance with the appropriate recognition criteria for assets, liabilities, income and expenses as set out in the IASB's Framework for the Preparation and Presentation of Financial Statements (the "Framework").

Where compliance with IFRS might result in users being misled by the financial statements, departure from IFRS is permitted provided the nature, reasons and impact of the departure is disclosed. There must be good reasons for not following the prescribed rules and departure should only occur where non-departure would conflict with the objectives of financial statements as set out in the Framework.

2.6 Going concern

Financial statements are prepared on a going concern basis except where there are material uncertainties which cast significant doubt over the entity's ability to continue to operate in the foreseeable future. Where there are uncertainties, the required disclosures should be made in accordance with IAS 1 and the accounts should be prepared on an alternative basis, e.g. break-up basis.

2.7 Accruals basis of accounting

IAS 1 states that items such as assets, liabilities, equity, income and expenses should be presented in the financial statements on an accruals basis. The accruals basis of accounting does not, however, apply to cash flow information.

2.8 Consistency of presentation and comparative information

To enable users to draw more meaningful information from an entity's financial statements, the presentation and classification of items in the financial statements should not change from one period to another unless a change is warranted in order to:

◆   reflect a change in circumstances; or
◆   comply with a new accounting standard.

Sometimes, entities change their year-end reporting date. This results in them having to report on either a long or short period. Likewise, when a new entity starts up, the first period of reporting is usually for a long or short period, say between six to 18 months (but not the usual 12 months). Where this is the case, the entity must report the reason for using a long or short period of reporting and, where comparative figures are presented, it should provide a disclosure, warning that the amounts stated will not be fully comparable.

Accounting standards state that prior period comparative information should be provided in the financial statements for all amounts reported, whether the amounts reported are on the face of the financial statements or in the notes and, if comparative figures are amended due to a change in accounting policy, then this must also be disclosed.

Test yourself 3.3

To which component of a complete set of financial statements does the accruals basis of accounting not apply?

The example below is an extract from the 2012 Next Plc consolidated financial statements, prepared under IFRS, which show prior year comparatives:

next plc

Consolidated Statement of Comprehensive Income

For the financial year ending 28 January

	Notes	2012 £m	2011 £m
Profit for the year		**474.8**	400.9
Other comprehensive income and expenses			
Exchange differences on translation of foreign operations		**(2.0)**	–
Gains on cash flow hedges		**15.6**	1.8
Actuarial (losses)/gains on defined benefit pension scheme	23	**(28.5)**	64.3
Tax relating to components of other comprehensive income	8	**4.5**	(15.5)
		(10.4)	50.6
Reclassification adjustments			
Transferred to income statement on cash flow hedges	5	**5.0**	(14.8)
Transferred to the carry amount of hedged items on cash flow hedges		**(5.9)**	4.7
Exchange gains transferred to income statement on disposal of subsidiary		**(0.6)**	–
		(1.5)	(10.1)
Other comprehensive (expense)/income for the year		**(11.9)**	40.5
Total comprehensive income for the year		**462.9**	441.4
Attributable to:			
Equity holders of the parent company		**463.0**	441.5
Non-controlling interest		**(0.1)**	(0.1)
Total comprehensive income for the year		**462.0**	441.4

When comparative amounts are reclassified, the entity is required to disclose:

◆ the nature of the reclassification;
◆ the amount of each item, or class of items, that has been reclassified; and
◆ the reason for the reclassification.

However, where it is impractical to reclassify prior period comparative amounts, IAS 1 says that the entity should disclose:

◆ the reason for not reclassifying the amounts; and
◆ the nature of the adjustments that would have been made if the amounts had been reclassified.

The equivalent standard in UK GAAP, FRS 28 "Corresponding Amounts", is silent on this matter of impracticability.

2.9 Content of financial statements

Each statement comprising a complete set of financial statements should include:

◆ the name of the reporting entity (e.g. XYZ Plc);
◆ whether the statements are for the entity or for the group;
◆ the statement of financial position date or period covered;
◆ the **presentation currency**, as defined in IAS 21 (covered later in this chapter);
◆ the level of rounding used in presenting amounts (e.g. £'000 or £m); and
◆ the level of **aggregation** used in presenting amounts.

presentation currency
is the currency in which the financial statements are presented.

aggregation
is a term used in IAS 1 to describe the grouping of immaterial assets and presenting the total as a single line item on the face of financial statements or in the notes. Aggregation is not permitted for material items or material classes of similar items.

Test yourself 3.4

What is the presentation currency and level of rounding used in the Tesco Plc Group income statement for the year ended 26 February 2011?

(See extract below)

Extract of the Tesco Plc Group results for the year ended 26 February 2011

Financial statements

Group income statement

Year ending 26 February 2011	notes	52 weeks 2011 £m	52 weeks 2010 £m
Continuing operations			
Revenue (sales excluding VAT)	2	60,931	56,910
Cost of sales		(55,871)	(52,303)
Gross profit		5,060	4,607
Administrative expenses		(1,676)	(1,527)
Profit arising on property-related items	3	427	377
Operating profit		3,811	3,457
Share of post-tax profits of joint ventures and associates	13	57	33
Finance income	5	150	265
Finance costs	5	(483)	(579)
Profit before tax	3	3,535	3,176
Taxation	6	(864)	(840)
Profit for the year		2,671	2,336
Attributable to:			
Owners of the parent		2,655	2,327
Non-controlling interests		16	9
		2,671	2,336
Earnings per share			
Basic	9	33.10p	29.33p
Diluted	9	32.94p	29.19p

Earnings per Share (or EPS) is a measure of net income of a company (less dividends paid on preference shares) divided by the number of shares in-issue. It is a frequently used indicator of a company's profitability and is often used by shareholders for comparing a company's financial health with a company with similar earnings.

2.10 Offsetting

non-current assets are assets that are likely to be held for more than 12 months.

IAS 1 states that the offsetting of assets and liabilities, and of income and expenses, is not allowed unless specifically required by an IFRS, for example, to reflect the true substance of a transaction or event. This is because the netting off of assets and liabilities can disguise transactions and therefore reduce the ability of stakeholders to get a true picture of the entity's assets and liabilities and assess its future cash flows.

Stop and think 3.2

Can you think of any circumstances in which it would be appropriate to offset financial assets and financial liabilities?

2.11 Statement of financial position (balance sheet)

The information within an entity's statement of financial position is intended to provide users with an understanding of its financial position as at a certain point in time.

The statement of financial position sets out the assets and liabilities of the reporting entity. Under UK GAAP, assets and liabilities are commonly presented using the following terms.

2.11.1 Assets
Non-current assets

◆ **Tangible non-current assets** (e.g. property, plant and machinery, fixtures and fittings, motor vehicles).

◆ **Intangible non-current assets** (e.g. **goodwill**, patents, trademarks, brand names, copyrights).

◆ Unquoted investments; (e.g. investments in unlisted subsidiary companies).

Current assets

◆ Current assets (e.g. inventory, trade receivables, investments traded on a stock exchange, cash at bank and in hand).

2.11.2 Liabilities
Liabilities due within one year

◆ Falling due in less than one year (e.g. trade payables, bank overdraft facility – provided the facility is not used for long-term financing).

Liabilities due in more than one year

◆ Falling due in more than one year (e.g. bank loans and other financing arrangements).

◆ **Shareholders' funds**.

IAS 1, however, uses slightly different terminology and expressly requires the statement of financial position to separate out non-current assets and liabilities from current assets and liabilities. Alternatively, entities reporting under IFRS may opt for a liquidity-based presentation of the financial position, provided this gives reliable and more relevant information than a current/non-current split between the assets and liabilities. Any such statement should present assets and liabilities in order of liquidity in a similar manner to the example below. Students should note, however, that this is not a common method of producing accounts.

tangible non-current assets
means assets which are capable of being physically touched (e.g. property; plant and machinery, fixtures and fittings, motor vehicles).

intangible non-current assets
are assets that you cannot touch or see and have no physical substance. Examples include goodwill, patents, copyrights, licenses, marketing rights, customer lists and customer relations.

goodwill
is a term used to refer to the value of an intangible asset such a brand or the value of the workforce, a client list, the value of having good customer relations and so on. Goodwill often arises when a company makes an acquisition insomuch as the purchase price reflects the book value plus a premium (which is the goodwill) for the company name, client list and other intangible attributes.

current assets
are assets that are readily realisable and likely to be held for less than 12 months (e.g. inventory, trade receivables, investments traded on a stock exchange, cash at bank and in hand).

liabilities due within one year
are those liabilities falling due in less than one year such as trade payables or bank overdrafts.

liabilities due in more than one year
are those liabilities falling due in more than one year such as bank loans and other financing arrangements.

Liquidity-based "consolidated statement of financial position" of HSBC Holdings plc as at 31 December 2011

Consolidated balance sheet at 31 December 2011

	Notes	2011 US$m	2010 US$m
Assets			
Cash and balance at central banks		129,902	57,383
Items in the course of collection from other banks		8,208	6,072
Hong Kong Government certificates of indebtedness		20,922	19,057
Trading assets	15	330,451	385,052
Financial assets designated at fair value	19	30,856	37,011
Derivatives	20	346,379	260,757
Loans and advances to banks		180,987	208,271
Loans and advances to customers		940,429	958,366
Financial investments	21	400,044	400,755
Assets held for sale	27	39,558	1,991
Other assets	27	48,699	41,260
Currents tax assets		1,061	1,096
Prepayments and accurued income		10,059	11,966
Intrests in associates and joint ventures	23	20,399	17,198
Goodwill and intangible assets	24	29,034	29,922
Property, plant and equipment	25	10,865	11,521
Deferred tax assets	10	7,726	7,011
Total assets		2,555,579	2,454,689
Liabilities and equity			
Liabilities			
Hong Kong currency notes in circulation		20,922	19,057
Deposits by banks		112,822	110,584
Customer accounts		1,253,925	1,227,725
Items in the course of transmission to other banks		8,745	6,663
Trading liabilities	28	265,192	300,703
Financial liabilities designated at fair value	29	85,724	88,133
Derivatives	20	345,380	258,665
Debt securities in issue	30	131,013	145,401
Liabilities of disposal groups held for sale	31	22,200	86
Other liabilities	31	27,967	27,964
Current tax liabilities		2,117	1,804
Liabilities under insurance contracts	32	61,259	58,609
Accruals and deferred income		13,106	13,906
Provisions	33	3,324	2,138
Deferred tax liabilities	10	1,518	1,093
Retirement benefit liabilities	7	3,666	3,856
Subordinated liabilities	34	30,606	33,387
Total liabilities		2,389,487	2,299,774

Equity			
Called up share capital	39	8,934	8,843
Share premium account		8,457	8,454
Other equity instruments		5,851	5,851
Other reserves		23,615	25,414
Retained earning		111,868	99,105
Total shareholders' equity		158,725	147,667
Non-controlling interests	38	7,368	7,248
Total equity		166,093	154,915
Total equity and liabilities		2,555,579	2,454,689

IAS 1 defines current assets as:

◆ cash and cash equivalents (as defined in IAS 7);

◆ assets held for collection, sale, or consumption within the entity's normal **operating cycle**;

◆ assets held primarily for the trading purposes; or

◆ assets that are realisable within 12 months of the reporting period.

All other assets should be classified as non-current (i.e. tangible and intangible long-term assets).

As noted above, current assets are commonly referred to in the statement of financial position under UK GAAP as cash at bank and in hand, trade receivables, inventory, etc. IAS 1 uses different terminology but does not prohibit the use of alternative descriptions in the financial statements provided the meaning is clear. For an example of this, see below:

shareholders' funds are all the assets of a company less all the liabilities. It is the equity amount in a company that is due to the owners (the shareholders).

operating cycle is the period of time from the acquisition of assets (materials or services) to their realisation in cash receipts. For a retailer this is the length of time inventory is held before receiving proceeds from its sale.

Consolidated Balance Sheet

next plc

As at 28 January

	Notes	2012 £m	2011 £m
Assets and liabilities			
Non-current assets			
Propertu, plant & equipment	11	581.9	592.4
Intangible assets	12	45.6	46.5
Interests in associates	13	6.1	5.1
Other investments	14	1.0	1.0
Defined benefit pension surplus	23	35.1	55.7
Other financial assets	17	44.6	24.3
		714.3	725.0
Current assets			
Inventories	15	371.9	368.3
Trade and other receivables	16	699.1	645.6
Other financial assets	17	12.5	4.1
Cash and short term deposits	18	56.4	49.3
		1,139.9	1,067.3

Current liabilities, per IAS 1, are those liabilities:

- ◆ expected to be settled within the entity's normal operating cycle;
- ◆ falling due within 12 months;
- ◆ held primarily for trading purposes; or
- ◆ which the entity has no unconditional right to defer payment beyond 12 months.

All other liabilities are non-current including long-term debt under an existing loan facility which is due to expire within 12 months of the year end. It is presumed that the loan will be refinanced and therefore remains a long-term obligation in the entity's books. However, if the entity breaches a **loan covenant**, resulting in the loan becoming repayable on demand on or prior to the statement of financial position date, the liability is treated as a current liability. This is still the case where the lender has agreed, after the statement of financial position date (i.e. the date of the statement of financial position) date but before the accounts sign-off, not to demand payment as a consequence of the breach. The liability is only classified as non-current if the lender agreed, on or before the statement of financial position date, to provide a period of grace lasting 12 months or more from the end of the reporting period, during which the entity may remedy the breach and within which the lender is unable to enforce repayment of the loan.

The extract below from the Next Plc consolidated statement of financial position shows the typical line items that appear under the headings "Current liabilities" and "Non-current liabilities".

loan covenant
is a restrictive measure placed on the borrower by the lender as a means of safeguarding the loan. Measures might include restricting the level of gearing of the borrower by insisting more equity is put into the company. If a company breaches its loan covenant then it may be forced to repay the loan or find an alternative lender who is likely to insist on a high rate of return on the loan to reflect the high level of gearing.

Current liabilities			
Bank loans and overdrafts	19	**(7.6)**	(125.2)
Bank loans and overdrafts	20	**(545.0)**	(544.6)
Other financial liabilities	21	(87.0)	(54.7)
Current tax liabilities		**(102.8)**	(108.4)
		(742.4)	(832.9)
Non-current liabilities			
Corporate bonds	22	**(652.1)**	(471.2)
Provisions	24	**(12.0)**	(13.3)
Deferred tax liabilities	8	**(15.4)**	(23.4)
Other financial liabilities	21	**(4.4)**	(2.6)
Other liabilities	25	**(205.2)**	(216.5)
		(889.1)	(727.0)
Total liabilities		**(1,631.5)**	(1,559.9)

The following items are presented on the face of the statement of financial position:

(a) property, plant and equipment;

(b) investment property;

(c) intangible assets;

(d) financial assets (excluding amounts shown under (e), (h) and (i));

(e) investments accounted for using the equity method;

(f) **biological assets**;

(g) inventories;

(h) trade and other receivables;

(i) cash and cash equivalents;

(j) assets held for sale;

(k) trade and other payables;

(l) provisions;

(m) financial liabilities (excluding amounts shown under (k) and (l));

(n) liabilities and assets for current tax, as defined in IAS 12 "Income Taxes";

(o) deferred tax liabilities and deferred tax assets, as defined in IAS 12;

(p) liabilities included in disposal groups;

(q) non-controlling interest, presented within equity; and

(r) issued capital and reserves attributable to owners of the parent.

biological assets
are living animals
and plants (IAS 41
"Agriculture").

Additional items may be presented, where relevant to the understanding of the financial position.

Below is the consolidated statement of financial position of Next Plc as at 28 January 2012 showing the relevant line items that one would expect to see presented on the face of the statement:

---

next plc

Consolidated Balance Sheet

As at 28 January

	Notes	2012 £m	2011 £m
ASSETS AND LIABILITIES			
Non-current assets			
Propertu, plant & equipment	11	**581.9**	592.4
Intangible assets	12	**45.6**	46.5
Interests in associates	13	**6.1**	5.1
Other investments	14	**1.0**	1.0
Defined benefit pension surplus	23	**35.1**	55.7
Other financial assets	17	**44.6**	24.3
		714.3	725.0

Current assets			
Inventories	15	**371.9**	368.3
Trade and other receivables	16	**699.1**	645.6
Other financial assets	17	**12.5**	4.1
Cash and short term deposits	18	**56.4**	49.3
		1,139.9	1,067.3
Total assets		**1,854.2**	1,792.3
Current liabilities			
Bank loans and overdrafts	19	**(7.6)**	(125.2)
Trade and other payables	20	**(545.0)**	(544.6)
Other financial liabilities	21	**(87.0)**	(54.7)
Current tax liabilities		**(102.8)**	(108.4)
		(742.4)	(832.9)
Non-current liabilities			
Corporate bonds	22	**(652.1)**	(471.2)
Provisions	24	**(12.0)**	(13.3)
Deferred tax liabilities	8	**(15.4)**	(23.4)
Other financial liabilities	21	**(4.4)**	(2.6)
Other liabilities	25	**(205.2)**	(216.5)
		(889.1)	(727.0)
Total liabilites		**(1,631.5)**	(1,559.9)
Net assets		**222.7**	232.4
EQUITY			
Share capital	26	**16.9**	18.1
Share premium account		**0.8**	0.8
Capital redemption reserve		**13.0**	11.8
ESOT reserve		**(141.1)**	(138.6)
Fair value reserve		**11.5**	(3.2)
Foreign currency translation reserve		**2.0**	4.6
Other reserves	27	**(1,443.8)**	(1,443.8)
Retained earnings		**1,763.4**	1,782.6
Shareholders' equity		**222.7**	232.3
Non-controlling interest		**–**	0.1
Total equity		**222.7**	232.4

Approved by the Board on 22 March 2012

Lord Wolfson of Aspley Gate   David Keens
Director   Director

A company's changes in equity should be presented in either the statement of financial position, the statement of changes in equity or in the notes. For each class of share capital, the following information should be provided:

◆   Number of shares authorised for issue.
◆   Number of shares issued and fully paid.

◆ Number of shares issued but not fully paid.

◆ Par value per share.

◆ Reconciliation of the number of shares outstanding at the start and end of the period.

◆ Description of any rights, preferences or restrictions attached to the share class.

◆ Details of **treasury shares** and its subsidiaries and associates.

◆ Shares held for issue under options and other contracts.

The financial statements should also disclose the nature and purpose of each category of reserve classified as equity.

Financial statements relating to limited partnerships and unit trusts, prepared under IFRS, should present the equivalent information as set out in the above bullet points.

2.12 Statement of comprehensive income (income statement)

The statement of comprehensive income includes all items of income and expenditure resulting in the profit or loss for the period. Other income is included in the "other comprehensive income" figure. Such items include:

◆ changes in revaluation surplus;

◆ actuarial gains and losses on defined benefit plans;

◆ gains and losses arsing from the translation of the financial statements of a foreign operation (IAS 21 "The Effects of Changes in Foreign Exchange Rates" – covered in more detail later in this chapter);

◆ gains and losses on re-measurement of **available-for-sale financial assets**; and

◆ gains and losses on **hedging** instruments in a **cash flow hedge** (IAS 39 "Financial Instruments: Recognition and Measurement" – also covered later in this chapter).

IAS 1 allows an entity to present either:

◆ a single statement of comprehensive income; or

◆ two statements:

   (i) an *income statement* showing the components of profit or loss; and

   (ii) a *statement of comprehensive income* that has the profit or loss figure from the bottom line of the income statement as the first line item and shows components of other comprehensive income underneath.

Below is a copy of the 2012 income statement (consolidated) and statement of comprehensive income (consolidated) of Next Plc. This is an example of the two-statement style of income presentation. Students will see that the profit figure of £474.8m from the bottom line of the income statement is used as the first line item of the comprehensive income statement.

treasury shares
are shares in a company held in the company's own name.

available-for-sale financial assets (AFS)
are all non-derivative financial assets designated on initial recognition as available for sale or any other instruments that do not fall into the following categories: (i) loans and receivables; (ii) held-to-maturity investments; or (iii) financial assets at fair value through profit or loss (IAS 39 Financial Instruments: Recognition and Measurement). Examples of AFS financial assets are debt instruments and certain types of listed and unlisted equity instruments.

hedging
is a risk management strategy in which an investment is undertaken to offset a position and reduce exposure to price, currency or other fluctuations, e.g. a forward contract is used to hedge against changes in foreign currency exchange rates.

cash flow hedge
is a hedge of the exposure to variability in cash flows that is (i) attributable to a particular risk associated with a recognised asset or liability (such as all or some future interest payments on variable rate debt) or a highly probable forecast transaction and (ii) could affect profit or loss.

Consolidated Income Statement

For the financial year ended 28 January

next plc

	Notes	2012 Underlying £m	Exceptional Items (Note 1) £m	Total £m	2011 Total £m
Continuing operations					
Revenue	3, 4	**3,441.1**	–	**3,441.1**	3,297.7
Cost of sales		**(2,395.8)**	–	**(2,395.8)**	(2,332.6)
Gross profit		**1,045.3**	–	**9,045.3**	965.1
Distribution		**(245.7)**	–	**(245.7)**	(223.2)
Administration expenses		**(201.3)**	–	**(201.3)**	(179.1)
Other (losses)/gains	5	**(1.1)**	3.1	**2.0**	2.2
Trading profit		**597.2**	3.1	**600.3**	565.0
Share of results	13	**1.5**	–	**1.5**	1.8
Operating profit	5	**598.7**	3.1	**601.8**	566.8
Finance income	7	**0.5**	6.1	**6.6**	0.9
Finance costs	7	**(28.9)**	–	**(28.9)**	(24.3)
Profit before taxation		**570.3**	9.2	**579.5**	543.4
Taxation	8	**(142.9)**	(2.4)	**(145.3)**	(150.3)
Profit from continuing operations		**427.4**	6.8	**434.2**	393.1
Profit from discontinued operations	2	**2.6**	38.0	**40.6**	7.8
Profit for the year		**430**	4.8	**474.8**	400.9
Profit for the year attributable to:					
Equity holders of the parent company		**430.1**	44.8	**474.9**	401.1
Non-controlling interest		**(0.1)**	–	**(0.1)**	(0.2)
Profit for the year		**430.0**	44.8	**474.8**	400.9

		Underlying		Total	Total
Basic earnings per share	10				
Continuing operations		**253.9p**		**257.9p**	217.6p
Discontinued operations		**1.5p**		**24.1p**	4.3p
Total		**255.4p**		**282.0p**	221.9p
Diluted earnings per share	10				
Continuing operations		**247.6p**		**251.6p**	212.3p
Discontinued operations		**1.5p**		**23.5p**	4.2p
Total		**249.1p**		**275.1p**	216.5p

Consolidated Statement of Comprehensive Income   next plc

For the financial year ended 28 January

	Notes	2012 £m	2011 £m
Profit for the year		**474.8**	400.9
Other comprehensive income and expenses			
Exchange differences on translation of foreign operations		**(2.0)**	–
Gains on cash flow hedges		**15.6**	1.8
Actuarial (losses)/gains on defined benefit pension scheme	23	**(28.5)**	64.3
Tax relating to components of other comprehensive income	8	**4.5**	(15.5)
		(10.4)	50.6
Reclassification adjustments			
Transferred to income statement on cash flow hedges	5	**5.0**	(14.8)
Transferred to the carrying amount of hedged items on cash flow hedges		**(5.9)**	4.7
Exchange gains transferred to income statement on disposal of subsidiary		**(0.6)**	–
		(1.5)	40.5
Other comprehensive (expense)/income for the year		**(11.9)**	40.5
Total comprehensive income for the year		**462.9**	441.4
Attributable to:			
Equity holders of the parent company		**463.0**	441.5
Non-controlling interest		**(0.1)**	(0.1)
Total comprehensive income for the year		**462.9**	441.4

The statements of income and comprehensive income comprise the following items:

(a) revenue;

(b) expenses;

(c) finance costs;

(d) share of the results of associates and joint ventures accounted for under the equity method;

(e) taxation;

(f) post tax profit or loss from continuing operations;

(g) post tax profit or loss from discontinued operations;

(h) profit or loss for the period;

(i) each component of other comprehensive income classified by nature (excluding amounts in (h));

(j) share of the other comprehensive income of associates and joint ventures accounted for using the equity method; and

(k) total comprehensive income.

The following items must be disclosed as allocations for the period:

◆ profit or loss for the period attributable to equity holders of the parent company;

◆ profit or loss for the period attributable to non-controlling interests;

◆ total comprehensive income attributable to the equity holders of the parent company; and

◆ total comprehensive income attributable to non-controlling interests.

In order to give a fair presentation of results, entities may present additional items in the statements provided these separate items are not extraordinary items. This is because the classification of extraordinary items is not permitted under IFRS and neither are they allowed under UK GAAP. Unusual items (referred to as "exceptional items" in FRS 3 "Reporting Financial Performance") may be presented on the face of the income statement.

With regard to material items, these should be separately disclosed, for example material amounts arising as a result of:

◆ write-downs of inventories to net realisable value or of property, plant and equipment to recoverable amount, as well as reversals of such write-downs;

◆ restructurings of the activities of an entity and reversals of any provisions for the costs of restructuring;

◆ disposals of items of property, plant and equipment;

◆ disposals of investments;

◆ discontinued operations;

◆ litigation settlements; or

◆ other reversals of provisions.

2.13 Statement of cash flows

The preparation and presentation of cash flow statements is governed by IAS 7 and is covered in Chapter 7.

2.14 Statement of changes in equity

The statement of changes in equity provides a snapshot of the composition of equity and how this has changed during the period. Typical components of the statement are:

◆ share capital;

◆ share premium;

◆ hedging reserve;

◆ fair value reserve;

◆ other reserves; and

◆ retained earnings.

Per IAS 1, the statement is required to display:

◆ total comprehensive income for the period, showing separately amounts attributable to the equity holders of the parent and to non-controlling interests;

◆ the effects of retrospective application; and

◆ reconciliations of the carrying amounts at the start and end of the period for each component of equity.

The following amounts may also be presented in the statement of changes in equity, or in the notes:

◆ amount of dividends recognised as distributions; and

◆ the related amount per share.

The 2012 Next plc company statement of changes in equity below gives an example of the key information available to users such as equity movement and dividends paid during the year.

Company Statement of Changes in Equity
For the financial year ended 28 January

	Share capital £m	Share premium account £m	Capital redemtion reserve £m	ESOT reserve £m	Value reserve £m	Other reserve £m	Retained earnings £m	Total equity £m
At January 2010	19.1	0.7	10.8	(78.2)	(2.6)	985.2	1,088.8	**2,023.8**
Profit for the year	–	–	–	–	–	–	–	**183.6**
Other comprehensive income/(expense) for the year	–	–	–	–	2.6	–	(0.8)	**1.8**
Total comprehensive income for the year	–	–	–	–	2.6	–	182.8	**185.4**
Shares issued	–	0.1	–	–	–	–	–	**0.1**
Shares purchased for cancellation	(1.0)	–	1.0	–	–	–	(165.3)	**(165.3)**
Shares purchased by ESOT	–	–	–	(95.9)	–	–	–	**(95.9)**
Shares issued by ESOT	–	–	–	35.5	–	–	(4.5)	**31.0**
Share option charge	–	–	–	–	–	–	11.8	**11.8**
Equity dividends paid	–	–	–	–	–	–	(129.6)	**(129.6)**
At January 2011	18.1	0.8	11.8	(138.6)	–	985.2	984.0	**1,861.3**
Profit for the year	–	–	–	–	–	–	179.1	**179.1**
Other comprehensive income for the year	–	–	–	–	–	–	–	**–**
Total comprehensive income for the year	–	–	–	–	–	–	179.1	**179.1**
Shares purchased for cancellation	(1.2)	–	1.2	–	–	–	(323.0)	**(323.0)**
Shares purchased by ESOT	–	–	–	(112.3)	–	–	–	**(112.3)**
Shares issued by ESOT	–	–	–	109.8	–	–	(42.2)	**67.6**
Share option charge	–	–	–	–	–	–	17.9	**17.9**
Equity dividends paid	–	–	–	–	–	–	(135.1)	**(135.1)**
At January 2012	16.9	0.8	13.0	(141.1)	–	985.2	680.7	**1,555.5**

The requirements of IFRS and UK GAAP have become increasingly more aligned in recent years, thanks largely to the progress made in respect of the global convergence of accounting standards. A set of financial statements is broadly the same under UK GAAP as it is under IFRS and the statement of changes in equity provides the same information as that provided under UK GAAP in the Statement of Total Recognised Gains and Losses (STRGL) (FRS 3). However, whilst the information presented in the statement of changes in equity is the largely the same, the statement is still different in that it shows the movement for each component of equity on the face of the statement under IAS 1. Entities reporting under UK GAAP tend to show the movements on components of equity in the notes.

2.15 Notes to the financial statements

The disclosure notes provide more detailed information in respect of items presented in the financial statements, such as a break-down of figures and supporting narrative. The notes also provide information on items that are not present on the face of the main statements. Under IAS 1, the main statements comprise the statement of financial position, the income statement, the statement of changes in equity and the statement of cash flows.

The kind of detailed and additional information that is required to be presented in the notes under IAS 1 includes, *inter alia:*

◆   confirmation of the basis of preparation of the financial statements and compliance with accounting standards, stating the standards applied, e.g. IFRS, UK GAAP or US GAAP;

◆   accounting policies adopted, judgements made and measurement basis applied;

◆   information required by other standards that is not presented on the face of the main statements;

◆   information that is not presented elsewhere in the financial statements, but is relevant and helps users understand them;

◆   disclosures in connection with contingent liabilities (see Chapter 5) and unrecognised contractual commitments;

◆   disclosures in respect of dividends, confirming:
    (a) dividends proposed or declared before the financial statements were authorised for issue but not recognised as a distribution to shareholders during the period, and the related amount per share; and
    (b) the amount of any cumulative preference dividends not recognised; and

◆   information that enables users of financial statements to evaluate the entity's objectives, policies and processes for managing capital and risk, including a confirmation of whether capital requirements are met.

If not cited elsewhere in the financial statements, e.g. in the opening pages of the annual report and accounts, the reporting entity should also include the following information about itself in the disclosure notes:

◆ domicile and legal form;

◆ country of incorporation/establishment;

◆ registered office address/principal place of business;

◆ description of principal activities; and

◆ if part of a group, the name of its parent and the ultimate parent of the group.

Students should be aware that the notes should always be cross-referenced to the relevant item in the financial statements.

Stop and think 3.3

A reporting entity's management may make various judgements when applying accounting policies to ensure the substance of a transaction, circumstance or event is properly reflected in the entity's financial statements. These judgements, which must be explained in the disclosure notes, may have a significant bearing on the amounts recognised in the financial statements. What kinds of judgements might be made by management when applying accounting policies?

3. Reporting the substance of transactions

Financial Reporting Standard (FRS) 5 "Reporting the Substance of Transactions" is a key accounting standard under UK GAAP, which requires entities to report the **commercial substance** of a transaction even if this differs from the exact legal form of the transaction. The standard sets out how to determine the substance of a transaction and whether assets and liabilities should be included in the statement of financial position. The standard also discusses appropriate disclosure requirements and how transactions should be reported in the other primary financial statements, namely the income statement and cash flow statement.

commercial substance
is concerned with economic rights and control rather than the exact legal form of a transaction.

The principal of substance over legal form has general application and applies to all transactions and arrangements that individually or collectively have a commercial effect. This means that any gains, losses, assets or liabilities arising from a series of interconnected transactions should be shown irrespective of their legal form. There are a few exceptions such as certain financial instruments (covered under FRS 26/ IAS 39) employment contracts, contracts for differences and insurance related transactions but for most transactions the principle of commercial substance over legal form must be complied with if an entity's accounts are to show a "true and fair view" under UK GAAP.

By ensuring that the commercial effect of a transaction takes precedence over legal form, FRS 5 effectively deals with "off statement of financial position financing", whereby entities use creative accounting practices to keep liabilities and financing arrangements off the statement of financial position in order to show the financial position in a more favourable light.

One of the principal objectives of FRS 5 is to ensure that whenever a single transaction or arrangement that covers a series of transactions results in an entity borrowing funds, then that borrowing should be reflected in the statement of financial position as a liability even if the financing arrangement has been structured so that there is no actual legal liability.

Assets and liabilities (refer to definitions in the previous chapter) should be recognised in an entity's statement of financial position if:

◆ there is satisfactory evidence that the asset or liability exists; and

◆ the monetary amount can be reliably measured.

An important factor in determining the economic substance of a transaction, is whether an entity assumes the risk and rewards associated with the transaction. If it is exposed to the risks and has access to the benefits relating to the assets or liabilities then the entity should recognise the relevant items in the statement of financial position. The difficulty is identifying the true commercial effect of a transaction and FRS 5 provides practical application notes in this respect by setting out the requirements of transactions that have specific features, namely:

◆ consignment inventory;

◆ sale and repurchase agreements;

◆ debt factoring;

◆ securitisation of assets;

◆ loan transfers;

◆ private finance initiative and similar contracts; and

◆ revenue recognition (see Chapter 2).

3.1 Consignment inventory

consignment inventory
is inventory that is delivered from the supplier to another party (e.g. the retailer) who assumes responsibility for selling the goods but is not required to pay the supplier until goods are sold.

Consignment inventory is the term given to inventory which is in possession of a party, e.g. a customer, who is not the legal owner. The inventory has not been sold but it also no longer forms part of the legal owner's inventory. In such circumstances, the risks and rewards of ownership effectively pass on to the other party. Consider, for example, a bicycle manufacturer delivering inventory to a bicycle retailer. The ownership remains with the manufacturer until the inventory is sold on by the retailer. This means that the retailer has no legal ownership of the bicycles upon receipt of the goods. However, the commercial substance is that risks and rewards of ownership have effectively been transferred from the manufacturer to the retailer in anticipation of onward sale of the assets. Pursuant to FRS 5, the retailer should recognise the asset(s) and record a corresponding liability to the manufacturer, as legal owner of the inventory. The retailer only purchases the inventory upon resale or consumption.

Consignment inventory arrangements are also common in the motor industry.

3.2 Sale and repurchase agreements

Companies sometimes enter into sale and leaseback arrangements, whereby the company sells assets to raise short-term finance and rents them back. The leaseback terms often provide for the seller to repurchase the assets after a period of time.

If the commercial substance of the transaction is (i) a genuine arm's length sale; and (ii) the leaseback results in an operating lease then the transaction is treated as a sale.

If the substance of the transaction is effectively a secured loan resulting in a finance lease then it should be accounted for as a secured loan because the risks and rewards of ownership remain with the seller.

3.3 Debt factoring

Debt factoring is where a number of debts are sold to a finance company (at a fixed percentage in order to help the business improve its cash flow) and replaced with one receivable, the factor (i.e. the finance company). Usually no more than 90% of the overall value of the debts is paid up front by the factor. Factoring may be one of two types, either recourse or non-recourse factoring. Recourse factoring means that if the debt is not recovered, the factoring company may recover the funds advanced to the business which sold the debt to it in the first place. This effectively means that whilst the debt has been sold, the seller has retained the risks and rewards of ownership and the debts must continue to be recognised in the books of the seller. With non-recourse debt factoring, if the factoring company fails to recover the debt, then it suffers the loss as there is no recourse to the seller of the debt. The seller has transferred the risks and rewards of ownership and so the debts no longer appear in its books.

debt factoring
is where a number of debts are sold to a finance company (at a fixed percentage in order to help the business improve its cash flow) and replaced with one receivable, the factor (i.e. the finance company).

3.4 Securitisation of assets

Securitisation is a method of raising finance by creating and issuing asset-backed securities, such as mortgage bonds. It is the income generated by the asset (e.g. the mortgage repayments) which acts as security. The assets are pooled, divided into smaller tiers according to their risk of default and sold to investors in affordable packages. Securitisation financing is common in jurisdictions which have a sophisticated finance industry.

securitisation
is a method of raising finance by creating and issuing asset-backed securities, such as mortgage bonds.

International Finance Centres, for example, use special purpose vehicles (legal entities formed for a specific purpose) to act as trustee for mortgage loan receivables, trusts and for other securitisations to collect receivables such as credit card balances and football match ticket sales.

The accounting treatment for the securitisation of assets is set out in FRS 5 under UK GAAP and in IAS 39 "Financial Instruments: Recognition and Measurement" under IFRS. Broadly speaking, derecognition of balance sheet items, that is to say the removal of assets or liabilities from the balance sheet, items depends on a number of items. These include transferring rights to cash flows from the asset, transferring the risks and rewards of ownership and relinquishing control

linked presentation is a provision under FRS 5 in UK GAAP which allows the finance amount of a securitisation transaction to be deducted from the gross amount of the asset it finances. The items are linked and the net figure is recognised on the face of the balance sheet. There is no concept of linked presentation under IFRS.

of the asset. With these types of non-recourse financing arrangements, **linked presentation** may be required in the financial statements if reporting under UK GAAP. Derecognition is not easily achieved because the risks and rewards of ownership cannot always be fully transferred.

3.5 Loan transfers

This is where a borrower transfers part of all of a loan to a third party. The commercial substance of the transaction depends on whether the risks and rewards of ownership of the loans have been transferred.

3.6 Private finance initiative and similar contracts

The private finance initiative was developed with the objective of giving the public sector a value for money service. Under a private finance initiative, a private sector business provides a service to the public sector. A typical private finance initiative contract might be for the provision of a property, such as a university or a hospital, and may include the provision of additional ancillary services in relation to the property such facilities management services which might include the provision of security, catering and cleaning services. Under FRS 5, the accounting treatment depends on the substance of the transaction, i.e. whether the risks and rewards in respect of the property remain with the public sector or are transferred to the private sector service provider.

3.7 Revenue recognition

Revenue recognition and measurement is covered in Chapter 2 of this Study Text (FRS 5 and IAS 18).

Making it work 3.1

Jersey law firm, Mourant du Feu & Jeune, acted as Jersey legal adviser on a securitisation transaction involving Permanent Financing (No.1) Plc, a deal which involved a £3.5 billion asset backed note issue. The transaction was named European Deal of the Year 2002 by International Securitisation Report, a leading securitisation industry journal. It concerned the securitisation of residential mortgage loans of up to £12 billion originated by Halifax plc, using a trust structure with a Jersey special purpose vehicle acting as trustee of the mortgage loans receivables trust. At the time, the transaction was the largest cross-border securitisation of residential mortgages launched anywhere.

Test yourself 3.5

Explain the main objectives of FRS 5.

Test yourself 3.6

What is the difference between recourse and non-recourse debt factoring?

4. Financial instruments

Financial instruments have traditionally been dealt with in the UK under FRS 26. More recently, IAS 39 "Financial Instruments: Recognition and Measurement" has been the main standard governing financial instruments. Its stated objective is to establish principles for recognising and measuring financial assets, financial liabilities and some contracts to buy or sell non-financial items. Other standards covering financial instruments include IAS 32 "Financial Instruments: Presentation" and IFRS 7 "Financial Instruments: Disclosures".

Financial instruments are effectively agreements, in respect of assets and loans, to which a monetary value can be applied. Financial instruments have their own unique characteristics and features and represent either debt or equity or a combination of both packaged as a tradable product. Financial instruments include:

◆ An entity's debt and its investments in debt.

◆ An entity's equity and its investments in equity.

◆ **Derivatives**.

◆ Loans and receivables.

◆ Cash and cash equivalents.

4.1 Derivatives

A derivative is a financial instrument that derives its value from something else such as an underlying asset or assets, for example an interest rate, commodity price or index. Derivative contracts are, typically, settled at a future date and are entered into at no, or minimal, initial investment. Examples of derivatives contracts include **hedging** instruments such as interest rate swaps, currency swaps, futures contracts (such as a commodity contract), forward contracts, options, caps, floors and collars.

A **swap** is where two parties agree at a specified date, or series of specified dates, to exchange cash flows (such as liabilities on outstanding debts). For example, one party swaps his fixed interest rate payments in exchange for the counterparty's floating (or variable) rate interest payments.

A **futures contract** is an agreement that obliges the holder to purchase or sell a specified amount of a financial product (e.g. commodity) at a specified price at a specified date in the future. Futures contracts are exchange traded products and are usually settled in cash. Sometimes, however, physical delivery of the product may be required.

derivative
is a financial instrument that derives its value from something else such as an underlying asset or assets, for example an interest rate, commodity price or index. Derivative contracts are, typically, settled at a future date and are entered into at no, or minimal, initial investment. Examples of derivatives contracts include interest rate swaps, currency swaps, futures contracts, forward contracts, options, collars, caps, floors and commodity contracts.

hedging
is a risk management strategy in which an investment is undertaken to offset a position and reduce exposure to price, currency or other fluctuations, e.g. a forward contract is used to hedge against changes in foreign currency exchange rates.

swap
is where two parties agree at a specified date, or series of specified dates, to exchange cash flows (such as liabilities on outstanding debts). For example, one party swaps his fixed interest rate payments in exchange for the counterparty's floating (or variable) rate interest payments.

futures contract
is a contract that obliges the holder to purchase or sell a specified amount of a financial product (e.g. commodity) at a specified price at a specified date in the future. Futures are typically exchange traded contracts.

forward contract
is an agreement that obliges the holder to purchase or sell a specified amount of a financial product (e.g. commodity) or foreign currency at a specified price at a specified date in the future. Unlike futures contracts, forwards are usually tailor-made contracts rather than exchange traded contracts.

A **forward contract** is an agreement that obliges the holder to purchase or sell a specified amount of a financial product (e.g. commodity) or foreign currency at a specified price at a specified date in the future. Unlike futures contracts, forwards are usually tailor-made contracts rather than exchange traded contracts. A forward effectively locks into the price at which an entity can purchase or sell at a specified date in the future and is therefore used by entities to hedge against adverse movement in price or foreign currency fluctuations.

An **option** is a contract that gives the option holder the right, but not the obligation, to buy or sell a set amount of a financial product at a set price (the strike price), during a set period of time. An option to buy is called a call option and an option to sell is called a put option. The option holder pays a premium to purchase the option from the option writer and would only exercise the option if the strike price is more favourable than the prevailing market price.

option
is contract that gives the option holder the right, but not the obligation, to buy (call option) or sell (put option) a specified amount of a financial product at a specified price (the strike price), during a specified period of time.

Making it work 3.2

Share options often form a part of executive remuneration and are intended to incentivise directors to maximise shareholder wealth. Directors may be awarded options to purchase a specified amount of their company's shares at a specified price during a specified period of time in the future. Michael Johnson, the Herbalife CEO, for example, earned US$77m by exercising his Herbalife share options in 2011. Most of the share options were awarded to him from 2003 to 2005 when Herbalife's shares were trading at under US$10 per share and 1.8m of them were exercised in 2011 when the price was around US$50 per share. Having purchased the shares at significantly less than market value, Johnson was able to resell the majority of the shares immediately for a gain of over US$40 per share.

Worked example 3.1: Accounting for an option

A company whose financial year end is 31 December 2011 buys a call option in June 2011 at a price of £0.50 per share. The option gives the company the right, but not the obligation, to purchase 200,000 shares issued in another company at a strike price of £5 per share between 1 May 2012 and 31 July 2012. At 31 December 2011, the option value is £2.

Upon purchasing the call option in June 2011, the company makes the following accounting entry in its books:

DR Call option £100,000 [200,000 shares at £0.50 per share]

CR Cash/bank £100,000

At the financial year end, it is necessary to recognise the *increase* in fair value of the options:

DR Call option £300,000 [200,000 shares x £2 = £400,000. £400,000 less £100,000 = £300,000]

CR income statement £300,000

On 10 May 2012, the company exercises the option to purchase the shares at the predetermined strike price when the market value is £7 per share. The option value remains unchanged from the 31 December 2011 value of £2.

The following accounting entries are required in order to recognise the fair value of the investment pursuant to IAS 39, to recognise the amount paid by the company and to derecognise the options:

DR Investment £1,400,000

CR Cash £1,000,000

CR Call option £400,000

An **interest rate cap** is an option contract which gives the holder (or purchaser) of the cap an upper predetermined limit (strike rate) on a floating exchange rate. The holder of the cap pays an option fee to the cap writer (or seller) and in return has the certainty that the applicable interest rate cannot go above the predetermined strike limit.

An **interest rate floor** is an option contract which gives the holder (or purchaser) of the floor a lower predetermined limit (strike rate) on a floating exchange rate. The holder of the floor pays an option fee to the floor writer (or seller) and in return has the certainty that the applicable interest rate cannot go below the predetermined strike limit.

An **interest rate collar** is a hedging instrument that sets the range of both upper and lower interest rate movements. To hedge against interest rate fluctuations, an entity simultaneously purchases an interest rate cap and sells an interest rate floor. The collar determines the range of interest rates which the holder is exposed to. The cap element of a collar can be used to protect against increases in floating rates of interest but the floor element limits the benefits if there is a fall in the floating rate.

interest rate cap
is an option contract which gives the holder of the cap an upper predetermined limit (strike rate) on a floating exchange rate. The holder of the cap pays an option fee to the cap writer and in return has the certainty that the applicable interest rate cannot go above the predetermined strike limit.

interest rate floor
is an option contract which gives the holder of the floor a lower predetermined limit (strike rate) on a floating exchange rate. The holder of the floor pays an option fee to the floor writer and in return has the certainty that the applicable interest rate cannot go below the predetermined strike limit.

interest rate collar
is a hedging instrument that sets the range of both upper and lower interest rate movements. To hedge against interest rate fluctuations, an entity simultaneously purchases an interest rate cap and sells an interest rate floor. The collar determines the range of interest rates which the holder is exposed to. The cap element of a collar can be used to protect against increases in floating rates of interest but the floor element limits the benefits if there is a fall in the floating rate.

Test yourself 3.7

What are the differences between futures and forwards?

Test yourself 3.8

Explain what is meant by a cap and a floor.

Stop and think 3.4

Why would an entity favour an interest rate collar over an interest rate cap?

4.2 Recognition of a financial asset or financial liability

IAS 39 states that financial assets or liabilities should be recognised at **fair value** and only recognised when the entity becomes subject to the contractual provision of an instrument. Prior to IAS 39, derivative contracts were not always recognised in an entity's financial statements where there was no initial investment with a monetary value attached. Under IAS 39, however, if a firm has entered into a derivative contract then this should be recognised in the statement of financial position because it has assumed the risks and benefits of the contractual arrangement.

Test yourself 3.9

Explain what is meant by fair value.

4.3 Derecognition of a financial asset

Derecognition of a financial asset arises where rights to cash flows from the asset cease because of termination or expiry of contract or because the financial asset has been transferred or sold, resulting in a transfer of the risks and rewards of ownership. In other words, the rights and obligations associated with the asset are no longer with the seller. If an asset is sold, but the seller retains the right to repurchase the asset at some point in the future, then derecognition depends on the agreed repurchase terms. If the seller is able to repurchase the asset at some point in the future at fair value then the seller has effectively transferred the risks and benefits of ownership to the buyer and derecognition is appropriate. If the repurchase price has already been fixed for some point in the future, then the seller retains the risks and rewards of ownership and derecognition would not be appropriate under IAS 39, irrespective of legal title to the asset.

The flow chart below sets out when a financial asset qualifies for derecognition.

IAS 39 Financial Instruments: Recognition and Measurement flow chart showing financial asset derecognition rules

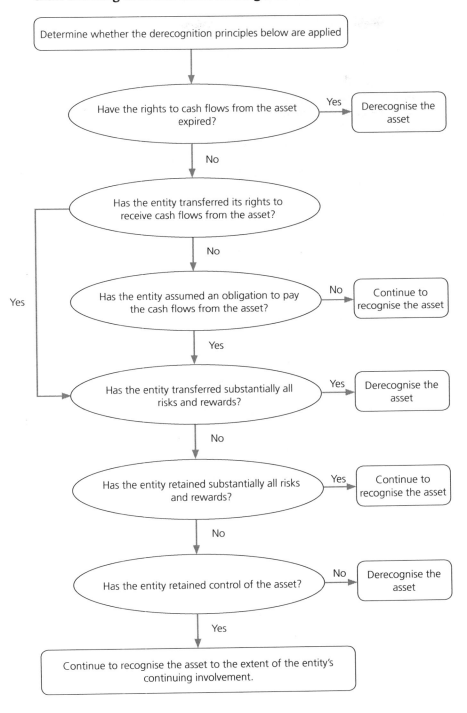

4.4 Derecognition of a financial liability

When an entity is no longer subject to a contractual obligation in respect of the instrument then derecognition is appropriate. If the entity still has an obligation then it must be reflected the statement of financial position.

4.5 Impairment of financial assets

IAS 39 specifies the rules in respect of impairment of financial assets and how impairment should be measured. At the end of each financial period, an entity is required to assess financial assets for impairment based on objective evidence that a financial asset or group of financial assets is impaired. If objective evidence of impairment exists then the amount of loss to be recognised is the difference between the carrying value of the asset and the present value of estimated future cash flows discounted at the financial instrument's original effective interest rate.

4.6 Hedge accounting

Under IAS 39 there are strict rules that apply to hedge accounting and its application, so entities are forced to consider whether it is worth investing the time assessing whether to apply hedge accounting under IAS 39 to a particular hedge. If hedge accounting is not applied, however, then the income statement may be exposed to greater volatility.

IAS 39 recognises three types of hedge:

◆ fair value hedge;

◆ cash flow hedge; and

◆ hedges of a net foreign investment.

fair value hedge
is a hedge of the exposure to changes in fair value of a recognised asset or liability or an unrecognised firm commitment or an identified portion of such an asset, liability or firm commitment that is attributable to a particular risk and could affect profit or loss.

cash flow hedge
is a hedge of the exposure to variability in cash flows.

A **fair value hedge** is a hedge of the exposure to changes in fair value of a recognised asset or liability or an unrecognised firm commitment or an identified portion of such an asset, liability or firm commitment that is attributable to a particular risk and could affect profit or loss.

A **cash flow hedge** is a hedge of the exposure to variability in cash flows that is (i) attributable to a particular risk associated with a recognised asset or liability (such as all or some future interest payments on variable rate debt) or a highly probable forecast transaction and (ii) could affect profit or loss.

Hedges of a net investment in a foreign operation are accounted for much like a cash flow hedge and are defined in IAS 21 "The Effects of Changes in Foreign Exchange Rates".

4.7 Future reporting of financial instruments

The IASB plans to replace IAS 39 using a phased in approach:

Phase 1: Classification and measurement
Phase 2: Impairment methodology
Phase 3: Hedge accounting

4.8 Classification and measurement

IFRS 9 "Financial instruments" was published by the IASB in November 2009 on the classification and measurement of financial assets. It was originally intended for the standard to apply to entities with a financial period commencing on or after 1 January 2013, with no requirement to restate the prior year comparative figures upon initial application, but has been pushed back two years and now applies to financial periods starting 1 January 2015 or later. For entities, keen to adopt the new standard, earlier application is allowed. The objective of the new standard is to improve the usefulness of financial information by simplifying the classification and measurement rules for financial instruments.

Test yourself 3.10

In respect of hedge accounting, what are the three types of hedge recognised by IAS 39?

5. The impact of foreign currency exchange rate changes

The UK accounting standards which govern the impact of foreign currency exchange rate changes are SSAP 20 "Foreign Currency Translation" and FRS 23 "The effects of changes in foreign exchange rates". IAS 21 "The Effects of Changes in Foreign Exchange Rates" is the international equivalent of FRS 23 and the two standards are essentially the same. The purpose of the standards is to prescribe how to account for transactions in foreign currencies and foreign operations. The standards explain the applicable exchange rates and the effects of foreign currency exchange rate changes in an entity's financial statements.

Whilst the accounting treatment of foreign transactions under FRS 23 and IAS 21 are broadly similar to the treatment under SSAP 20, FRS 23 and IAS 21 do not deal with accounting for hedges of a net investment in a foreign operation. Net investment hedging is, instead, covered under FRS 26 "Financial Instruments Measurement" and IAS 39 "Financial Instruments: Recognition and Measurement".

FRS 23 (IAS 21) principally deals with:

◆ the translation of foreign currency transactions and balances;
◆ the translation of results and financial position of foreign subsidiaries for consolidation purposes; and
◆ the translation of foreign currency results into the presentation currency (i.e. the currency in which the financial statements are reported).

5.1 Functional currency

The **functional currency** is the currency of the primary economic environment in which an entity operates. This is usually the environment in

functional currency
means the currency of the primary economic environment in which an entity operates.

which it generates and spends cash, such as the currency in which its goods and services are denominated and paid for or the currency used to pay for labour, material and other costs associated with the provision of goods and services. The functional currency might also be determined by (i) the country where competition and regulations largely determine the selling prices of an entity's goods and services; and (ii) the currency in which funds are generated from financing activities (evidenced by the currency of an entity's debt instruments and issued equity).

An entity must determine its functional currency and measure its performance and financial position in that currency. All other currencies are treated as foreign currencies. Entities cannot change functional currency unless there is a change in circumstances, events or conditions that warrants a change in functional currency. If an entity's circumstances or activities change, then it will need to reassess its functional currency and any change in functional currency will need to be disclosed in the entity's annual report and accounts.

presentation currency
is the currency used for the presentation of financial statements.

hyperinflationary economy
is an economy where inflation is extremely high and out of control resulting in rapid price rise increases and depreciation of the currency.

Entities are able to choose the currency used for the presentation of financial statements. Under FRS 23 and IAS 21 this is commonly referred to as the **presentation currency**. Where the presentation currency differs from the functional currency, the functional currency should be translated into the presentation currency.

FRS 23 and IAS 21 are closely linked with FRS 24 and IAS 29 which are the standards governing inflation. If the functional currency of an entity is that of a **hyperinflationary economy**, then the financial statements need to be restated in accordance with FRS 24/IAS 29.

Test yourself 3.11

In the context of FRS 23 and IAS 21, what should a subsidiary of a multinational group do if its circumstances or activities change?

5.2 Foreign currency transactions

Transactions in a foreign currency should be translated into the functional currency at the **spot rate** of exchange on the date of the transaction. For practical purposes, both FRS 23 and IAS 21 allow an approximate rate to be used such as the weekly or monthly average rate, provided there have been no significant fluctuations of the currency during the relevant period.

spot rate
is the market fx rate used in transactions with immediate delivery.

5.3 Translation of monetary and non-monetary items at the statement of financial position date

◆ Foreign currency denominated monetary items should be converted at the closing rate of exchange.

◆ Non-monetary foreign currency items valued on an historic cost basis should be converted at the exchange rate on the date the transaction took place (i.e. the historic rate of exchange).

◆ Non-monetary foreign currency items held at fair value should be converted at the exchange rate prevailing at the most recent valuation date, i.e. when the fair values were last determined.

5.4 Recognition of foreign exchange differences

Exchange differences are recognised by an entity in the income statement in the period in which they occur with the exception of exchanges differences on monetary items forming part of a net investment in a foreign operation, which are recognised in the group accounts. The exchange gains or losses are recognised in the income statement upon disposal of the foreign entity.

Foreign currency dividends paid to a parent from its foreign subsidiary may result in exchange gains or losses in the financial statements of the parent entity. These exchange differences should be recognised in the income statement of the parent entity and should not be reversed out on consolidation.

exchange differences are gains and losses arising from settlement or from converting monetary items back to one currency from another, using different exchange rates to those used for the initial recognition.

5.5 Consolidation of group entities

Entities within a group may have different functional currencies because the functional currency is determined at entity level and not at group level. Each entity within the group should translate its individual results and financial position into the presentation currency of the group so that consolidation may take place in the presentation currency.

Chapter summary

◆ An entity should adopt accounting policies that are appropriate for its particular circumstances and which will give a true and fair view.

◆ An entity should regularly review its accounting policies and change them if appropriate.

◆ An entity should make sufficient disclosures in its financial statements to enable users to understand the policies adopted and how they have been applied.

◆ Accounting policies are principles, bases, conventions, rules and practices for recognising, selecting measurement bases for, and presenting assets, liabilities, gains, losses and changes to shareholders' funds.

◆ Estimation techniques are the methods used by an entity to implement accounting policies and arrive at estimated values, corresponding to the measurement bases selected for assets, liabilities, gains, losses and changes to shareholders' funds, e.g. measuring depreciation of non-current assets, measuring obsolescence of inventory, measuring work-in-progress, measuring the fair value of financial assets and liabilities.

◆ Comparability of financial information should be taken into account when considering a change in policy. However, the main criteria are relevance and reliability of financial information.

◆ The following disclosures should be made under FRS 18:

- specific disclosures in respect of the accounting policies adopted;
- specific disclosures in respect of accounting policy changes;
- description of estimation techniques used in applying the policies;
- details of any information relevant to the assessment of an entity's status as a going concern, if it is known that the entity has going concern issues; and
- particulars of any true and fair view override.

◆ Broadly speaking, the practice for determining accounting policies is the same under both UK GAAP and IFRS.

◆ Under IAS 8, any expected and imminent changes in accounting policy need to be disclosed.

◆ IAS 1 provides guidance on the form and content of the financial statements and the underlying accounting concepts selected and applied by management. It also requires financial statements to fairly represent the position, performance and cash flows of an entity.

◆ A complete set of financial statements prepared in accordance with IAS 1 should include a statement of financial position, a statement of comprehensive income, a statement of changes in equity, a statement of cash flows and disclosure notes that support the financial statements.

◆ IAS 1 states that financial statements should present the financial position, financial performance and cash flows of an entity fairly and accurately.

◆ Financial statements are prepared on a going-concern basis except where there are material uncertainties which cast significant doubt over the entity's ability to continue to operate in the foreseeable future.

◆ IAS 1 states that items such as assets, liabilities, equity, income and expenses should be presented in the financial statements on an accruals basis. The accruals basis of accounting does not, however, apply to cash flow information.

◆ When comparative amounts are reclassified, the entity is required to disclose the nature of the reclassification, the amount of each item, or class of items, that has been reclassified as well as the reason for the reclassification.

◆ Financial statements should state the following information: company name, whether the statements are for the company or the group, the relevant reporting date/period, the presentation currency, the level of rounding, the level of aggregation.

◆ Offsetting is prohibited unless specifically required by an IFRS.

◆ The statement of financial position must either separate out non-current assets and liabilities from current assets and liabilities or, if more relevant, a liquidity-based statement of financial position must be provided.

◆ Current assets are described in IAS 1 as cash and cash equivalents; assets held for collection, sale, or consumption within the entity's normal operating cycle; assets held primarily for the trading purposes and assets that are realisable within twelve months of the reporting period.

◆ Current liabilities are liabilities expected to be settled within the entity's normal operating cycle; falling due within 12 months; held primarily for trading purposes; or which cannot be deferred beyond 12 months.

◆ The statement of comprehensive income presents profit and loss for the period as well as other comprehensive income such as revaluation surpluses. The statement of comprehensive income may be presented either as one statement or two statements comprising an income statement and a statement showing other comprehensive income.

◆ When the presentation of financial statements is amended or items in the financial statements are re-classified, comparative amounts shall be reclassified unless the reclassification is impractical. When comparative amounts are reclassified, the disclosures should explain the nature of the reclassification; the amount of each item, or class of items, that has been reclassified; and the reason for the reclassification.

◆ The statement of changes in equity provides a snapshot of the composition of equity and how this has changed during the period.

◆ The disclosure notes provide more detailed information in respect of items presented in the financial statements, such as a break-down of figures and supporting narrative. The notes also provide information on items that are not present on the face of the financial statements.

◆ The objectives of FRS 5 "Reporting the Substance of Transactions" is to require an entity's financial statements to report the economic substance of a transaction into which it has entered rather than looking purely at legal form. The standard sets out how to determine the substance of a transaction and its affect on assets and liabilities. It helps entities determine whether assets and liabilities should be included in the statement of financial position and discusses appropriate disclosure requirements. The standard also discusses how transactions should be reported in the other primary financial statements, namely the income statement and cash flow statement.

◆ Economic (or commercial) substance is concerned with economic rights and control rather than the exact legal form of a transaction.

◆ Consignment inventory is the term given to inventory which is in possession of a party who is not the legal owner.

◆ Debt factoring is where a number of debts are sold to a finance company (at a fixed percentage in order to help the business improve its cash flow) and replaced with one receivable, the factor (i.e. the finance company).

◆ Securitisation is a method of raising finance by creating and issuing asset-backed securities, such as mortgage bonds. It is the income generated by the asset (e.g. the mortgage repayments) which acts as security. The assets are pooled, divided into smaller tiers according to their risk of default and sold to investors in affordable packages.

◆ Linked presentation is a provision under FRS 5 in UK GAAP which allows the finance amount of a securitisation transaction to be deducted from the gross amount of the asset it finances. The items are linked and the net figure is recognised on the face of the statement of financial position. There is no concept of linked presentation under IFRS.

◆ The objective of IAS 39 is to establish principles for recognising and measuring financial assets, financial liabilities and some contracts to buy or sell non-financial items.

◆ A derivative is a financial instrument that derives its value from something else such as an underlying asset or assets, for example an interest rate, commodity price or index. Derivative contracts are, typically, settled at a future date and are entered into at no, or minimal, initial investment.

◆ Hedging is a risk management strategy in which an investment is undertaken to offset a position and reduce exposure to price, currency or other fluctuations, e.g. a forward contract is used to hedge against changes in foreign currency exchange rates.

◆ IAS 39 states that financial assets or liabilities should be recognised at fair value and only recognised when the entity becomes subject to the contractual provision of an instrument.

◆ Under IAS 39, derecognition of a financial asset arises where rights to cash flows from the asset cease because of termination or expiry of contract or because the financial asset has been transferred or sold, resulting in a transfer of the risks and rewards of ownership.

◆ Under IAS 39, when an entity is no longer subject to a contractual obligation in respect of the instrument then derecognition of the financial liability is appropriate. If the entity still has an obligation then it must be reflected the statement of financial position.

◆ Under IAS 39, an entity is required, as at the statement of financial position date, to assess financial assets for impairment based on objective evidence that a financial asset or group of financial assets is impaired.

◆ The UK accounting standards which govern the impact of foreign currency exchange rate changes are SSAP 20 "Foreign Currency Translation" and FRS 23 "The Effects of Changes in Foreign Exchange Rates". IAS 21 "The Effects of Changes in Foreign Exchange Rates" is the international equivalent of FRS 23 and the two standards are essentially the same.

◆ FRS 23 sets out the standard accounting practice for (i) translating foreign currency transactions and balances; (ii) translating foreign subsidiaries for consolidation purposes; and (iii) translating foreign currency results into the presentation currency for reporting purposes.

◆ Functional currency means the currency of the primary economic environment in which an entity operates. All other currencies are treated as foreign currencies. Groups do not have a functional currency. Functional currency is always determined at entity level.

◆ Transactions in a foreign currency should be translated into the functional currency at the spot rate on the date of the transaction. For practical purposes, both FRS 23 and IAS 21 allow an approximate rate to be used such as the weekly or monthly average rate, provided there have been no major currency fluctuations during the relevant period.

◆ The presentation currency is the currency in which the financial statements are presented in the annual report and accounts. Foreign currency monetary items should be converted to the presentation currency at the closing rate at the statement of financial position date.

◆ Exchange differences are recognised by an entity in the income statement in the period in which they occur.

◆ Foreign currency dividends paid to a parent from its foreign subsidiary may lead to exchange gains or losses in the financial statements of the parent entity.

Chapter four
Events after the reporting period

List of topics

1 Events after the reporting date: Terminology and accounting treatment

Introduction

This chapter discusses International Accounting Standard 10 in respect of events after the reporting period and explains the terminology used in the standard. Students will gain an understanding of the types of circumstances (occurring between the end of the reporting period and the date the financial statements are authorised for issue) which give rise to adjustments to the financial statements. Students will also learn which types of events do not lead to the adjustment of figures within the financial statements but do warrant disclosure of additional information with a view to helping users of accounts evaluate the circumstances and make informed decisions.

1. Events after the reporting date: Terminology and accounting treatment

IAS 10 originally dealt with both events after the reporting date and with contingencies. Contingencies are now covered under IAS 37 "Provisions, Contingent Liabilities and Contingent Assets" (see Chapter 5).

The purpose of IAS 10 is to set out:

◆ when it is appropriate for entities to adjust their financial statements for events after the reporting period; and

◆ the disclosures required regarding:

(i) the date on which the financial statements have been approved for issue; and

(ii) events after the reporting period.

events after the reporting period are those events, whether favourable or unfavourable, that have occurred between the date of the statement of financial position and the date when the financial statements were authorised for issue.

The standard defines "**Events after the Reporting Period**" as those events, favourable and unfavourable, that occur between the date of the statement of financial position and the date when the financial statements are authorised for issue.

Under the standard, two types of events can be identified:

◆ those that show evidence of the conditions that existed at the date of the statement of financial position which are **adjusting events** after the reporting period; and

◆ those that are indicative of conditions that arose after the date of the statement of financial position which are **non-adjusting events** after the reporting period.

Material adjusting events should be reflected in the financial statements by adjusting the amounts recognised. An adjusting event includes an event that provides evidence that the reporting entity is no longer a going concern. If this is the case, the entity should not prepare its accounts on a going-concern basis.

Non-adjusting events, as the name suggests, should not trigger a change in accounting treatment. This is because the events occurred after the reporting period and there is no evidence to justify a change in accounting treatment as at the statement of financial position date. Non-adjusting events also include dividends declared after the reporting period. This is because the liability to make the dividend payments did not exist at the statement of financial position date.

Non-adjusting events may require disclosure if material and if it is expected that they would affect the economic decisions made by users of the financial statements. The disclosures under IAS 10 are:

◆ the nature of the event; and

   (i) an estimate of the financial effect; or

   (ii) a statement that a reasonable estimate of the financial effect cannot be made.

Disclosures in the financial statements should also be updated to reflect conditions existing at the reporting date in relation to which new information exists.

Examples of material adjusting events after the reporting period include:

◆ a court case settlement confirming the existence of a present obligation as at the end of the reporting period, in which case a provision will need to be recognised in accordance with IAS 37 "Provisions Contingent Liabilities and Contingent Assets" instead of the disclosure of a contingent liability in the notes;

◆ the discovery of material misstatements or fraud that show the financial statements to be inaccurate;

◆ the bankruptcy of a major customer which results in trade receivables being non-recoverable; and

adjusting events are events after the reporting period that provides further evidence of conditions that existed at the end of the reporting period. An event that raises going concern issues for the entity is an adjusting event.

non-adjusting events are events after the reporting period that is indicative of a condition that arose after the end of the reporting period.

◆ the presence of persuasive evidence that the entity can no longer continue as a going concern.

Examples of non-adjusting events after the reporting period include:

◆ a fall in the market value of investments between the statement of financial position date and the date when the financial statements are approved for issue;

◆ an announcement that part of the business is no longer viable and will cease to operate;

◆ the sale of a major subsidiary; and

◆ flood damage to material assets.

Stop and think 4.1

Why should the decline in the market value of investments not be treated as an adjusting event after the reporting period?

Chapter summary

◆ The purpose of IAS 10 is to prescribe when it is appropriate for accounts to be adjusted after the reporting period and to set out the required disclosures to be made in the accounts.

◆ Events after the reporting period are those events, whether favourable or unfavourable, that have occurred between the statement of financial position date and the date when the financial statements were authorised for issue.

◆ Two types of events can be identified under the standard – adjusting events and non-adjusting events.

◆ Adjusting events are events after the reporting period that provide evidence of conditions that existed at the end of the reporting period.

◆ Non-adjusting events are events after the reporting period that are indicative of conditions that arose after the end of the reporting period.

◆ An adjusting event includes an event that provides evidence that the reporting entity is no longer a going concern. If this is the case, the entity should not prepare its accounts on a going-concern basis.

◆ Dividends declared after the reporting period are non-adjusting events.

Chapter five
Provisions, Contingent Liabilities and Contingent Assets

List of topics

1   Provisions
2   Contingent liabilities
3   Contingent assets

Introduction

At a company's financial period end, assets and liabilities not yet received or incurred but which relate to transactions and events during the reporting period may need to be recognised in the accounts. The amount and timing of these transactions may not be known with certainty at the statement of financial position date and may rely upon the occurrence or non-occurrence of uncertain future events not wholly within the company's control. The recognition criteria and accounting treatment of such items is covered under the international accounting standard, IAS 37, "Provisions, Contingent Liabilities and Contingent Assets". **Provisions**, **contingent liabilities** and **contingent assets** are only recognised in the accounts if the appropriate criteria are met.

This chapter explains what is meant by the terms provisions, contingent liabilities and contingent assets. The recognition criteria and accounting treatment is discussed and an example is given of how IAS 37 prohibits the misuse of provisions in financial statements. The chapter also explains how companies might use deceptive accounting practice, such as profit smoothing, in order to give the impression that there is greater financial stability and less volatility than might actually be the case. The chapter outlines what is meant by a constructive obligation and highlights, from an accounting perspective, the significance of a company merely having the intent to transact as opposed to having an actual obligation to transact. The measurement of provisions is briefly discussed and the application of a discount factor to reflect the timing of future cash flows is explained. Students will also learn what is meant by the term onerous contract.

provision
is a liability of uncertain timing or amount.

contingent liability
is a possible obligation to transfer economic benefit as a result of a past transaction or event and whose existence will be confirmed only by the occurrence or non-occurrence of uncertain future events not wholly within the entity's control. A contingent liability may also be a present obligation which is not recognised either because it is unlikely payment of the liability will materialise or because the amount cannot be measured reliably.

contingent asset
is a possible asset that arises from past events and whose existence will be confirmed only by the occurrence or non-occurrence of uncertain future events not wholly within the entity's control.

What is the objective of IAS 37?

The objective of the IAS 37, the international accounting standard which covers the accounting treatment and recognition criteria for provisions, contingent liabilities and contingent assets, is to ensure that the appropriate recognition criteria are applied and that any relevant information in connection with provisions, contingent liabilities and contingent assets is included in the disclosure notes of the financial statements to enable users of accounts to better understand the nature, scale and timing of these accounting items.

1. Provisions

A provision is defined as a liability of uncertain timing or amount. A provision may only be made in the accounts where there is a **legal** or **constructive obligation**. If there is merely intent and not an obligation then a provision may not be recognised under IAS 37. Companies are not allowed to simply provide for potential future expenditure in order to smooth profits and **window dress** the financial statements. There has to be a present obligation, at the statement of financial position date, which is **probable** and which may be reliably estimated in monetary terms.

If:

◆ no present obligation (legal or construed) exists;

◆ the outflow of resources to settle the obligation is improbable; and

◆ a reliable estimate cannot be made of the amount of the obligation

then no provision may be made in a company's financial statements under IAS 37. This standard prevents a company's board from making general provisions in a good year in order to be able to release the amount back to the income statement in a bad year, thereby smoothing profits.

published policies
undertaken to accept certain responsibilities which have created an expectation from a third party.

legal obligation
an obligation that derives from a contract, law or other form of enactment.

constructive obligation
an obligation to a third party which has been construed due to an entity having created a valid practice expectation

window dressing
describes the use of deceptive accounting practices to present the reporting entity in a better light.

probable obligation
an obligation is probable if it is more likely than not to occur.

Worked example 5.1: Profit smoothing:

A listed company reports profits for the years ended 31 July 2009, 2010, 2011 and 2012:

	2009 £'000	2010 £'000	2011 £'000	2012 £'000
Profit	450	500	1,100	200

The company likes to be in a position to report steady growth which it believes will satisfy shareholders and other stakeholders and attract further inward investment. However, it has had exceptional results in 2011 and a relatively poor result in 2012 which may lead shareholders to believe there is volatility and undue risk.

If it were not prevented by accounting standards, the company may have been tempted to smooth the profits by creating general provisions for possible or unknown expenses in 2011. Then, when these expenses did not arise the following year, the company could have released them back to the income statement as set out in the example below:

	2009 £'000	2010 £'000	2011 £'000	2012 £'000
Original profit	450	500	1,100	200
General provision	–	–	(500)	–
Release of provision	–	–	–	500
Reported profit	450	500	600	700

The example shows that the company could, if allowed, have achieved a steady improvement in its reported results by massaging the figures. IAS 37 prohibits irresponsible use of provisions in financial statements and stops the misrepresentation of the financial position and performance of the company. In order to use provisions, there must be an obligation which can be reliably estimated and there must be a probable likelihood (greater than 50% chance) that this obligation will need to be settled. The company, in the above example, cannot simply provide for a future expense which does not exist in order to window dress the accounts.

1.1 Provisions and the restructuring of operations

Companies often use provisions for the restructuring of operations. Restructuring may have a significant impact on the operations of a business, be it through the sale or termination of a business, the closure of a branch, cessation of operations in a particular jurisdiction or the restructuring of its management team. A provision for restructuring costs may only be recognised where management has a legal or constructive obligation to restructure. The business must have a detailed and formal restructuring plan which sets out the parts of the business affected, the locations concerned, details of the employees subject to termination payments, expenditure and timings. The business must have also raised a valid expectation in those affected by the restructuring, for example by communicating the plan or having already commenced the restructuring. A mere intent to restructure is insufficient.

1.2 How to measure the value of a provision

With regard to the measurement of provisions, if the pre-requisites for the recognition of a provision in a company's financial statements exist, i.e. there is an obligation of an uncertain timing or amount, the amount recognised as a provision shall be a best estimate as at the statement of financial position date.

constructive obligation
this is an obligation to a third party which has been construed due to an entity having either:
- set a precedent through past practice;
- published policies; or
- undertaken to accept certain responsibilities

and, in doing so, has created a valid expectation on the part of a third party. Examples of a constructive obligation:
- A company has previously made generous redundancy payments in excess of the statutory requirement;
- Land contamination by a chemical company if the company's policy is to clean up even if it is not legally obliged to do so;
- A retailer has a returns policy for unused and undamaged goods returned within, say, 4 weeks;
- A marketing company has undertaken to give out cash prizes and laptops to 10% of participants of a recent survey and the undertaking was communicated to all participants before they undertook the survey;
- A company has a restructuring plan in place and has created a valid expectation by those affected that the restructuring will be carried out.

Stop and think 5.1

What should an entity consider when determining the best estimate of a provision?

Where the time value of money could have a material impact on the future cash flows, the provision should be discounted to reflect the value of the expenditure that is expected to be required to settle the liability. This will depend on when the expenditure is going to be incurred. The time value of money works on the principle that one pound today is worth more than one pound tomorrow because the value of money is eroded by inflation. If a discount factor is applied to reflect the fact that payment is unlikely to be made for, say, a further 11 months after the statement of financial position date, a £1 million pound obligation might, for example, show as a £980,000 provision as at the statement of financial position date. There are special rules in respect of selecting the appropriate discount rate which preparers of the accounts need to follow. This is intended to prevent the over or understatement of provisions.

At the end of each reporting period, provisions need to be reviewed and adjusted to show the current best estimate. This might mean that some provisions are reversed as payment of the obligation is no longer probable.

Test yourself 5.1

Explain what you understand by the term provision and, in this context, give at least one example of a constructive obligation.

2. Contingent liabilities

A contingent liability is a possible obligation to transfer economic benefit as a result of a past transaction or event and whose existence will be confirmed only by the occurrence or non-occurrence of uncertain future events not wholly within the entity's control. As the obligation is only possible (i.e. less likely than not to occur) then it is a contingent liability and not recognised in the accounts as a provision.

A contingent liability might also be a present obligation. However, if the amount of the present obligation cannot be reliably measured or it is unlikely that the entity will have to transfer economic benefit in order to satisfy the obligation then the contingent liability is not recognised as a provision in the accounts. Instead, a disclosure should be made for each class of contingent liability as at the statement of financial position date setting out the nature of the contingent liability, estimations of the possible economic outflows and timings and amounts of these outflows. If there is any possibility of reimbursement then this should also be disclosed. There is no requirement for disclosure where it is virtually certain that the business will not have to make a payment.

Contingent liabilities might arise when a firm anticipates very high legal expenses as a result of a major court case. The outcome of the court case is unknown at the statement of financial position date and therefore the firm does not know whether to account for the legal costs or not. Under IAS 37, a firm must assess whether it is at fault in any way and if it is probable that it will have to pay anything as a result. A firm could have a very large contingent liability or zero liability if it is deemed likely to win the court case.

The International Accounting Standards Board (IASB) proposes to update IAS 37 in order to increase transparency but the proposed changes are on hold as there are concerns that major court cases may be prejudiced by the proposed rules which might reveal how much a company is willing to pay to settle a case.

Under the proposed rules, the contingent liability would be a weighted average of all possible outcomes (win, loss, settlement, dismissal, etc.) and would be aggregated with any other cases so that the potential liability of any one case is not shown.

Stop and think 5.2

IAS 37 is about increasing transparency. Can you think of any shortcomings of the accounting standard and give an example of a possible future liability or scenario which might result in a company's accounts reporting an unrealistic figure?

3. Contingent assets

A contingent asset is a possible asset that arises from a past transaction or event and whose existence will be confirmed only by the occurrence or non-occurrence of uncertain future events not wholly within the entity's control.

Contingent assets should not be recognised in the accounts, until the realisation of income is almost certain to occur, for example the settlement of a court case resulting in compensation owing for breach of contract. At this point, the asset is no longer a contingent asset as economic benefit is probable.

Stop and think 5.3

Should a future operating loss be recognised as a provision?

Test yourself 5.2

What are the key differences between a provision and a contingent liability?

Test yourself 5.3

Should a provision be accrued in the following circumstances?

An company rewards its staff for professional level examination passes and the rewards are documented in the company's staff handbook creating an expectation on behalf of staff that an exam pass will lead to a financial reward.

A company providing fund administration is to provide training to its staff to update them on recent changes in legislation governing collective investment funds;

A firm has entered into an onerous contract.

onerous contract
is a present obligation where the unavoidable costs of fulfilling the contract are higher than the economic benefits that are expected to be received. Onerous contracts can arise where a firm undertakes a contract to supply a product or service and the cost of the raw materials or human resource costs more than originally anticipated.

Chapter summary

◆ IAS 37 enhances the transparency of financial statements and helps prevent misleading accounting practice and profit smoothing because organisations preparing accounts under international accounting standards are not able to use general provisions to smooth out volatility.

◆ A provision may only be made in the financial statements where there is a present obligation (either legal or construed), where the outflow of economic resources is probable (more than 50% chance) and if the obligation can be measured or estimated with reasonable reliability.

◆ A constructive obligation is an obligation to a third party which has arisen due to an entity having either (i) set a precedent through past practice; (ii) having published a policy; or (iii) having undertaken to accept certain responsibilities and in so doing has created an valid expectation by third parties.

◆ Provisions may need to be discounted to reflect the time value of money and to help ensure provisions are free from material misstatement.

◆ Contingent liabilities often arise when a firm is involved in legal proceedings and the outcome is not known at the statement of financial position date. The AISB has set out new and slightly controversial proposals in respect of IAS 37 which might lead to firms having to account for lawsuits before the outcome of a specific case is known. However, the contingent liability would be a weighted average of all possible outcomes in order to disguise the potential liability of any one case.

◆ Contingent assets should not be recognised unless economic benefit is virtually certain.

Part
Three

In this part, students will learn about the key ratios used for measuring liquidity, profitability, efficiency and gearing. Students will also gain an understanding of how some key ratios, such as return on capital employed and earnings per share, interlink with other performance indicators and turnover ratios. Students will learn that a single performance indicator will not tell the whole story and that ratios should be considered in aggregate and in context of the business environment and markets in which an organisation is operating.

Students will also gain an insight into cash flow statements and will learn how to prepare cash flow statements and make adjustments for non-cash items such as depreciation, inventory, receivables and payables in order to determine the net cash inflow or outflow from operating activities. Students will learn about the main purpose and functions of the cash flow statement and will be able to interpret cash flow statements using them to assess liquidity, solvency and the financial adaptability of a business.

Learning outcomes

At the end of this part, students should be able to:

- discuss and explain the main profitability ratios;
- explain what is meant by the terms working capital and overcapitalisation;
- assess liquidity and explain the difference between the quick ratio and the current ratio;
- calculate and explain the main efficiency ratios;
- explain the relationship between ROCE, operating profit margin and net asset turnover;
- explain why ratios are likely to be different for companies in different industry sectors and give examples of industry sectors where non-current asset turnover and net asset turnover might vary;
- discuss the significance of inventory turnover and explain the benefits and disadvantages of both high and low inventory turnover;
- understand the importance of receivable and payable payment periods;
- distinguish between debt and equity and explain why a company might choose one type of financing over another;
- calculate the various gearing ratios;
- understand the term public offering;
- explain the implications of loan covenants;
- define what is meant by the term primary financial statement;
- prepare a cash flow statement showing net cash flows from operating, investing and financing activities;
- reconcile operating profit to net cash flow from operating activities; and
- explain the purpose and functions of the cash flow statement.

Chapter six
Financial Ratio Analysis

List of topics

1 Profitability ratios
2 Liquidity ratios
3 Efficiency ratios
4 Gearing ratios
5 EPS and other key investor ratios

Introduction

Financial ratios enable users of accounts to establish the relationship between items in the statement of financial position and income statement and provide users with meaningful information about a company's activities, typically in respect of liquidity, profitability, earnings, leverage and financial stability. The ratios help analysts, shareholders and other stakeholders to identify financial strengths and weaknesses of a company, to benchmark companies against like companies in the same or similar industry and to compare performance and financial position over time.

In this chapter, students will learn about five categories of ratios and what to consider when calculating and interpreting each type of ratio. In the section on profitability ratios, the difference between net and gross profit margin is explained and students will learn a number of different methods to calculate a company's return. Liquidity ratios will also be explained and the key difference between the current ratio and the quick ratio outlined. Students will learn why liquidity is so important for a business and also why it is not realistic for a well run business to maintain high levels of cash. Efficiency ratios and their link to profitability are also discussed, for example, the return on capital employed measures both efficiency and profitability. Students will gain an understanding of how net asset turnover, net profit margin and return on capital employed inter-relate and how inventory turnover, receivables and payables periods impact the cash flows of a business. Gearing ratios are also discussed and the impact on gearing of financing decisions. Students will also gain an understanding of the earnings per share ratio and other shareholder investment ratios such as the price earnings ratio, dividend cover and dividend yield.

1. Profitability ratios

Profitability ratios measure a company's ability to generate earnings over expenditure. A high ratio indicates the company is performing well.

Ratios are used to compare a company's performance with other similar companies and to compare a company's performance in one period with a prior period. For example, a company might use profitability ratios to compare its fourth quarter performance with that of a competitor, or it may compare its own quarter two ratio with its quarter two ratio in the prior year. Profitability ratios might also be used for quarter-on-quarter comparison (e.g. Q2 v Q3) but care must be taken to be aware of the impact of seasonal variations which will impact the figures.

For example, ice-cream sales in Britain in Q3 (July to September) should always be better than Q4 (October to December) ice-cream sales. It follows that profit on ice-cream sales is likely to be greater in Q3 than Q4 and that comparing summer profitability with winter profitability may not provide as useful management information as comparing like with like. It would be far more useful to compare profitability of Q3 in 2012 with Q3 in 2011.

1.1 Net profit margin (return on sales)

Return on sales (or profit margin) measures profit on sales after tax. The higher the ratio, the more profit the business will make for each £1 of sales. For example, a business with a 25% margin will make 25p for each £1 of sales whereas a business with a margin of 10% will make 10p for each £1 of sales. As with all ratios, the profit margin ratio of a company is more meaningful if compared with like companies in the same industry as it enables investors and other users to make informed decisions by comparing "apples with apples" rather than "apples with oranges".

The formula for net profit margin is:

$$\frac{\text{Net profit after tax}}{\text{Sales}} \times 100$$

Care should be taken not to confuse increased profits of a company with increased net profit margin. Whilst both measures are closely linked, an absolute rise in profits does not always mean the profit margin is improving. The company may simply have sold more goods at the existing margin rather than the margin itself improving.

 The profit before tax figure may also be used in place of profit after tax to calculate the net profit margin. For example, the profit before tax figure may be more appropriate where the effects of a taxation need to be stripped out to provide a more meaningful comparison of either (i) two companies on different tax rates; or (ii) of a company's year on year net profit where there has been a change in the rate of taxation from one year to the next.

1.2 Gross profit margin

The gross profit margin measures the gross profit a business makes on sales and is calculated as follows:

$$\frac{\text{Sales} - \text{cost of sales}}{\text{Sales}} \times 100$$

Students should note that an increase in gross profit margin will not necessarily lead to an increase in the net profit margin.

Worked example 6.1

Income statement extract of Profit Margin Ltd for the year ended 31 March 2012 (with prior year comparative):

	2012	2011
	£	£
Sales	500,000	700,000
Cost of sales	(200,000)	(400,000)
Gross profit	300,000	300,000
Administration expenses	(50,000)	(60,000)
Legal fees	(60,000)	(20,000)
Other expenses	(90,000)	(80,000)
Net profit	100,000	140,000

Net profit margin = net profit/sales
2012: Net profit margin = 100,000/500,000 = 20%
2011: Net profit margin = 140,000/700,000 = 20%

Gross profit margin = gross profit/sales
2012: Gross profit margin = 300,000/500,000 = 60%
2011: Gross profit margin = 300,000/700,000 = 43%

Expenses as a percentage of sales:
2012: 200,000/500,000 × 100 = 40%
2011: 160,000/700,000 × 100 = 23%

The gross profit margin of Profit Margin Ltd has increased from 43% to 60% because cost of sales has fallen relative to sales. The increase in the gross profit margin has not translated into an increase in the net profit margin, however, because expenses have risen relative to sales (from 23% to 40%).

return on capital employed (ROCE) is a measure of a company's success at achieving a return on capital invested. It is calculated by multiplying operating profit margin by net asset turnover.

As we shall find out in more detail when we look at the **return on capital employed** ratio, profit margin is closely linked with asset turnover. For example, if a company has a high asset turnover then its sales volumes will also be high but the company may have cut its prices (and therefore its margin) to generate the increased sales. By multiplying the profit margin by asset turnover we are able to establish the return on the capital employed by the company.

1.3 Return on capital employed (ROCE) (see also efficiency ratios)

ROCE is a measure of a company's success at achieving a return on capital invested. It is probably the single most important profitability and efficiency ratio as it reflects the profit as a percentage of the amount of capital employed. There are a number of ways of calculating ROCE but the most common method is to divide a company's return or earnings by net capital employed. The ratio is calculated as follows:

$$ROCE = \frac{\text{Profit on ordinary activities before interest and taxation (PBIT)}}{\text{Total assets (TA) less current liabilities (CL)}} \times 100$$

$$= \text{PBIT}/(\text{TA}-\text{CL}) \times 100$$

Using profit before interest and taxation (PBIT) is preferred to profit after tax because the profit after tax figure will be affected by tax rate variations. This means year-on-year comparative figures for profitability will be skewed by non-operational variations. If students only have the profit-after-tax figure they can calculate PBIT by adding back the tax and the interest on the long-term loan capital.

PBIT might also be described as earnings before interest and taxation (EBIT) so the formula might be presented as follows:

$$ROCE = \frac{\text{Earnings}}{\text{TA}-\text{CL}} \times 100$$

The ROCE formula might also be set out as:

$$ROCE = \frac{\text{Earnings}}{\text{Capital employed}} \times 100$$

$$= \frac{\text{Earnings}}{\text{Shareholders' funds} + \text{debt}} \times 100$$

or

ROCE = operating profit margin x net asset turnover

This means that the relationship between ROCE, profit margin and asset turnover may be described as:

$$\frac{\text{PBIT}}{\text{Capital employed}} = \frac{\text{PBIT}}{\text{Sales}} \times \frac{\text{Sales}}{\text{Capital employed}}$$

Assuming all else stays the same, a company's ROCE will fall if either profit margin or if net asset turnover falls. Likewise, a company's ROCE will increase if either profit margin or net asset turnover increases. However, if a company decides to increase its profit margin to make a greater return then it needs to be aware that selling goods at a higher value may lead to reduced sales which could equally lead to a fall in ROCE or ROCE staying the same. Alternatively, in the hope of improving its return, a company might choose to boost net asset turnover by reducing its profit margin and selling its products at a cheaper price. The main reasons for ROCE changing includes changes to asset values, sales figures or expenses.

Worked example 6.2

ABC Plc
30 June 2012
£'000

Sales	5,000
Profit before interest and tax	200
Capital employed	1,500

ROCE = 200,000/1,500,000 = 13.3%
Profit margin = 200,000/5,000,000 = 4%
Net asset turnover = 5,000,000/1,500,000 = 3.3 times

ABC Plc has a ROCE of 13.3% for the period ended 30 June 2012. In order to meet targets in the next quarter, ABC's management team believes the best way to increase the company's return is by pushing up the prices of its products and operating at a much higher profit margin.

The figures for the quarter ended 30 September 2012 are as follows:

ABC Plc
30 September 2012
£'000

Sales	2,000
Profit before interest and tax	200
Capital employed	1,500

ROCE = 200,000/1,500,000 = 13.3%
Profit margin = 200,000/2,000,000 = 10%
Net asset turnover = 2,000,000/1,500,000 = 1.3 times

The management strategy of ABC Plc of putting up prices and operating at a higher profit margin has failed to improve the company's ROCE. This is because the higher prices led to reduced net asset turnover. Profit has remained the same, hence ROCE is the same.

Students need to understand that the ROCE ratio may be presented in a number of different ways and in the examination may be required to calculate ROCE from limited information. The profit before interest and tax figure may not be given but students need to know how to calculate this using the profit after tax or profit after tax and dividends figure. Students should also appreciate that earnings means the same as profit for the purposes of the calculation. If the total assets and current liabilities figures from the top half of the statement of financial position are not provided then students can use the figures from the bottom half of the statement of financial position (shareholders' funds and debt). Students should also be aware that capital employed could be described as net capital employed or gross capital employed. The important distinction is that current liabilities are deducted from gross capital employed to get net capital employed because:

Gross capital employed = non-current assets + investments + current assets
and
Net capital employed = non-current assets + investments + current assets – current liabilities
= non-current assets + investments + **working capital**
= total assets less current liabilities

Care also needs to be taken with the non-current assets figure as some **intangible non-current assets**, such as goodwill, need be deducted from non-current assets in calculating the ratio, unless the intangible has been purchased or has a sale value. Furthermore, non-current asset investments may be undervalued especially if they have not undergone a recent revaluation exercise. For example, if property is shown in the statement of financial position with a lower carrying cost than its true market value, the ROCE will show a higher percentage return.

working capital
is a measure of how a company meets its short-term obligations (i.e. current liabilities) with its current assets and is calculated by deducting current liabilities from current assets.

intangible non-current assets
assets which have no physical substance, e.g. goodwill, copyright.

Worked example 6.3: ROCE

Using the information provided, calculate the return on capital employed of ROCE Plc for the year ended 31 December 2011.

ROCE Plc
Balance as at 31 December 2011

	2011 £'000	2011 £'000	2010 £'000	2010 £'000
Non-current assets		5,680		5,680
Current assets:				
Inventory	200		350	
Receivables	1,250		300	
Cash at bank and in hand	50		350	
		1,500		1,000
Payables: amounts falling due within one year		(300)		(400)
Net current assets		1,200		600
Total assets less current liabilities		6,880		6,280
Payables: amounts falling due after more than one year				
8% loan stock 2018		(100)		100
		6,780		6,180

Share capital	500	500
Share premium	50	50
Income statement	6,230	5,630
	6,780	6,180

After taxation of £160,000 and dividends of £50,000 the retained profit for the year ended 31 December 2011 was £600,000. Profit on ordinary activities after taxation was £500,000 for the year ended 31 December 2010 and taxation was £127,500.

Solution

31 December 2011:

$$\text{ROCE} = \frac{\text{Profit on ordinary activities before interest and taxation (PBIT)}}{\text{Total assets (TA) less current liabilities (CL)}} \times 100$$

$$= \text{PBIT}/(\text{TA-CL}) \times 100$$

$$= \frac{\text{Retained profit + dividends + taxation + interest (on loan stock)}}{\text{TA–CL}} \times 100$$

$$= \frac{£600,000 + £50,000 + £160,000 + £8,000 \text{ (w1)}}{£6,880,000} \times 100$$

$$= \frac{£818,000}{£6,880,000} \times 100$$

$$= 11.9\%$$

Working 1: 8% loan stock 2018: 8% × £100,000 = £8,000

31 December 2010:

$$\text{ROCE} = \frac{\text{Profit on ordinary activities before interest and taxation (PBIT)}}{\text{Total assets (TA) less current liabilities (CL)}} \times 100$$

$$= \text{PBIT}/(\text{TA–CL}) \times 100$$

$$= \frac{£500,000 + £127,500 + £8,000}{£6,280,000} \times 100$$

$$= \frac{£635,500}{£6,280,000} \times 100$$

$$= 10.1\%$$

The company's profitability has risen from 10.1% in 2010 to 11.9% in 2011. The company appears to be performing efficiently with relative returns exceeding the 8% interest payable on the loan stock. This indicates that the company might benefit from borrowing more long-term money in order to generate greater returns. Further analysis should be undertaken to determine the reason for the 20% increase in profitability as measured by the increase in ROCE. Stakeholders should, therefore, review the full annual report and financial statements in order to establish if the company has taken on increased risk with a view to generating greater returns. A comparison should also be undertaken of ROCE of the company with the ROCE earned by similar-sized companies in the same business sector.

Stop and think 6.1

What might cause the ROCE to vary from one year to another?

1.4 Return on investment (ROI)

ROCE might also be referred to as return on investment or ROI which describes profit in relation to the amount of capital invested. A widely used formula for determining the return of a particular investment is:

$$ROI = \frac{\text{Average annual accounting profit}}{\text{Investment}} \times 100$$

The average investment amount is usually used and is calculated by taking account of the scrap value of the investment at the end of its economic useful life:

$$\text{Average investment} = \frac{\text{Initial investment} - \text{scrap value}}{2}$$

required rate of return
the minimum percentage return that investors expect to receive on an investment. Investors should consider all investments whose rate of return meets or exceeds the required rate of return.

hurdle rate
is the minimum rate of return which the company will accept on a particular project or investment. If the project goes according to plan, the rate of return will exceed the hurdle rate. The hurdle rate is also used as a benchmark for determining when investment managers are entitled to incentive fees.

If the expected rate of return on the investment is greater than the **required rate of return** then the investment should be undertaken. If, however, there are several mutually exclusive investment options which are all expected to generate a return above the company's **hurdle rate**, then the investment which generates the highest rate of return should be chosen. If the investments are not mutually exclusive, then the company should, of course, consider undertaking all investments available where the expected rate of return exceeds the required rate of return.

1.5 Return on equity (ROE)

The return on equity ratio considers the return that shareholders get on their investment. The ratio is calculated as:

$$\frac{\text{Earnings}}{\text{Equity}} \times 100$$

The ratio measures a company's efficiency: the higher the ratio the more efficient a profitable the company is likely to be. Like many ratios, care should be taken to only compare the ROE ratio of a company with a similar company in the same industry sector and to be aware of the level of gearing of that company. For example, companies which are highly geared, i.e. have a high proportion of debt to equity, are likely to have a higher ROE ratio. For example,

Company A has raised £10m in equity and generates £1m in earnings. It's ROE is 10%. Company B has financed itself with £10m in equity plus £8m in debt. It therefore has more funds available to it than Company A, which it can use to generate additional profits. If Company B's earnings are, say, £1.6m, then its ROE is 1.6/10 x 100 = 16%.

1.6 Return on total assets (ROA)

ROA measures how a company's assets are being used to generate profit. The ratio is calculated by dividing net profit after tax by assets. Bank's often find this ratio a useful measure of return because, unlike the return on equity ratio, it takes account of debt funding.

$$\frac{\text{Net income}}{\text{Total assets}} \times 100$$

$$= \frac{\text{Profit after tax}}{\text{Total assets}} \times 100$$

For example, Company A has net income of £3m and total assets of £15m. Its ROA is therefore 20%. Company B has net income of £3m and total assets of £20m. Its ROA is therefore 15%.

Company A has a greater ROA because it generates the same net income as Company B from less assets.

A high ratio indicates a well run, profitable business. The asset return will, however, depend on the type of business.

1.7 Earnings per share (EPS)

Earnings per share is a measure of net income of a company (less dividends paid on preference shares) divided by the number of shares in issue. It is a frequently used indicator of a company's profitability and is often used for comparing a company's financial health with a company with similar earnings.

The EPS ratio is calculated as follows:

$$EPS = \frac{\text{Earnings} - \text{preference dividends}}{\text{Number of shares}}$$

See Section 5 towards the end of this chapter for more information on EPS.

Test yourself 6.1

Explain, with examples, the relationship between ROCE, profit margin and asset turnover. (See worked example 6.2 above.)

2. Liquidity ratios

Liquidity ratios help a company determine its ability to pay its short-term debt obligations by using its liquid assets. If a company's liquidity ratios show that a company has insufficient cover to meet its short-term obligations then it should take appropriate action which might include bringing this to the attention of its shareholders and other stakeholders such as the financial regulator (if the company is subject to supervisory oversight).

current ratio
is a measure of short-term liquidity which shows a company's ability to meet short-term obligations from short-term assets.

quick ratio
is a measurement of short-term liquidity which focuses on those items that can be turned into cash easily and quickly; therefore it does not include inventory which may not be easily realisable at full net book value.

The most common liquidity ratios are the **current ratio** and the **quick ratio** ("acid test"). There are, however, a number of other liquidity ratios and the most common of these are discussed below.

2.1 Current ratio

The current ratio is a measure of a company's ability to repay liabilities due within one year out of current assets. It is calculated by taking the current assets of a company and dividing them by the current liabilities. A ratio of 1 or greater means the company has full cover.

The formula is:

$$\frac{\text{Current assets}}{\text{Current liabilities}}$$

Worked example 6.4

The statement of financial position of a company shows the following assets and liabilities:

	£'000
Non-current assets	500
Current assets	
Inventory	200
Trade Receivables	50
Cash and bank and in hand	100
	350
Current liabilities (falling due within 1 year)	
Trade payables	70
Bank loan	10
Accruals	30
Tax	50
Net current assets	190

The current ratio of the company is:

$$\frac{\text{Current assets}}{\text{Current liabilities}}$$

= 350/160 = 2.2:1

The ratio is over 2 which means the company has sufficient cover to meet its liabilities due within one year. However, this ratio does not take account of the fact that inventory may not be easily converted into cash in a timely manner. If the inventory cannot be easily sold, then the quick ratio (or "acid-test") may be a more reliable method of calculating a company's ability to meet payables falling due within one year and other liabilities due within one year.

2.2 Quick ratio (or "acid-test")

The quick ratio measures a company's ability to meet liabilities due within one year out of the assets that are the most liquid and, therefore, the most quick and easy to realise (i.e. convert into cash). Inventory is not always considered to be quick and easy to realise and therefore is deducted from the current assets figure in calculating the quick ratio. The quick ratio is, therefore, a more conservative ratio than the current ratio.

A ratio of 1 or greater means the company has full cover.

The formula is:

$$\frac{\text{Current assets} - \text{inventory}}{\text{Current liabilities}}$$

Worked example 6.5

Using the statement of financial position figures for the company in the above example, the quick ratio would be as follows:

$$\frac{\text{Current assets} - \text{inventory}}{\text{Current liabilities}}$$

$$= \frac{350 - 200}{160}$$

$$= 150/160 = 0.9:1$$

The ratio is less than 1 which means the company, when subjected to the acid-test, has insufficient cover to meet its liabilities due within one year. If inventory can be converted to cash in a timely manner then the company may be able to demonstrate sufficient liquid cover to meet its short-term obligations.

2.3 Liquidity ratio (or cash ratio)

The liquidity or cash ratio measures a company's ability to meet liabilities due within one year out of cash and cash equivalents (including invested funds) and is a more conservative measure of short-term liquidity compared with the current and quick ratio. Its uses are limited, so this ratio is less frequently used by financial analysts, compared with the current and quick ratio. Whilst liquidity is an important measure of a company's ability to meet short-term debt obligations, it is not realistic for a company to maintain high cash levels. A company is likely to generate better returns for its shareholders if it utilises its cash elsewhere.

A ratio of 1 or greater means the company has full cover. However, a very high ratio may not be good for shareholders as it could be an indicator of poor asset utilisation. A ratio of less than 1 does not necessarily mean a company has insufficient cover. For example, a company may have a significant level of other current assets which it deems to be sufficiently liquid to mitigate the risk of running out of funds. A company might also have a high level of non-current assets, such as a transport company, and may not need as much liquidity as, say, an on-line retail company. A liquidity ratio of 0.6 to 1.0 might be acceptable in the transport industry, whereas a ratio of greater than 1.0 to 1.5 would normally be required in the retail industry.

Stop and think 6.2

Why do you think a retail company might need greater liquidity than a logistics company?

The formula for the liquidity or cash ratio is:

$$\frac{\text{Cash and cash equivalents}}{\text{Current liabilities}}$$

Worked example 6.6

Using the statement of financial position figures for the company in the above example, the liquidity ratio would be as follows:

$$\frac{\text{Cash and cash equivalents}}{\text{Current liabilities}}$$

$$= 100/160 = 0.6:1$$

The ratio is less than 1 which means the company has insufficient cash to meet its liabilities due within one year.

2.4 Cash and cash equivalents/current assets

This is a measure of cash as a percentage of total current assets and is calculated by dividing cash by current assets.

This is a measure of cash as a percentage of total current assets and is calculated by dividing cash by current assets. Cash and cash equivalents are the most liquid of current assets so a business with a high cash and cash equivalents ratio to current assets is considered healthy in terms of liquidity.

The formula is:

$$\frac{\text{Cash and cash equivalents}}{\text{Current assets}} \times 100$$

i.e.

$$\frac{\text{Cash and cash equivalents}}{\text{Receivables, inventory, cash and cash equivalents, other current assets}} \times 100$$

Worked example 6.7

Using the statement of financial position figures for the company in the above example, the cash and cash equivalents as a percentage of current assets would be as follows:

$$\frac{\text{Cash and cash equivalents}}{\text{Current assets}} \times 100$$

= 100/350 = 28.6%

2.5 Cash flow ratio

This ratio measures a company's net cash inflow from operating activities as per the company's cash flow statement to its total debts and helps determine the cash position of the company compared with a prior period or with like companies. However, because the formula measures cash inflow to total debts, which includes liabilities falling due in over one year, it is perhaps less useful than cash ratios which are based on short-term liquidity requirements.

The formula is:

$$\frac{\text{Net cash inflow from operating activities}}{\text{Total debts}} \times 100$$

2.6 Net working capital/total assets

This is a measure of net current assets divided by total assets and is calculated as follows:

$$\frac{\text{Current assets} - \text{current liabilities}}{\text{Total assets}} \times 100$$

Worked example 6.8

Using the statement of financial position figures for the company in the above example, the net working capital as a percentage of total assets would be as follows:

$$\frac{\text{Current assets} - \text{current liabilities}}{\text{Total assets}} \times 100$$

$$= \frac{\text{Net current assets}}{\text{Total assets}} \times 100$$

$$= \frac{350 - 160}{850} \times 100$$

$$= 190/850 = 22.4\%$$

3. Efficiency ratios

Efficiency ratios enable users of accounts to determine if a company is improving in efficiency. An improvement in efficiency usually results in increased profitability. Accordingly, some ratios may be described as both efficiency ratios and profitability ratios.

3.1 Return on capital employed (ROCE)

As explained in the earlier section on profitability ratios, ROCE is a measure of a company's success at achieving a return on capital invested. It is probably the single most important profitability and efficiency ratio as it reflects the profit as a percentage of the amount of capital employed.

There are a number of ways of calculating ROCE but the most common method is to divide a company's return or earnings by net capital employed. The ratio is calculated as follows:

$$\text{ROCE} = \frac{\text{Profit on ordinary activities before interest and taxation (PBIT)}}{\text{Total assets (TA) less current liabilities (CL)}} \times 100$$

$$= \text{PBIT}/(\text{TA}-\text{CL}) \times 100$$

The ROCE is calculated by analysts to determine how well a company is performing and is sometimes compared with prior year performance in a company's annual report. For a supermarket, the ROCE might be in the region of 11%.

Please refer back to the more detailed description of ROCE covered in the section on profitability ratios.

3.2 Net asset turnover

$$\text{Net asset turnover} = \frac{\text{Sales}}{\text{Net assets}} = \frac{\text{Sales}}{\text{Capital employed}} = X \text{ times}$$

This ratio is expressed as the number of times net assets are turned over and expresses the ability of a business to generate sales from capital employed. A high number (relative to like companies in the same industry) might indicate that more investment is needed, whilst a low number indicates the business is not utilising its assets efficiently.

Test yourself 6.2

What is the relationship between operating profit margin, net asset turnover and ROCE? (See worked example 6.2 above.)

3.3 Non-current asset turnover

The non-current asset turnover ratio is a measurement of how effective a company is at generating turnover from non-current asset investments (e.g. property, plant and equipment) at its disposal.

It is calculated by dividing sales (i.e. sales less cost of sales) by non-current assets.

$$\frac{\text{Sales}}{\text{Non-current assets}}$$

This ratio is particularly relevant for manufacturing companies and companies that have substantial investment in non-current assets. To measure efficiency, the ratio should be compared with companies from the same industry or with its own prior year figures. A fall in net sales is likely to result in a fall in the efficiency ratio (unless non-current assets also fall in value, e.g. due to depreciation). If sales do not change from one year to the next and yet the ratio falls, it may indicate a fall in efficiency or that the company is over-invested in non-current assets which are failing to generate efficient returns. It may also be a result of the company having upgraded its plant and equipment which may result in higher turnover being generated in future years.

Worked example 6.9

Efficient Manufacturing Company Limited had non-current assets on 31 August 2011 of £200,000 before depreciation. It invested £700,000 to upgrade plant and machinery on 1 June 2012. The annual depreciation is charge is 25%. Sales for the years ended 31 August 2011 and 31 August 2012 are set out below.

	2012	2011
	£'000	£'000
Sales	2,000	1,500

Calculate the non-current asset turnover for the years ended 31 August 2011 and 31 August 2012.

Solution:

2011:

$$\text{Non-current asset turnover} = \frac{\text{Sales}}{\text{Non-current assets}}$$

$1,500,000/(200,000 \times 75\%) = 1,500,000/150,000 = 10$ times

The company has a high non-current asset turnover ratio which indicates the company's assets are effective at generating turnover.

2012:

$$\text{Non-current asset turnover} = \frac{\text{Sales}}{\text{Non-current assets}}$$

Working 1:

$$\begin{aligned}
\text{Non-current assets} &= (£150,000 \times 75\%) + (£700,000 - (£700,000 \times 25\% \\
&\quad \times 3/12)) \\
&= £112,500 + £700,000 - £43,750 \\
&= £768,750
\end{aligned}$$

$$\frac{\text{Sales}}{\text{Non-current assets}} = \frac{£2,000,000}{£768,750} = 2.6 \text{ times}$$

Whilst the non-current asset turnover ratio has fallen significantly, implying a fall in efficiency may not be due to a fall in turnover. It is possible that the fall in the efficiency ratio could be attributed to over-investment in plant and machinery, but it is perhaps more likely that the fall is due to the non-current asset investment being made in the final quarter of the financial year. The non-current assets figure has increased significantly year on year, but the assets have not been held long enough to generate increased sales for the year ended 31 August 2012. In the case of Efficient Manufacturing Company Limited, it therefore cannot be assumed that efficiency has fallen simply because the non-current asset turnover ratio has fallen. The company should consider calculating the ratio for the nine months to 31 May 2012 and annualizing the resultant figure which might be a fairer comparative on which to evaluate efficiency:

$$\begin{aligned}
\text{Non-current assets} &= (£150,000 - (£150,000 \times 25\% \times 9/12)) \\
&= £150,000 - £28,125 \text{ (depreciation charge for the} \\
&\quad \text{9 months)} \\
&= £121,875
\end{aligned}$$

$$\frac{\text{Sales}}{\text{Non-current assets}} = \frac{(£2,000,000 \times 9/12)/£121,875}{£121,875} = 12.3 \text{ times}$$

In this example, we see that efficiency of Efficient Manufacturing Company Limited increased for the nine months ended 31 May 2012 when compared with the prior year.

3.4 Inventory turnover

Inventory turnover measures how efficient a company is at converting inventory to revenues and shows how often inventory is turned over or used during the period under review. A quick rate of turnover (high ratio) indicates that inventory is tightly controlled (e.g. management has decided to use **just in time procurement**) or that cash may not be available to place larger inventory orders. A low turnover rate may be a result of poor sales volumes or a relatively large order of inventory having previously been placed. Long turnover periods might mean excessive inventory leading to higher storage costs and increased risk of being left with obsolete inventory which may never be sold. Low inventory turnover implies either a downturn in trading or **overcapitalisation** which can lead to a lower return on investment.

The inventory turnover formula used to calculate how many times the company has sold the value of its inventory during the year is:

$$\frac{\text{Cost of sales}}{\text{Inventory}}$$

The inventory days formula used to show the number of days it takes to turn over the inventory (i.e. the number of days that cash is tied up in inventory) is:

$$\text{Inventory days} = \frac{\text{Inventory}}{\text{Cost of sales}} \times 365 = \text{X days}$$

The average inventory (at cost) figure is used in the calculation. One method commonly used for calculating average inventory, where inventory movement is fairly consistent throughout the year, is to add the opening inventory value to closing inventory and divide by two:

$$\text{Average inventory} = \frac{\text{opening inventory} + \text{closing inventory}}{2}$$

just in time procurement (JIT) is a term used to describe a procurement policy whereby inventory is delivered just before it is needed. It relies on close customer and supplier relations to ensure the inventory arrives "just in time". JIT production methods are commonly used in the motor industry and other manufacturing industries enabling flexible manufacturing processes which keep inventory levels to a minimum.

overcapitalisation is an over-investment in working capital which can lead to excessive inventory, high receivable/low payable level and an unnecessarily large amount of cash. Overcapitalisation can result in a lower return on investment and the unnecessary use of long-term funds to meet short-term obligations.

Test yourself 6.3

What are the disadvantages of slow inventory turnover?

The manufacturing industry controls inventory turnover tightly by using just in time procurement methods. This minimises stockholding which reduces inventory costs and improves the quick ratio.

3.5 Sales to net working capital

The sales to net working capital ratio shows the amount of net current assets required to generate sales and, therefore, helps a business to control its cash levels. Whilst it is important for a business to have liquidity, any excess cash should be used to keep financing needs to a minimum and thereby reduce the overall cost of capital. If a company uses long-term capital to fund short-term obligations it should expect lower investment returns.

working capital
is a measure of how
a company meets its
short-term obligations
(i.e. current liabilities) with
its current assets and is
calculated by deducting
current liabilities from
current assets.

The ratio is also known as net working capital turnover because it is a measure of how efficiently **working capital** is turned over.

The formula is:

$$\frac{\text{Sales}}{\text{Net working capital}} \times 100 = \frac{\text{Sales}}{\text{CA-CL}} \times 100$$

Broadly speaking, a high ratio indicates the company has a strong ability to use working capital efficiently to maintain sales and a low ratio indicates inefficiency and overcapitalisation. As with the analysis of all ratios, other factors should be taken into account, such as the macro economic climate, and ratios should not be looked at in isolation.

Stop and think 6.3

What are the possible shortfalls of sales to net working capital ratio?

3.6 Receivables days

This is a measure of the average time it takes receivables to pay for goods they have received on credit. An increase in receivables days is a sign that the quality of the receivables is decreasing and could, if not addressed, lead to a business having cash flow difficulties. In a financial services company, receivables days which exceed 90 days usually have to be discounted for the purposes of short-term liquidity calculations as it becomes increasingly less certain that the receivables will pay in full in a timely manner. In the retail clothing business, the average receivables payment period is often significantly shorter and credit terms of no more than 30 days are not unusual. Broadly speaking, the lower the receivables days, the better the cash position for the business.

A business with a tightly run credit control department will regularly monitor the average debtor payment period and look for movements in the trend so that increases in receivables days are effectively managed in a timely manner.

The ratio is calculated as follows:

$$\frac{\text{Trade receivables}}{\text{Sales}} \times 365 = \text{X days}$$

3.7 Payables days

This efficiency and performance ratio measures the average time it takes a business to pay its payables. It is calculated by dividing trade payables by purchases.

$$\frac{\text{Trade payables}}{\text{Purchases}} \times 365 = \text{X days}$$

If the purchases figure is not available then the cost of sales figure would be used.

If the ratio is over 90 days in, say, the financial services industry, it could mean that the business is struggling to generate sufficient cash to settle its invoices in a timely manner. A high ratio could also imply unethical practice. For example, in the food retail industry a major supermarket chain might intentionally delay payment to suppliers who are dependent on the supermarket for the business.

Worked example 6.10

If a supermarket has purchases of £30 million and £5 million of payables, how long does it take on average to pay its suppliers?

Solution:

$$\text{Payables days} = \frac{\text{Trade payables}}{\text{Purchases}} \times 365 = 5/30 \times 365 = 61 \text{ days}$$

Stop and think 6.4

What might the implications be if a company's payables payment period were to decrease significantly from one year to the next?

4. Gearing ratios

Gearing ratios measure the solvency of a company and focus on the extent to which businesses use long-term **debt financing** compared with **equity financing**. **Gearing** is therefore a measurement of long-term debt to shareholder funds. The various gearing ratios indicate the ability of a business to fund its debt and interest payments for its continuing operations. A company that is highly geared or leveraged has a high proportion of debt to equity, whereas a company with a low gearing ratio has a relatively low level of debt compared with equity.

A highly geared company might be considered more risky than a company without gearing because the highly geared company will have regular interest payments to service the debt and, in times of increasing interest rates, businesses with high levels of borrowing with variable rate interest payments may find themselves faced with uncomfortably large monthly outgoings in order to service the debt. This means there is likely to be less money available for distribution to equity holders in the form of dividends.

A company that is funded only by equity will have no interest payments. Instead, it will pay out a dividend to the owners of the company but only if it can afford to do so. Dividends are paid out at the discretion of the board whilst interest payments on long-term debt financing are a contractual payment. Whilst equity might be less risky than debt, it may prove more costly for the company to raise equity finance because the raising of equity will involve a **public offering**. Many companies will be funded by both debt and equity.

debt financing
occurs when a company raises finance by issuing bonds, bills or notes and, in exchange, promises to repay the lender the interest and capital on the loan.

equity financing
is capital raised by selling shares in the company, typically by public offering. Investors buy the shares and become shareholders or owners of the company's equity.

gearing
is a measurement of long-term debt to equity and measures the extent to which a company is leveraged by comparing borrowed funds to shareholder funds.

The merits and drawbacks of each type of financing would need to be taken into account should the company require further financing.

Lenders of finance are particularly interested in a company's gearing ratios since a high gearing ratio might indicate a company's inability to repay the debt. It is therefore, not unusual, for lenders to restrict a company's level of gearing through the use of **loan covenants**.

Stop and think 6.5

Can you think of any benefits of debt over equity as a source of financing?

public offering
is an offer to the public for subscriptions for sale of shares in a company in accordance with the terms of the offering document.

loan covenant
this is a restrictive measure placed on the borrower by the lender as a means of safeguarding the loan. Measures might include restricting the level of gearing of the borrower by insisting more equity is put into the company. If a company breaches its loan covenant then it may be forced to repay the loan or find an alternative lender who is likely to insist on a high rate of return to reflect the high level of gearing. In effect, a loan covenant is a charge over a non-current asset.

There are a number of gearing ratios, the most commonly used ones being:

4.1 Debt to equity

$$\text{Gearing} = \frac{\text{Debt}}{\text{Equity}} = \text{D/E}$$

This ratio measures debt to equity by taking the total debt figure from the statement of financial position and dividing it by the total equity. When comparing companies of similar nature and in the same industry, a low debt to equity ratio indicates less risk than a high debt to equity ratio.

4.2 Debt to debt plus equity (or debt ratio or gearing ratio)

This gearing ratio is much like the debt to equity ratio but measures debt to total assets.

$$\text{Gearing} = \frac{\text{Debt}}{\text{Equity} + \text{Equity}} \times 100 = \frac{\text{Debt}}{\text{Total assets}} \times 100 = \text{D/(D+E)} \times 100$$

This ratio might also be expressed as Debt/Total capital employed × 100 and is often referred to as the main gearing ratio.

This measures debt as a proportion of total assets. Again, assuming everything else is equal, a lower gearing ratio indicates less risk. A high ratio indicates greater vulnerability to economic downturns because the company may have to continue to pay fixed interest payments on the debt when earnings fall.

4.3 Interest cover (or interest times covered)

$$\text{Interest cover} = \frac{\text{Profit before interest and taxation (PBIT)}}{\text{Interest paid}}$$

This ratio measures a company's ability to meet its interest payments from earnings. An interest cover of 4 indicates that a company has sufficient earnings to meet its interest payments four times. A ratio of 2, means the earnings will cover interest 2 times. Higher interest cover ratios, therefore, indicate that a company is better placed to meet its interest obligations. Interest cover of less than 1 or slightly less than 1 means the company is likely to have difficulty in servicing its debt.

When analysing **leverage** ratios, care should be taken not to simply state that a debt to equity ratio of, say, 180% means that a company is highly geared. A company's leverage should always be compared to that of similar companies in the same industry and commentary made in a relevant context. Analysts and users of financial statements should take into account the risk profile of the company and its investment policy. For example, it may not be unusual for a collective investment fund whose investment policy is specialist and alternative investments to be highly geared. A company with a high proportion of non-current assets is also more likely to have a high level of gearing, e.g. a construction company or a company that hires out plant and machinery, and so it would not be appropriate to compare the gearing of a plant hire company which might have financial gearing of 200% or more with that of a retail clothes store or financial services company which is less likely to need to raise finance to fund non-current asset investments and therefore might have a gearing level of no more than 100%.

leverage
describes the use of debt and borrowed funds by a business with a view to increasing the return on an investment. A business that is highly leveraged will have a high debt to equity (or gearing) ratio.

5. Earnings per share (EPS) and other key investor ratios

Earnings per share is a measure of net income of a company (less dividends paid on preference shares) divided by the number of shares in issue. It is a frequently used indicator of a company's profitability and is often used by shareholders for comparing a company's financial health with a company with similar earnings.

The EPS ratio is calculated as follows:

$$\frac{\text{Earnings} - \text{preference dividends}}{\text{No of shares}}$$

For the purposes of the calculation earnings means profit after tax.

Worked example 6.11

A company has net income of £20 million for the year ended 30 June 2012 and has eight million shares in issue.

What is the basic EPS of the company?

Answer:

EPS = Earnings/No of shares

= £20m/8m = £2.50 per share

Worked example 6.12

A company has net income of £20 million for the year ended 30 June 2012. The company has eight million shares at the start of the financial year and, on 1 October 2011, issues a further 2 million shares. The company pays out dividends on preference shares of £1 million. What is the year end EPS?

Answer:

$$EPS = \frac{Earnings - preference\ dividends}{No\ of\ shares}$$

Earnings = £20m
Preference dividends = £1m
Weighted average number of shares = (8m × 3/12) + ((8m + 2m) × 9/12)
= (8m × 3/12) + (10m × 9/12)
= 2m + 7.5m = 9.5m

$$EPS = \frac{£20m - £1m}{9.5m}$$

= £19m/9.5m = £2 per share

Test yourself 6.4

Company A has earnings of £13 million and Company B has earnings of £12 million. Company A pays out dividends on preference shares of £1m. Company B pays preference dividends of £1.5m. Company A has 4 million shares in issue whereas Company B has 4 million shares in issue for the first half of the financial year and 2 million for the remaining six months. Which company has the highest earnings per share?

A company with greater overall earnings than another company is not necessarily more profitable because the company which has less earnings might have a higher EPS, i.e. it generates more earnings per share. Another consideration with profitability measures is to be aware that two companies may have the same EPS and so it is important for analysts and investors to take other factors and other profitability ratios into account when making an investment decision. For example, if Company A and Company B in the above example had the same EPS then the company with the least paid up share capital might be considered the better investment choice because it would have generated the same EPS despite less money having being invested in the company by the shareholders.

5.1 Price Earnings ratio (P/E ratio)

The price to earnings ratio is a measure of earnings growth and is calculated by dividing the market value per share by the EPS.

$$\text{P/E ratio} = \frac{\text{Market value per share}}{\text{EPS}} = \frac{\text{Market value per share} \times \text{number of shares}}{\text{Total earnings}}$$

$$= \frac{\text{Market capitalisation}}{\text{Total earnings}}$$

The P/E ratio is viewed as an important measure by many shareholders because it indicates how long it will take for them to receive back their initial investment in the company. For example, if a company has a market capitalisation of £85 million and net profit of £5 million then the P/E ratio would be 17. As with many other ratios, the P/E ratio requires a comparative to be meaningful but, simplistically speaking, the P/E ratio would suggest, rightly or wrongly, to shareholders that it will take 17 years for their investment in the company to be paid off by earnings.

Worked example 6.13

Parnings Erice plc has the following income statement figures for the year ended 31 March 2012.

	£'000
Operating profit	50,000
Tax	(24,000)
Profit after tax	26,000
Dividend for the year	(10,000)
Retained profit	16,000

Parnings Erice plc has ten million ordinary £1 shares in issue with a market value of 350p per share. The company has no preference shares, hence the dividend for the year is on ordinary shares. Calculate the P/E ratio for Parnings Erice plc.

Solution: There are no dividends on preference shares to deduct from earnings for the purposes of the EPS calculation.

$$\text{EPS} = \frac{\text{Profit after tax}}{\text{No of shares}}$$

$$= \frac{£26,000,000}{10,000,000} = £2.60$$

P/E ratio = £3.50/£2.60 = 1.3

The P/E ratio is not without its shortcomings and one of the main drawbacks is that it is calculated using the earnings figure which is subject to manipulation by management. Analysts may, therefore, use their own projection of future earnings in the calculation rather than relying on past performance as a measure of future performance.

A low P/E ratio of a company might indicate to investors that its shares are value for money but it could also mean that earnings are expected to fall, hence why analysts might use their own earnings forecasts to calculate the P/E ratio. Analysis of earnings growth should, therefore, take a number of financial and non-financial factors into account and not rely solely on the P/E ratio.

5.2 Dividend cover

The dividend cover ratio measures a company's ability to maintain dividend payments. It shows how many times the dividends can be paid out of profits. For example, a dividend cover of two times means that a company can afford to pay dividends twice out of profits. Put another way, it means profits attributable to shareholders were twice the dividend level.

Dividend cover is a key shareholder investment ratio because most shareholders like to receive regular and stable dividend payments. If the dividend cover is two times or less then shareholders might become anxious if profits fall as this may mean their expected dividend payment is under threat. A dividend cover of three or four times will provide shareholders with more comfort that profits are sufficient to cover a healthy dividend payment. The ratio serves, therefore, as a useful measure of sustained profitability:

Dividend cover = EPS/dividend per ordinary share

5.3 Dividend yield

Dividend yield is a key investor ratio as it highlights the return on the shares, i.e. how much an investor receives in dividend payments relative to his or her investment:

$$\text{Dividend yield} = \frac{\text{Annual dividend per ordinary share}}{\text{Market value of share}} \times 100$$

Worked example 6.14

A company's annual dividend is 80p per share and the ex dividend share price is £16 per share.

Dividend yield = £0.80/£16 = 5%.

5.4 Dividend payout ratio

The dividend payout ratio measures the proportion of earnings paid out as dividends and is measured as:

$$\frac{\text{Total annual dividend}}{\text{EPS}} \times 100$$

Chapter summary

◆ For ratios to be meaningful, they should always be considered in context and compared with prior period ratios and/or with ratios of similar companies in the same industry sector.

◆ Key profitability ratios include net profit margin, gross profit margin, return on capital employed, return on equity, return on assets and earnings per share.

◆ An increase in gross profit margin may not translate into an increase in the net profit margin if expenses increase relative to sales.

◆ The main liquidity ratios include the current ratio, the quick ratio and the cash ratio. Other liquidity ratios covered in this chapter are the cash and cash equivalents as a percentage of current assets, the cash flow ratio and net working capital to total assets. The quick ratio is a more conservative measure than the current ratio because the quick ratio measures a company's ability to meet liabilities due within one year out of the most liquid assets (and therefore the quickest to convert to cash). Inventory value is deducted from the current assets figure in the quick ratio calculation.

◆ Efficiency ratios comprise return on capital employed (which is covered in more detail in the profitability ratios section of this chapter), net asset turnover, non-current asset turnover, inventory turnover, sales to net working capital receivables (or debtor), debtor days and payables (or creditor) days.

◆ Net asset turnover multiplied by the operating profit margin gives the return on capital employed. An increase in profit margin does not necessarily lead to a greater return because increasing the margin might lead to reduced sales and slower asset turnover. Return on capital employed is dependent on both profit margin and net asset turnover.

◆ Working capital is a measure of how a company meets its current liabilities with its current assets.

◆ Overcapitalisation is an over-investment in working capital which can lead to cash being tied up in inventory and generally high cash levels which could otherwise have been invested elsewhere to produce a higher return.

◆ Gearing (or leverage) ratios measure the solvency of a business and focus on the extent to which businesses use long-term debt financing compared with equity financing. An increase in gearing is usually linked to an increase in risk. A reduction in the gearing level does not necessarily mean that debts have been paid off by the company. It could mean that the company has taken on additional equity funding, thereby reducing the voting powers of existing shareholders who chose not to take up the offer for more shares.

◆ Banks and other lenders of finance are very interested in leverage ratios because a high level of gearing might indicate a company's inability to repay its loan. Lenders often impose loan covenants on borrowers, which restrict a company's gearing level, and help to safeguard the loan.

◆   EPS and other investor ratios help investors to assess the financial health of a company compared to a company with similar earnings because the company with greater overall earnings may have a lower EPS.

◆   The P/E ratio measures earnings growth and is calculated by dividing the market value per share by the EPS. This is a key shareholder investment ratio because it indicates how long it will be before they will get back their initial investment in the company. A low P/E ratio might indicate that shares are value for money, or it could mean that earnings are forecast to fall. As with all ratios, other factors (including non-financial factors) should be taken into account when making an investment decision.

Chapter seven
Cash flow statements

List of topics

1   Preparation of cash flow statements
2   Interpretation of cash flow statements

Introduction

Cash is important for the running of any business. Stakeholders like to see profit but a company will not be viable over time if it is unable to generate and obtain cash. A company will need cash to settle amounts payables and to pay employees, tax authorities and shareholders. If payments are not made, deliveries from suppliers will cease and banks will call in their loans and employees will stop working. If tax authorities are not paid, the company may be forced into administration and if shareholders do not receive their dividend, they may no longer invest in the company. It is therefore important that businesses are aware of their cash flows and that stakeholders have access to cash flow reports and other information to help them assess cash generation and absorption as well as the financial position of the business in terms of liquidity, solvency and financial adaptability.

In this chapter, students will gain an understanding of how cash flow statements are prepared and will learn to reconcile operating profit to net cash flow from operating activities. The chapter will also discuss how to interpret cash flow statements and establish if an organisation's cash flows are being well managed.

1. Preparation of cash flow statements

The **statement** of **cash flows** is a **primary financial statement** in the annual report and accounts and is concerned with cash flows from **operating activities**, **investing activities** and **financing activities**. The statement shows changes in cash and cash equivalents over a financial period and therefore serves as an analytical tool to enable users of accounts to review the prior period's cash movements and period-end cash position assess the viability of a business in terms of liquidity, solvency and financial adaptability. Unlike the

cash flow statement
is a primary financial statement found in the annual report and accounts and is concerned with cash flows from operating activities, investing activities and external sources of finance. The statement shows changes in cash and cash equivalents over a financial period and therefore serves as an analytical tool to enable users of accounts to review the past year's cash movements and year-end cash position and assess the viability of a business in terms of liquidity, solvency and financial adaptability.

primary financial statements
are the statement of financial position, income statement and cash flow statement. These three primary statements provide the key information to users of accounts in order for them to assess financial performance and the financial position of the organisation.

operating activities are the main income producing activities of a business and include other activities that are neither investing nor financing activities.

investing activities refers to acquisitions and disposals of investments which are not classified as cash equivalents.

financing activities describe the raising of finance in the form of debt or equity and includes short- and long-term borrowings as well as proceeds from the issuance of ordinary shares.

statement of income, the cash flow statement only reports transactions that have a cash flow and does not include accounting entries such as accruals. Accordingly, the cash flow statement provides additional information to supplement the other two primary financial statements, namely the statement of financial position and the income statement. The preparation of cash flow statements is governed by International Accounting Standard 7 (IAS 7).

Cash flow statements comprise three main sections showing all the cash items which generate the net increase or decrease in cash and cash equivalents:

◆ net cash generated from/(used in) operating activities;
◆ net cash generated from/(used in) investing activities;
◆ net cash generated from/(used in) financing activities.

Opening and closing cash positions need to be reconciled based on the effect of these activities. The first main section of the cash flow statement, the net cash inflow or outflow from operations, is calculated by taking the operating profit and adjusting it for depreciation and movements in items such as stock, receivables and payables. This is known as the reconciliation of operating profit to net cash flow from operating activities. The examples below show the main adjustments required, namely:

◆ Depreciation (add back to operating profit).
◆ Increase in inventory (deduct from operating profit).
◆ Increase in receivables (deduct from operation profit).
◆ Increase in payables (add to operating profit).
◆ Decrease in inventory (add to operating profit).
◆ Decrease in receivables (add to operating profit).
◆ Decrease in payables (deduct from operating profit).

Worked example 7.1

A company has a profit before tax of £600,000 for the period ended 30 June 2012. A depreciation charge of £20,000 has been applied to non-current assets, receivables and payables have increased by £150,000 and £80,000 respectively and inventory has decreased by £65,000. What is the net cash flow from operating activities that will appear in the company's cash flow statement for the period ended 30 June 2012?

Answer:

	£
Profit before tax	600,000
Add back depreciation	20,000
Operating profit	620,000
Decrease in inventory	65,000
Increase in receivables	(150,000)
Increase in payables	80,000
Net cash inflow from operating activities	**£615,000**

Worked example 7.2

A company has operating profit of £110,000 for the year ended 31 March 2012. During the year receivables have decreased by £20,000 from £80,000, payables have decreased by £95,000 and inventory has increased by £40,000. What is the net cash flow from operating activities for the year ended 31 March 2012?

Answer:

	£
Operating profit	110,000
Increase in inventory	(40,000)
Decrease in receivables	20,000
Decrease in payables	(95,000)
Net cash outflow from operating activities	**£(5,000)**

Worked example 7.3

A company has operating profit of £950,000 for the year ended 31 December 2011. During the year receivables have increased by £9,000, payables have decreased by £35,000 and stock inventory levels have increased by £50,000. What is the net cash flow from operating activities for the year ended 31 December 2011?

Answer:

	£
Operating profit	950,000
Increase in inventory	(50,000)
Increase in receivables	(90,000)
Decrease in payables	(35,000)
Net cash inflow from operating activities	**£775,000**

reconciliation of operating profit to net cash flow from operating activities is a note in the financial statements which shows non-cash item adjustments made to operating profit in order to determine the net cash flow from operating activities. The non-cash reconciling items include depreciation, movement in inventory and movement in receivables and payables. The reconciliation does not form part of the primary cash flow statement but may be presented alongside to the cash flow statement or as a separate note in the financial statements.

Operating activities

Operating activities are those activities which generate revenue such as receipts from the sale of goods and services and receipts from royalties. Operating activities are also those activities directly linked to creating a product or the provision of a service, for example, payments to suppliers and employees.

Taxes attributable to income, for example corporation tax, are usually also treated as operating cash flows unless they specifically relate to an investing or financing activity. Likewise, cash flows relating to dividends and interest may also be classified as operating activities provided the classification remains consistent from one reporting period to the next. Other examples of operating cash flows include receipts from the sale of goods, receipts from royalties, supplier payments and payments to employees.

Investing activities

Cash flows from investing activities, the second main section of the cash flow statement, include the acquisition and disposal of investments (both non-current as well as current assets such as investments in securities) that are not classified as liquid assets. In other words, they cannot be easily and quickly converted into cash without a material loss in value.

Financing activities

Financing activities include the issuance of ordinary shares to raise equity finance, repayment of short- and long-term borrowings, proceeds from short- and long-term borrowings and finance leases. Cash flows relating to dividends paid to equity holders are also included in the financing activities section of the cash flow statement. Dividends received, however, could be classified as either operating activities or investing activities depending on the business activities of the recipient.

It is also possible for cash flows relating to the same transaction to be separately classified. For example, interest on a financing lease might be classified an operating activity whilst capital repayments are financing activities.

Cash Rich Plc
Cash flow statement for the year to 31 March 2012

	2012 f'000	2011 f'000
Cash flows from operating activities		
Net profit for the year	1,224	1,050
Net gain on financial assets at fair value through profit or loss	(200)	(180)
Decrease/(increase) in receivables	(55)	10
Increase in payables	225	100
Amortisation of investments	50	67
Net cash flow from operating activities	**1244**	**1047**
Cash flows from investing activities		
Purchase of assets at fair value through profit or loss	–	(100)
Decrease/(increase) in current investments	15	(5)
Interest received	100	60
Net cash flow from investing activities	**115**	**(45)**
Cash flows from financing activities		
Dividends paid	(1,074)	(1,000)
Net cash flow from financing activities	**(1,074)**	**(1,000)**
Net increase in cash and cash equivalents	**285**	**2**
Cash and cash equivalents at beginning of year	**615**	**613**
Cash and cash equivalents at end of year	**900**	**615**

In order to see how the cash balances have moved, it is useful to also look at the statement of financial position, the income statement and the statement of changes in equity:

Income statement for the year ended 31 March 2012

	2012 f'000	2011 f'000
Income		
Net gain on financial assets at fair value through profit or loss	200	180
Advisory fees	1,000	900
Investment income (including interest received)	180	160
Gain on foreign exchange	5	–
Other income	50	40
Total income	**1,435**	**1,280**
Expenses		
Administration fees	10	8
Advisory and management fees	100	90
Amortisation	50	60
Operating costs	15	20
Accounting and Audit fees	5	5
Director fees	13	21
Legal and professional fees	10	15
Bank charges	1	1
Loss on foreign exchange	–	4
Sundry expenses	7	6
Total operating expenses	**211**	**230**
Net profit for the year	**1,224**	**1,050**

Statement of financial position as at 31 March 2012

	2012 f'000	2011 f'000
Assets		
Non-current assets		
Financial assets at fair value through profit or loss	700	600
Intangible assets	150	200
Current assets		
Investments	15	30
Receivables	255	200
Cash and cash equivalents	900	615
Total assets	**2,020**	**1,645**
Liabilities		
Current liabilities		
Payables	920	695
Equity		
Share capital	250	250
Retained earnings	850	700
Total equity and liabilities	**2,020**	**1,645**

Statement of changes in equity for the year ended 31 March 2012

	Share capital	Retained earnings	2012 £'000	2011 £'000
Opening balance	250	700	950	900
Net profit for the year	–	1,224	1,224	1,050
Dividends paid	–	(1,074)	(1,074)	(1,000)
Closing balance	250	850	1,100	950

The operating activities section of the statement cash flows of Cash Rich Plc shows an increase in receivables indicating that debt collection may need a review.

Investing activities have generated more cash than the prior year but this has not been reinvested. The directors may, therefore, wish to consider if it is in the best interests of the company to reinvest some of the cash or whether to increase the dividend payment to shareholders. The company could also use cash to buy back shares or reduce payables.

The financing activities section shows the company is able to generate sufficient cash to pay a healthy dividend which is likely to be welcomed by shareholders. The positive cash flow also provides creditors and lenders of finance with comfort that it should be able to repay its debts as they fall due which, in turn, places the company in a strong position should it need to negotiate additional financing.

Stop and think 7.1

What might a net cash outflow from operating activities indicate to analysts?

2. Interpretation of cash flow statements

Whilst the income statement shows revenues and expenses, many of which have been accrued and have not resulted in a cash flow, the statement of cash flows shows actual cash inflows and outflows of a business during the reporting period. A business may have reported a sizeable profit evidenced by the income statement but it could have liquidity issues (e.g. resulting from credit sales which are no longer recoverable) which are more clearly explained by the statement of cash flows.

Cash is an easy concept to understand and investors take comfort if they see positive cash flows. Students should note, however, that net cash outflows do not necessarily warrant a red flag. Cash outflows from operating activities could, for example, be due to a planned increase in the level of inventories to cater for growth and improved sales. Likewise, cash outflows from investing activities might be simply due to the purchase of assets which are expected to lead to positive cash flows in the future. Analysts will look at trends over time and will want comfort that the business is able to sustain itself.

By providing additional information to the statement of income and statement of financial position, the cash flow statement enables a business to better assess liquidity, solvency and financial adaptability.

It is important for a business to have short term funds available to ensure it remains solvent. The cash flow statement helps a business understand the affect of short- and long-term borrowings on its cash flow items by separating out the financing activities and showing the movements for the financial period. It also provides users of accounts with a snapshot of the opening and closing balances of cash and cash equivalents and therefore helps a business identify if it has surplus cash which could be invested elsewhere to maximise shareholder wealth or which could be used to pay off capital on the interest bearing loans. Excess cash could also send a message to investors that the company is in a healthy position to invest in growth of the business and pay dividends.

Test yourself 7.1

What are the main functions of the cash flow statement?

The operating activities section of the statement indicates how well the core business activities of a company are doing and a positive net cash inflow implies a company is stable. If the core operational activities are generating positive cash flows, the company may be able to operate without having to seek additional finance from external sources.

The section on investing activities shows the extent of expenditure incurred in order to acquire new investments. It also shows cash received from existing investments. A high level of investment, such as capital expenditure to purchase property, plant and equipment, signals the company has sufficient cash and is confident of future growth.

In the financing activity disclosures, the repayment of loans indicates the company is generating sufficient cash flows to meet its long-term obligations. The financing activity disclosures also enable users to distinguish between outgoings used to service debt finance and outgoings to equity holders in the form of dividend payments. The financing activity inflows are likely to be borrowings or proceeds from the issuance of equity shares.

The financing activity inflows are likely to be borrowings or proceeds from the issuance of equity shares, for example:

	£
Cash flows from financing activities	
Plus:	
Proceds from loan borrowings	10,000
Proceeds from the issurance of equity shares	80,000
Additional capital drawdown	10,000
Less:	
Loan repayments	(5,000)
Dividends	(10,000)
Equals:	
Net cash flow from financing activities	**85,000**

The above example shows that the company has raised additional finance through a combination of debt and equity resulting in cash inflows of £100,000. The company has also paid out £5,000 to service its debt and £10,000 in dividends. Whilst the business has attracted inward investment, analysts may question whether the payment of the dividend was in the best interests of the company, for had the dividend not been paid, additional capital may not have needed to have been drawn down and the loan of £10,000 would not have been required. The company may be seeking finance for its investing activities or it could be facing negative cash flows from its operating activities.

Stop and think 7.2

In what way might a statement of cash flows add value for stakeholders and other users of accounts?

Test yourself 7.2

What do the operating, investing and financing cash flows of Cash Rich Plc in section 7.1 tell you about the company?

Chapter summary

◆ The cash flow statement is a primary financial statement and shows the movements in cash and cash equivalents over a financial period which helps stakeholders assess a business in terms of liquidity, solvency and financial adaptability.

◆ The preparation of the cash flow statement is governed by IAS 7. There are three main sections covering operation, investing and financing activities.

◆ The reconciliation of operating profit to net cash flow from operating activities may either be adjoined to the cash flow statement or disclosed as a separate note in the annual report and financial statements. The reconciliation statement shows adjustments to profit for non-cash items such as depreciation and for movements in inventory, receivables and accounts payable.

◆ The operating activities section indicates how well the core operating activities are going and a net positive cash inflow implies the company is stable and may not need to seek any additional finance from external sources.

◆ Cash flows from investing activities include the acquisition and disposal of investments that are not classified as liquid assets. It also shows cash received from existing investments. This section indicates possible future growth of the company.

◆ The financing section shows cash flows relating to share issues, short and long-term borrowings as well as the repayment of capital under finance lease arrangements. Cash flows from some activities such as financing lease repayments might be separately classified so that interest payments are treated as operating activities and capital repayments are classified as financing activities. This section of the cash flow statement helps users distinguish between outgoings to repay debt and outgoings to fund equity dividends.

Part Four

Chapter 8
Trust accounting

Chapter 9
Reporting requirements of companies, trusts and other offshore vehicles

In this part, students will learn about trust income and capital and the significance of the income and capital split in the context of life interest trusts. Students will also learn about the main financial statements comprising the accounts of a life interest trust and will gain an understanding of which accounting items might be classified as income and which might be treated as capital.

Other types of offshore vehicles are also covered in this part of the study text, including companies, limited partnerships and foundations. Students will gain an understanding of how international finance centres are used for tax planning purposes and how sometimes they might be misused for illicit practices.

Learning outcomes

At the end of this part, students should be able to:

◆ explain the concept of a trust;

◆ understand the role of the trustee of a trust;

◆ explain the difference between income and capital;

◆ explain the term "discretionary trust";

◆ outline the key features of a life interest trust;

◆ understand some of the key requirements of the Companies Act 2006 in respect of UK public and private companies;

◆ explain the requirements that might be required for conversion from a private to public company;

◆ explain some of the key features of Jersey public and private companies;

◆ summarise the similarities and differences between Guernsey and BVI limited companies;

◆ discuss the different types of share capital and explain the difference between equity and debt financing and the impact of debt financing on gearing and taxation;

◆ discuss the uses of cell companies;

◆ summarise the key differences between trusts, companies, partnerships and foundations;

◆ outline the characteristics of offshore financial centres and explain the uses, misuses and private uses of offshore jurisdictions;

◆ explain the European Savings Directive on tax information exchange and transparency; and

◆ understand the basics of taxation, anti-avoidance rules and how UK resident, non-domiciled, individuals might benefit from offshore international finance centres.

Chapter eight
Trust accounting

List of topics

1 Trusts: Income and capital
2 Trusts: Preparation and interpretation of non-complex financial statements

Introduction

In this chapter, students will learn about trusts, trustees, trust income and trust capital. Students will also gain an insight into discretionary trusts and life interest trusts and will learn the importance of segregating income from capital. The chapter also explains what is meant by the terms "life tenant" and "remaindermen" in the context of life interest trusts.

The chapter also introduces accounting for a life interest trust and students will learn how to prepare a life tenant's account and how to treat certain items of income and expenditure.

1. Trusts: Income and capital

1.1 Trusts

A **trust** is a legal arrangement whereby one or more persons, known as the trustee(s), are entrusted with the legal ownership of the assets of another party, the settlor, and to hold those assets (which might include property, investments and cash) "on trust" for the benefit of one or more beneficiaries. A trust has no separate legal personality and therefore cannot contract in its own name. Instead, a trustee will be appointed to manage the affairs of the trust and contract in its name, i.e. as trustee of the trust.

Trusts are often used for estate planning purposes, for example where a high net worth individual wishes for his spouse, children and descendants to benefit from his estate but does not want the children to be spoilt by receiving large sums of cash at an early age, as this may discourage them from working hard and completing their education. The assets are settled on trust and the trustees are empowered to invest the funds on behalf of the beneficiaries and make

trust
is a legal arrangement whereby one or more persons, known as the trustee(s), are entrusted with the legal ownership of the assets of another party, the settlor, and to hold those assets (which might include property, investments and cash) "on trust" for the benefit of one or more beneficiaries.

trust deed
is a legal document setting out the terms of the trust and includes details of the interested parties, such as the settlor, trustees and beneficiaries as well as details of the trustee's powers – such as powers to invest and powers to distribute capital and income.

forced heirship
is essentially a feature of civil law jurisdictions and Islamic countries which do not recognise the full freedom of testation. This means, for example, that an individual making his will may not be able to leave an equal proportion of his assets to his surviving children and spouse. In order to prevent all the assets going to the eldest child, the individual may use a foundation or trust and thereby avoid the forced heirship rules.

fiduciary duty
is the legal obligation of a fiduciary to act in the best interests of another party.

distributions of capital and/or income to them, at their discretion or as set out in the **trust deed**.

Offshore trusts are also commonly used for the avoidance of **forced heirship**, for the avoidance of probate and for tax planning purposes.

1.2 Trustee

A trustee is an individual or corporate body (e.g. a limited liability company) which takes legal ownership of the assets of a trust fund and manages the trust fund for the benefit of the beneficiaries. A trust may have one of more trustees depending on the trust law governing the trust. For example, a Jersey trust may have one or more trustees, whereas in Guernsey the minimum requirement is typically two trustees. The trustee may be liable for damages if it does not carry out its **fiduciary duty** in a proper manner. The trustee's duty includes the maintenance of accurate records in order to be able to report the beneficiaries as and when required. A trustee is usually entitled to receive payment for its services and the terms will be set out in the trust deed.

1.3 Trust income and capital

The segregation of trust capital from trust income is an important consideration for trustees, for failure to properly distinguish between income and capital can result in adverse tax consequences. It is also important to separate out income and capital if the beneficiaries of income differ from the beneficiaries of capital, for example with life interest trusts.

1.4 Trust income

Income describes the money earned from an asset and trust income is mostly likely to be interest on bank deposits, property rental income, profits from trading and dividends received from investments. Everyday expenditure incurred to maintain trust assets, such as property management fees, are charges on income.

1.5 Trust capital

Trust capital represents the cash and non-cash assets initially settled on trust as well as capital subsequently settled on trust. In other words, it is the money, investments, property and other assets put into the trust. Profits derived from the sale of an investment are treated as capital and expenses relating to these assets, such as administration costs in relation to the sale of the asset, are charges on capital.

1.6 Discretionary trusts

A discretionary trust is a trust where the trustees have absolute discretion over the trust funds and may determine how much of the trust fund may be paid out to one or more of the beneficiaries.

1.7 Life interest trusts

Life interest trusts (also known as interest-in-possession trusts) are often set up as part of one's estate planning, so that when a person dies his or her surviving spouse is entitled to the income from the trust fund for life and, thereafter, the capital is typically passed on to the children, who would be known as the **remaindermen**. The beneficiary of the income is known as the life tenant, e.g. the surviving spouse, and is entitled to the income arising on the trust fund net of expenses, such as the trustee fees. By splitting out income and capital and ensuring capital is not eroded by only paying income, and not capital, to the life tenant, the trustees can ensure that the capital value of the trust fund is preserved for the surviving children. This is not to say that the trustees cannot pay capital to the life tenant – this will depend on the terms of the trust deed. Difficulties can arise when large expenses, such as trustee or legal fees, arise in respect of the trust. If the expenses are incurred in connection with income payments to the life tenant, for example, the remaindermen may expect to see the trustees paying such costs from the income of the trust fund and not from capital.

remaindermen
is the term given to beneficiaries who receive the remaining capital upon termination of a life interest trust, e.g. after the death of the life tenant.

Income arising on a trust might include, *inter alia*, bank deposit interest, dividends from shares held or property rental income. Revenue expenses typically include professional fees (e.g. legal fees, accountancy fees, registered office fees, company secretarial fees, trustee fees), bank charges and income distributed to the life tenant during the year.

The balance due to the life tenant may be found in the statement of financial position. The statement of financial position of a life interest trust is a snapshot of the trust's financial position showing its assets and liabilites at a specific point in time, for example:

◆ fixed asset investments held by the trust such as freehold property and quoted investments;

◆ current assets such as receivables and cash at hand/bank; and

◆ payables such as amount due to life tenant and other current liabilities.

Worked example 8.1

The income account on a life interest trust account shows an amount due to the life tenant of £50,000 as at 6 April 2010. The net income of the trust for the year ended 5 April 2011 was £40,000 of which a half was paid out in distributions to the Life Tenant during the year. What is the current liability of the life interest trust as at 5 April 2011?

Answer

	£
Opening balance due to life tenant	50,000
Net income of trust for the year	40,000
	90,000
Distributed to life tenant during year	(20,000)
Closing balance due to life tenant	**70,000**

The current liability of the Life Interest Trust as at 5 April 2011 is £70,000.

2. Trusts: Preparation and interpretation of non-complex financial statements

Trustees of a trust are responsible for ensuring accurate accounting records are maintained and that financial statements, if required by the trust deed, are clearly presented. The annual accounts for a trust typically include the following statements:

◆ Income account.

◆ Capital account.

◆ Statement of financial position.

◆ Schedule of investments.

The income account is mostly likely to show interest on bank deposits, property rental income and dividends received from investments. It will also show expenses paid out such as bank charges, overdraft interest, income tax, legal fees, accountancy fees, administration and other professional fees. Any income distributions will also appear on the income statement. With life interest trusts, the income due to the life tenant is shown in the life tenant's account.

The capital account shows the cash and non-cash assets initially settled on trust as well as additional settled funds. It also shows the increase in capital from investments, including gains and losses on realisation, and items of capital expenditure such as capital gains tax and inheritance tax. Certain professional fees may also be charged to capital if they relate to expenditure of a capital nature, for example, fees incurred in relation to the administration of an estate. Any capital distributions will also appear on the capital account. If a trust has separate funds (e.g. one fund for each beneficiary), the capital account should clearly show the capital balances by fund.

The statement of financial position shows fixed and current assets held by the trust including investments, property, bank balances and any receivables owing money to the trust (perhaps from a related party). It also shows the liabilities such as a bank overdraft, payables and, in the case of a life interest trust, the amount due to the life tenant.

The schedule of assets typically lists quoted and other investments, the amount of shares held, the book value and market value of those shares, additions, disposals and gain and losses on disposal of the shares.

Worked example 8.2

The income account of a life interest trust showed an amount due to the life tenant of £100,000 as at 1 January 2011. The net income for the trust for the financial year ended 31 December 2011 was £15,000 of which £10,000 had already been distributed to the life tenant during the year.

Prepare the life tenant's account for the year ended 31 December 2011 and state how much was due to the life tenant as at 31 December 2011.

Explain how would this be reflected in the statement of financial position of the life interest trust?

Answer: £100,000 + £15,000 – £10,000 = £105,000 would be due to the life tenant and this would be reflected as a current liability in the trust's statement of financial position as at 31 December 2011.

The Life Tenant's Account for the year ended 31 December 2011 would look like this:

	£
Balance as at 1 January 2011	100,000
Net income for the year	15,000
Amount available for distribution	115,000
Amount distributed in year	(10,000)
Balance as at 31 December 2011	105,000

Worked example 8.3

The Liam Johnson Life Interest Trust was established on 7 June 1991 under the laws of Jersey. The appointed trustees are ABC Trustees Limited. The terms of the trust are to pay income to the life tenant, Mrs Linda Johnson, during her life and upon her death to pay the capital to the children, Miss Sinead Johnson, Mr Joseph Johnson and Mrs Sarah Lemmer.

The following balances have been extracted from the ledgers of the Life Interest Trust Account for the 12 months ending 5 April 2012.

	DR £	CR £
Balances at 5 April 2012		
Quoted investments (market value)	500,000	
Freehold property (market value)	450,000	
Bank balances		
Capital	31,598	
Income	3,751	

Trust capital transactions for the reporting period

Investment management expenses	1,500	
Legal fees	1,000	
Accountancy fees	1,200	
Gain on sale of investments		500

Trust revenue transactions for the reporting period

Rental income		20,000
Income from quoted investments (dividends)		23,800
Bank interest		958
Trustee fees	2,500	
Accountancy fees	150	
Bank charges	175	
Distributions to life tenant	35,000	

Other balances b/f as at 6 April 2011

Life interest trust fund		971,542
Due to life tenant		10,074
	1,026,874	1,026,874

Assume, for the purposes of this example, that there is no taxation.

1. Prepare the income account for the Liam Johnson Life Interest Trust for the year ended 5 April 2012

Solution:

Liam Johnson Life Interest Trust
Income Account for the year ended 5 April 2012

	2012 £	
Income		
Rental income	20,000	
Income from quoted investments	23,800	
Bank interest	958	44,758
Expenses		
Trustee fees	2,500	
Accountancy fees	150	
Bank charges	175	
		(2,825)
Net income for the year		41,933

The figure for net income for the year is used for preparing the life tenant's account. The life tenant's account and the capital account are integral parts of the statement of financial position.

Students will see from the life tenant's account below that the balance is £17,007. In other words, the trust has a liability to Mrs Linda Johnson of this amount. The trustees are, therefore, in a position to distribute more income to Mrs Linda Johnson if required.

2. Prepare the life tenant's account as at 5 April 2012
Solution:
Liam Johnson Life Interest Trust
Life tenant's account – Mrs Linda Johnson 2012

	£
Balance as at 6 April 2011	10,074
Net income for the year	41,933
	52,007
Less: Amount distributed during the year	(35,000)
Balance as at 5 April 2012	**17,007**

3. Prepare the capital account as at 5 April 2012
Solution:
Liam Johnson Life Interest Trust

Capital account	2012
	£
Balance as at 6 April 2011	971,542
Add: Gain on sale of investments	500
	972,042
Less: Investment management expenses	1,500
Legal fees	1,000
Accountancy fees	1,200
	(3,700)
Balance as at 5 April 2012	968,342

It is important that expenses are appropriately apportioned between capital and income depending on the nature of the work undertaken. Students will note from the capital account that £1,000 of legal fees and £1,200 of accountancy fees have been apportioned to capital. As mentioned earlier in this chapter, difficulties can arise if large expenses arise in respect of the trust. In, this example the fees are not high relative to the value of the trust fund. However, if and when the expenses incurred are in connection with income payments to the life tenant, the remaindermen (Miss Sinead Johnson, Mr Joseph Johnson and Mrs Sarah Lemmer) may expect to see the trustees paying such costs from the income of the trust fund and not from capital.

4. Prepare the statement of financial position as at 5 April 2012
Solution:

Liam Johnson Life Interest Trust
Statement of financial position as at 5 April 2012

	2012
	£
Capital account	968,342
Life tenant's account – Mrs Linda Johnson	17,007
	985,349
Represented by:	
Quoted investments	500,000
Freehold property	450,000
Bank balances	
Capital	31,598
Income	3,751
	985,349

The statement of financial position clearly shows the split between the capital account and income due to the life tenant. The bank balances are also separated out into capital and income.

Chapter summary

- A trust is a legal arrangement whereby one or more persons, known as the trustee(s), are entrusted with the legal ownership of the assets of another party, the settlor, and to hold those assets (which might include property, investments and cash) "on trust" for the benefit of one or more beneficiaries.

- A trust has no separate legal personality and therefore cannot contract in its own name. Instead, a trustee will be appointed to manage the affairs of the trust and contract in its name, i.e. as trustee of the trust.

- A trustee is an individual or corporate body (e.g. a limited liability company) which takes legal ownership of the assets of a trust fund and manages the trust fund for the benefit of the beneficiaries.

- Income describes the money earned from an asset and trust income is mostly likely to be interest on bank deposits, property rental income and dividends received from investments.

- Trust capital represents the cash and non-cash assets initially settled on trust as well as capital subsequently settled on trust.

- A discretionary trust is a trust where the trustees have absolute discretion over the trust funds and may determine how much of the trust fund may be paid out to one or more of the beneficiaries.

- The beneficiary of the income of a life interest trust is known as the life tenant.

◆ The beneficiary of the capital of a life interest trust, upon death of the life tenant, is known as the remainderman.

◆ The accounts of a life interest trust typically include an income statement, a capital statement, a statement of financial position (balance sheet) and a schedule of investments.

Chapter nine

Reporting requirements of companies, trusts and other offshore vehicles

List of topics

1 Public and private limited companies
2 Share and loan capital
3 Implications of gearing and taxation
4 Corporate and private offshore vehicles
5 Accounting methods
6 Legitimate uses, misuses and private uses of offshore jurisdiction
7 Tax jurisdictions
8 Partnerships

Introduction

In this chapter students will learn about the key differences between public and private limited companies in the UK as well as the key features of limited companies in offshore jurisdictions such as Jersey, Guernsey and the British Virgin Islands. The differences between limited partnerships and limited liability partnerships are also discussed.

Students will also learn about share and loan capital and will gain an understanding of what is meant by ordinary shares, preference shares, authorised share capital, issued share capital, called up share capital, paid up share capital, retained profits and share premium. The implications of gearing and taxation are discussed in the context of a company raising finance and the need for the directors to strike the balance of debt and equity finance.

Students will also learn about various corporate and private offshore vehicles, such as cell companies, trusts and foundations and examples will be given of how offshore vehicles have been used for illicit purposes.

1. Public and private limited companies

Companies have their own legal personality which is separate from the legal personalities of the individuals who own and manage the company. Limited companies, therefore, offer protection to the owners of the business and this is why sole traders often form companies to limit their liability for debts. A company contracts in its own name.

It is possible to form an unlimited company but these are less common as the benefits, which include not having to file financial statements with Companies House, rarely outweigh the downside of unlimited liability.

In the UK, the Companies Act 2006 sets out the requirements of limited companies. Limited companies are either public or private and may be limited by shares or by guarantee, for example:

◆ Public limited companies (or plcs) may issue shares to the general public and each shareholder's liability is limited to the amount unpaid on the shares.

◆ Private companies limited by shares may only issue shares to a restricted circle of persons, which does not include the general public. Each member's liability is limited to the amount unpaid on their shares.

◆ Private companies limited by guarantee, unlike private companies limited by shares, do not have share capital. The members are guarantors whose liability is limited to the amount they undertake to contribute to the company's assets if it is wound up.

There are also other types of company – protected cell companies and incorporated cell companies – which offer limited liability, if desired. These types of company are discussed later in this chapter in the section on corporate and private offshore vehicles.

1.1 UK Public limited companies

As the shares of a public company are offered to the general public, many public companies choose to be listed on a stock exchange. The Companies Act 2006 sets out a number of requirements in respect of UK public companies, for example:

◆ The Memorandum of Association must state that the company is a public company.

◆ The certificate of incorporation, issued by Companies House, states that the company is a public company.

◆ The company's name must end with "public limited company" or "plc." or Welsh equivalent.

◆ There must be at least two shares in issue and the minimum issued share capital requirement is £50,000 of which 25% of the nominal amount must be paid up on each share.

◆ There must be at least two directors.

◆　A public company is required to have a company secretary.

◆　A public company requires a trading certificate.

1.2 UK Private limited companies

The Companies Act 2006 sets out a number of requirements in respect of UK private companies, for example:

◆　A private limited company is a company that is not a public company.

◆　Its name must end with "limited" or "Ltd" or Welsh equivalent. There are, however, exceptions to the rule, e.g. companies with charitable status or whose objects are the promotion of commerce, art, science, education, religion or similar have an exemption from this requirement and as long as they:

    (i)　apply income to promote their objects;

    (ii)　prohibit the payment of dividends to members; and

    (iii)　require their assets on winding up to be transferred to another body with objects similar to their own or to a charitable organisation. (for example: Hospice Aid UK, Science Alive).

◆　A private company only requires a minimum of one shareholder.

◆　A private company only needs a minimum of one director.

1.3 Re-registration of a UK private company as public

A private company may re-register (with the Registrar of Companies, Companies House) as a public company limited by shares provided certain conditions are met including requirements in respect of the company's share capital (it must have share capital and must meet the requirements of s. 91 of the Companies Act 2006) and it's net assets (s.92). The company would also need to make the necessary changes to its name and Articles of Association to reflect the fact that it will be a public company.

1.4 Re-registration of UK public company as private

A public company may re-register as a private limited company upon special resolution and filing of the necessary documents to the Registrar of Companies. Certain conditions have to be met and the change of status may not proceed if an application has been made to cancel the special resolution (or where such an application has been made, it has to have been withdrawn). The company must make the necessary changes to its name and Articles of Association to reflect the fact that it will be a private company limited by shares or limited by guarantee, as appropriate.

1.5 Offshore companies

Offshore companies are, in many ways, similar to UK companies, although companies limited by guarantee or unlimited companies are less common. An important point to note is that offshore international finance centres expect service providers to have carried out a minimum level of due diligence before the submitting incorporation documents to the companies registry. Such due diligence needs to be carried out on the underlying customer and the respective businesses in which they are involved. The risks associated with the customer and the business activities are expected to be properly documented and assessed as to how the risks may impact the service provider. This is not to say that the international finance centre will not conduct its own due diligence but it expects the first level of checks to have been appropriately undertaken by the local service provider.

1.6 Jersey public limited companies

A Jersey public company is a company with:

(i)   more than thirty members; or

(ii)   which has at least two members and states in the Memorandum of Association that it is a public company.

The company's name must end with the word "Limited" or abbreviation "Ltd" or with the words "avec responsabilité limitée" or the abbreviation "a.r.l.". Alternatively, a public limited company may choose the name to end with the words "public limited company" or with the abbreviation "PLC" or "plc". A public company must have at least two directors. An important distinction between Companies (Jersey) Law 1991 and the Companies Act 2006 in the UK is that the minimum age requirement for a director in Jersey is 18, whereas it is only 16 in the UK.

A Jersey public company may issue an offering document (or prospectus) in respect of offering its shares for subscription to the general public. It is required to file audited financial statements with the Registrar of Companies within seven months of the financial period end. A Jersey public company undertaking a regulated activity, for example a public company which is a collective investment fund (as defined by Article 3 of the Collective Investment Funds (Jersey) Law 1988) will also be subject to additional requirements of the Jersey Financial Services Commission. Such requirements include adhering to any relevant certificate or permit conditions and Codes of Practice.

1.7 Jersey private limited companies

A Jersey private company is a company that is not a public company and whose Memorandum of Association states that it is a private company. A private company limited by shares requires only one member. The company's name must end with the word "Limited" or abbreviation "Ltd" or with the words "avec responsabilité limitée" or the abbreviation "a.r.l.". Companies (Jersey) Law 1991 also states that a private company must have at least one director and, as is the requirement for public companies, he or she must have attained the age of 18 or over. There is no requirement for private companies to file audited financial statements with the Registrar of Companies but accounting records do need to be maintained and accounts prepared to enable the company to establish its financial position at any point in time. Unaudited financial statements may also need to be filed with the tax authorities.

1.8 Guernsey limited companies

Guernsey companies are governed by The Companies (Guernsey) Law, 2008. The Companies (Guernsey) Law, 2008, does not distinguish between public and private companies. As well as limited liability companies, it is possible to have a mixed liability company in Guernsey which can be a hybrid of guarantee members and shareholders. The shareholders can have either unlimited or limited liability. With limited companies, a member's liability is limited to the amount unpaid on his or her shares. A company that is limited by shares must have the following words or abbreviations at the end of its name: "Limited", "With limited liability", "Ltd.", "Avec responsibilité limitée" or the abbreviation "ARL". A Guernsey company must have at least one director and at least one member and its objects are unrestricted unless otherwise specified in the company's Memorandum of Association. The accounts of the company must be audited unless the company is exempt under s.256 of Companies (Guernsey) Law, 2008. The company is exempt if the members pass a waiver resolution in the financial year before the financial year to which it relates, or if it is in respect of the company's first financial year, in that financial year.

Test yourself 9.1

How might a Guernsey limited company seek an exemption under Companies (Guernsey) Law, 2008, from the requirement to have its financial statements audited?

1.9 British Virgin Islands limited companies

Companies in the BVI are governed by the British Virgin Islands Business Companies Act 2004. A BVI public company must have at least five members and the company name must end with the appropriate corporate suffix, e.g. "Limited", "Corporation", "Incorporated", "Société Anonyme", "Sociedad Anonima" or abbreviations "Ltd", "Corp", "Inc" or "S.A.". Private trust companies must also use the designation "PTC" immediately before the suffix. Companies established for a charitable purpose or whose objects are non-commercial may apply for an exemption from having to use the corporate name ending. A key feature of BVI companies is that, with the exception of restricted purpose companies, they are not required to state their objects. This gives corporate capacity and flexibility and effectively removes the *ultra vires* doctrine. Directors are, nevertheless, required to act in good faith and exercise due care and skill in the exercise of their functions. BVI companies must have at least one director, although there is no requirement to have a director appointed immediately on registration.

Case law: Salomon v. A. Salomon & Co. Ltd. [1897]

Salomon v. *A. Salomon & Co. Ltd.* is a landmark case in UK company law and established the principle of corporate personality. In other words, the company is liable for its own debts, not the owners or the directors.

Mr Aron Salomon ran his own business as a sole trader manufacturing boots and shoes. He set up a limited company, A Salomon & Co Ltd and sold the business to the company in 1892 in return for £29,000 in cash, a £10,000 secured debenture and 20,001 shares in the company which was considered to be worth considerably more than the value of the business. There were seven subscribers in total, Mr Salomon, his wife and their five children. He made two of his sons directors of the company. The company went into liquidation a year later and there were £11,000 in trade payables but Mr A Salomon was a secured creditor who had preferential rights over the trade payables.

The payables alleged the company was a sham and without substance. However, the House of Lords judgment stated that Mr Salomon was perfectly entitled to take advantage of the provisions and avail himself of the corporate veil and not be liable for the debts of the company.

In the judgment, Lord Macnaghten said:

'*When the memorandum is duly signed and registered, though there be only seven shares taken, the subscribers are a body corporate "capable forthwith", to use the words of the enactment, "of exercising all the functions of an incorporated company". Those are strong words. The company attains maturity on its birth. There is no period of minority – no interval of incapacity. I cannot understand how a body corporate thus made "capable" by statute can lose its individuality by issuing the bulk of its capital to one person, whether he be a subscriber to the memorandum or not. The company is at law a different person altogether from the subscribers to the memorandum; and, though it may be that after incorporation the business is precisely the same as it was before, and the same persons are managers, and the same hands receive the profits, the company is not in law the agent of the subscribers or trustee for them. Nor are the subscribers as members liable, in any shape or form, except to the extent and in the manner provided by the Act.... The unsecured payables of A. Salomon and Company Limited, may be entitled to sympathy, but they have only themselves to blame for their misfortunes. They trusted the company, I suppose, because they had long dealt with Mr. Salomon, and he had always paid his way; but they had full notice that they were no longer dealing with an individual, and they must be taken to have been cognisant of the memorandum and of the articles of association.*'

2. Share and loan capital

Companies need to raise money in order to fund their operating and financing activities. Short-term financing is usually in the form of cash in the bank and at hand, bank overdrafts, supplier credit, etc. Long-term financing is achieved by either issuing *equity* shares (to shareholders as members of the company) or issuing *debt* such as loan stock (to the lenders as payables of the company). The directors of the company need to carefully consider the implications of issuing equity or debt because this can affect, amongst other things, ownership and control, the level of *gearing*, risk and level of taxation.

2.1 Share capital

Share capital represents the amount of cash and non-cash considerations raised by a company in return for issuing shares. Share capital is the investment in the company by its shareholders. There are varying types of share capital and each type of share capital carries different rights and obligations, the most common of which are ordinary share capital and preference share capital.

2.1.1 Ordinary shares
Holders of ordinary (or equity) shares are members of a company who receive voting rights and dividend entitlements (which are not guaranteed and depend on the company's financial performance). Ordinary shareholders rank last in line for dividend payments and for the repayment of capital if the company goes into liquidation. As the holders of ordinary shares normally carry more risk than preference shareholders and lenders, they hope to benefit from dividend growth and increasing share prices.

2.1.2 Preference shares
Holders of preference shares are members of a company who are entitled to dividends (if declared) ahead of ordinary shareholders. The preference share dividends are usually fixed percentage dividends. For example, a 5% £1 preference share entitles the holder to a 5p dividend. Preference shares do not usually carry voting rights. They rank ahead of ordinary shareholders but after loan stock in the event of a liquidation.

2.1.3 Capital requirements
Companies are often required to maintain a minimum level of share capital to safeguard against risk and ensure they are better placed to survive reduced levels of business and exposure to market risk, operational risk and credit risk. For example, a bank must maintain the minimum level of capital stipulated in the Basel requirements and by the relevant supervisory authorities. A well capitalised bank or financial institution is better placed to survive a market downturn or financial crisis than a bank with no safety buffer.

2.1.4 Authorised share capital
Authorised share capital represents the amount of share capital that a firm is allowed to issue. The concept of authorised share capital is less common than it used to be and many jurisdictions now allow companies to issue an unlimited

equity
Is capital raised by selling shares in the company, typically by public offering. Investors buy the shares and become shareholders or owners of the company's equity.

debt
financing occurs when a company raises finance by issuing bonds, bills or loan notes and, in exchange, promises to repay the lender the interest and capital on the loan.

gearing
measures long-term debt to equity and measures the extent to which a company is leveraged by comparing borrowed funds to shareholder funds.

number of shares if the company's Memorandum of Association permits. For example, this is now the case with BVI Business Companies under the BVI Business Companies Act 2004.

2.1.5 Issued share capital

The issued share capital is the nominal value of all shares which have been issued and taken up by the members. For example, a company that issues 100,000 shares of £1 each has an issued share capital of £100,000. A company cannot issue more than the authorised amount of share capital, which for some companies is an unlimited number of shares.

2.1.6 Called up share capital

Called up share capital is the amount that has been requested for payment in exchange for the shares that have been issued. This occurs when a company does not initially require all the funds from a share issue and so only calls up a set amount to begin with, e.g. 60% of the total. For example, a company issues 200,000 £1 shares but only calls up 60p per share. The issued share capital is £200,000 but the called up share capital is only £120,000. The company may call up the outstanding 40% when investments are identified or funds are required for other purposes.

Stop and think 9.1

A company allots 500,000 shares at £1 per share but only calls up 80p per share. What is the amount of called up share capital and how would the company record the transactions in the company books?

2.1.7 Paid up share capital

Paid up share capital is the amount of called up share capital that has been paid. If any called up capital has not been paid up then it is treated as a receivable on the asset side of the company's statement of financial position (i.e. money owing to the company) and is termed "Called up capital not paid".

2.1.8 Retained profits

Retained profits are also a source of financing for companies and form part of shareholders' equity. Retained profits represent the net profits from prior periods of trading after dividends and taxation and which are available for reinvestment in the business.

2.1.9 Share premium

Sometimes shares are issued at a premium. This means that shares are sold at a higher price than the nominal or carrying value. For example:

A company issues 2 million ordinary shares of £1 each at £1.20 per share. Assuming the share capital is fully paid up, the bookkeeping entries are:

DR	Cash	£2,400,000
CR	Share capital	£2,000,000
CR	Share premium	£400,000

2.2 Loan capital

Loan capital is a type of long-term debt in the form of loan stock or debentures. A company may raise money by accepting loans from investors and issuing loan notes, bonds or debentures in return which entitle the lenders to a fixed interest payment. Debentures are secured loans which rank ahead of shareholders and trade payables in the event the company enters into liquidation. Lenders therefore normally carry less risk than shareholders.

Loan capital is often preferred to equity because issuing debt does not affect ownership and control of the company. In other words, if a company issues more shares to raise finance, existing shareholders may find their shareholdings are diluted if they do not take up the share offer. Raising funds by issuing debt does not create this issue. It does, however, create gearing and tax implications which directors need to take into consideration when determining how to raise finance.

In Chapter 6, students will recall that a company that is highly geared or leveraged has a high proportion of debt to equity whereas a company with a low gearing ratio has a relatively low level of debt compared with equity.

A highly geared company might be considered more risky than a company without gearing because the highly geared company will have regular interest payments to service the debt and, in times of increasing interest rates, businesses with high levels of borrowing with variable rate interest payments may find themselves faced with uncomfortably large monthly outgoings in order to service the debt. This means there is likely to be less money available for distribution to equity holders in the form of dividends.

Lenders of finance are particularly interested in a company's gearing ratios since a high gearing ratio might indicate a company's inability to repay the debt. It is, therefore, not unusual for lenders to restrict a company's level of gearing through the use of loan covenants. Most entities aim to strike a good balance of debt to equity which reflects their specific risk appetite and investment strategy.

The interest element on debt is usually deductible for corporation tax purposes, which reduces the net rate of taxation and thereby the company's cost of capital.

3. Implications of gearing and taxation

The interest payments on the debt instruments are allowable for corporation tax purposes which makes debt an attractive form of finance.

Companies raise finance in order to generate greater returns. The choice of equity or debt can influence a number of key investor ratios, such as return on equity and **EPS** (see Chapter 6). If a company chooses to issue ordinary shares to raise finance, rather than debt, there will be more shares in issue which means the earnings per share is likely to fall.

loan covenant
a restrictive measure placed on the borrower by the lender as a means of safeguarding the loan. Measures might include restricting the level of gearing of the borrower by insisting more equity is put into the company. If a company breaches its loan covenant then it may be forced to repay the loan or find an alternative lender who is likely to insist on a high rate of return on the loan to reflect the high level of gearing.

EPS (or earnings per share)
is a frequently used indicator of a company's profitability and is often used by shareholders for comparing a company's financial health with a company with similar earnings.

Issuing debt as a source of finance, however, leads to a company to increasing its gearing. This can, however, have a positive impact on the company's EPS ratio. This is because the additional funds can be used to generate greater profits without increasing the number of shares in issue. Companies need to be able to service the interest charge on the debt and directors need to be mindful that the larger the interest charge, the less profit after interest (which will impact the return on equity ratio).

Companies which are highly geared are also at risk of not being able to pay their debts as they fall due and lenders of debt finance (e.g. banks) may impose loan covenants restricting the activities of the company if gearing exceeds a pre-determined limit.

4. Corporate and private offshore vehicles

There are various types of corporate and offshore vehicles such as limited companies (covered earlier in this chapter), cell companies, partnerships (covered later in this chapter), trusts (see Chapter 8), foundations as well as other special purpose vehicles. Offshore structures are often a combination of more than one type of vehicle, for example, a trust with one or more underlying companies or special purpose vehicles.

4.1 Companies

Companies are incorporated in offshore jurisdictions for a number of uses, including:

◆ trading;

◆ investing;

◆ holding real estate;

◆ holding intellectual property rights;

◆ holding super yachts, aircraft; and

◆ holding and investing in works of art and other chattels.

4.2 Cell companies

A **cell company** is a private or public company which is able to segregate its assets and liabilities between different cells. Each cell may be used to carry out distinct and independent businesses. Whilst protected cells of a protected cell company have no separate legal personality, they are treated as separate legal entities limiting the ability of creditors from seeking the assets of one cell to pay off the debts of another. Whilst cell companies typically have limited liability, a cell company can be an unlimited or guarantee company.

Protected cell companies (PCCs) were developed in Guernsey in the late 1990s and other offshore jurisdictions (including Cayman Islands, Jersey, Isle of Man, Mauritius, Bermuda and St Vincent and The Grenadines) have since developed

cell company
is a private or public company which is able to segregate its assets and liabilities between different cells. Each cell may be used to carry out distinct and independent businesses and the assets of each cell can be ring-fenced.

their own types of cell companies such as segregated portfolio companies in the Cayman Islands and both incorporated cell companies (ICCs) and PCCs in Jersey.

Protected cells have no separate legal personality and therefore transact through the overarching cell company. The cells enable assets to be segregated and ring-fenced and are often used in collective investment schemes in preference to umbrella funds. They are also used frequently in captive insurance schemes. **Ring-fencing** is a protective measure to prevent the assets of a ring-fenced cell from being used to pay off the debts of another cell. With PCCs, it is usual for the directors to have a legal obligation to properly separate cellular assets. That said, the legislation in some jurisdictions, e.g. Jersey, permits a cell to invest in another cell of the same cell company (but not in the cell company itself).

With incorporated cells (ICs) of an incorporated cell company, each cell has its own separate legal personality. Accordingly, each cell has its own board of directors (also permitted for cells of a PCC in some jurisdictions) and is able to contract and sue in its own name. The IC is not a subsidiary of the ICC. ICC structures, therefore, enable assets to be legally separated rather than relying on the actions of the directors to properly separate the cellular assets.

Having separate legal personality is an important factor for stakeholders to consider because an ICC/IC structure is less likely to face challenges from payables than a PCC/PC structure whose ring-fencing capability is less substantive and might not be recognised by foreign court.

ring-fencing
is a protective measure to prevent the assets of a ring-fenced cell from being used to pay off the debts of another cell.

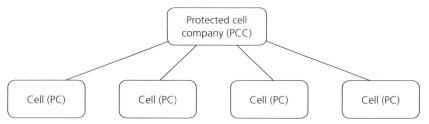

4.3 Foundations

A foundation is an organisation and is similar to a company in that it is a legal entity which can own assets and contract in its own name. Foundations are typically established by a one-off donation by an individual or business, known as the "founder" and run by the foundation's "council", in accordance with the foundation's charter, by-laws and regulations for non-profitable, charitable, scientific, humanitarian or philanthropic purposes. They are also used as an alternative vehicle to offshore trusts and companies.

Foundations are versatile offshore vehicles and have been a success story in a number of jurisdictions, particularly Liechtenstein, Panama, Malta and the Netherlands Antilles. Foundations may be established for a specified or unlimited period and, in some jurisdictions, the founder has the right to change the purpose of the foundation or revoke the foundation, although this may result in adverse tax implications.

In Liechtenstein, a foundation is known as a "Stiftung" and in the Netherland Antilles as a "Stichting".

4.4 Benefits of foundations

◆ versatile offshore vehicles;

◆ protect the assets against creditor claims;

◆ simpler concept for clients to understand compared with trusts;

◆ can last for an indefinite period;

◆ confidentiality;

◆ succession planning;

◆ avoidance of **forced heirship** rules;

◆ protect assets in times of political instability to avoid expropriation of assets;

◆ probates may be avoided;

◆ the founder can also be the **guardian** and oversee the function of council, potentially influencing its decisions;

◆ often no fiduciary duty imposed on council (unlike for trusts and companies); and

◆ can be used to mitigate tax liabilities.

4.5 Drawbacks of foundations

◆ may have investment restrictions, e.g. a foundation might be prohibited from acquiring, holding or disposing of immoveable property in some jurisdictions;

◆ may not be able to carry out activities of a commercial nature if not incidental to the attainment of the foundation's objects;

◆ absence of court judgments and so tax mitigation is uncertain;

◆ founder surrenders ownership of assets; and

◆ professional fees are incurred.

forced heirship
essentially a feature of civil law jurisdictions and Islamic countries which do not recognise the full freedom of testation. This means, for example, that an individual making his will may not be able to leave an equal proportion of his assets to his surviving children and spouse. To prevent the assets going exclusively to the eldest child, the individual may use a foundation or trust to avoid the forced heirship rules.

guardian
is the person who empowered to oversee the foundation's council and performs a similar function to the protector of a trust. The founder might choose to appoint a guardian to a foundation, which may be himself, to ensure the foundation is run in an appropriate manner and in accordance with the foundations charter.

Key differences between a foundation, trust and company:

Vehicle	Source of funds	Management	Benefit
Foundation	Founder**	Council	Beneficiaries*
Trust	Settlor	Trustee	Beneficiaries
Company	Subscribers	Directors	Shareholders

*A foundation can exist without beneficiaries and, unlike trusts, the beneficiaries of a foundation are not owed a fiduciary duty by the foundation council.
**As with a "declaration of trust", the founder of a foundation may remain anonymous.

5. Accounting methods

There are two main accounting methods:

◆ Cash basis.
◆ Accruals basis.

5.1 Cash basis

The cash basis of accounting is where income is only accounted for when received and expenses accounted for when physical payment is made.

5.2 Accruals basis

Under the accruals basis of accounting, non-cash transactions should be accounted for in the financial statements in the reporting period to which they relate rather than in the period when cash changes hands. The accruals basis should only reflect those items which meet the definition of an **asset** or **liability**.

asset
the right or other access to future economic benefits controlled by an entity as a result of past transactions or events.

liability
is the obligation of an entity to transfer economic benefits as a result of past transactions or events.

An example of the accruals basis of accounting is the depreciation of non-current assets. Depreciation is defined by International Accounting Standard 16 (IAS 16) "Property, Plant and Equipment" as the "systematic allocation of the depreciable amount of an asset over its useful life".

Entities should depreciate non-current assets, such as plant and equipment, on an annual basis and review the residual value and useful life of the assets at the financial year end. The principal purpose of the depreciation charge is to recognise the cost of a non-current asset over the reporting period and to match the cost against the revenue being generated through the use of that asset.

The depreciation charge is an accounting entry, not a cash expense, and helps ensure non-current assets are recorded at fair value, to reflect wear and tear, rather than being maintained in the books at an unrealistic historic value.

Motor vehicles and computer equipment are two types of non-current asset which become obsolete over a relatively short period of time. As with many other fixed assets, they are subject to an annual depreciation charge in an entity's financial statements. The shorter the useful life of the asset, the higher the depreciation charge relative to the life of the asset, e.g.:

Asset 1:	Asset 2:
Value £10,000	Value £10,000
Useful life 10 years	Useful life 5 years
Straight line depreciation	Straight line depreciation
Annual depreciation charge:	
£10,000/10yrs = £1,000 p.a.	£10,000/5yrs = £2,000 p.a.

Asset 1 and Asset 2 are both valued at £10,000, but as Asset 2 has a shorter useful life than Asset 1, the annual depreciation charge is higher.

6. Legitimate uses, misuses and private uses of offshore jurisdictions

Whilst in the large majority of cases, international finance centres in offshore jurisdictions are used for legitimate reasons by multinational organisations, families and private individuals (for tax and estate planning, wealth management, financial expertise, etc.), offshore jurisdictions are also, on occasions, used for tax evasion and other illegitimate purposes.

A number of international finance centres, such as Jersey and Guernsey, are on the **EU white list of third country equivalence**. They have been assessed by the **International Monetary Fund (IMF)** as being either compliant or largely compliant with international standards in respect of their **AML/CFT** framework. They have also demonstrated a greater degree of compliance with international standards than some of the world's largest economies. Certain other international finance centres, with less robust regulatory frameworks, are more exposed to being abused by criminals.

For example, the UK's National Audit Office report of 16 November 2007 on "Managing Risk in the Overseas Territories" stated that "capacity limitations in the offshore financial sector have limited Territories' ability to investigate suspicious activity reports, and, in the case of the Turks and Caicos Islands, Anguilla and Montserrat, resources are below the critical mass necessary to keep up with increasingly sophisticated international standards and products in offshore financial services".

Indeed, the following characteristics of international finance centres are likely to be attractive to money launderers:

◆ no tax information exchange agreements with other jurisdictions;

◆ absence of Memoranda of Understandings (MoUs) with other jurisdictions;

◆ capacity limitations and lack of robust AML/CFT measures;

◆ little client due diligence undertaken;

◆ poor standards of money laundering reporting;

◆ absence of court cases leading to criminal convictions for money laundering and financial crime;

◆ use of **shelf companies** to facilitate fast-track incorporations and give the impression of corporate longevity;

◆ secrecy laws;

◆ good transport links;

◆ independent government that withstands external pressure; and

◆ use of a major currency.

There have been a number of high-profile cases in recent years in connection with the misuse of offshore jurisdictions, including the German tax probe into Liechtenstein and laundering of money through Jersey.

EU white list
is a list of jurisdictions considered to have the equivalent anti-money laundering controls as EU member states.

International Monetary Fund (IMF)
is an organisation of nearly 200 countries, "working to foster global monetary cooperation, secure financial stability, facilitate international trade, promote high employment and sustainable economic growth, and reduce poverty around the world."
(Source: www.imf.org)

AML/CFT
means anti-money laundering and countering of financing of terrorism.

shelf companies
a term given to companies which are inactive and have been put 'on the shelf'. As a shelf company is already formed, financial service providers keep them until they have a client wishing to have immediate use for the company. The service provider can simply transact in the company's name on behalf of the client and transfer the beneficial ownership of the company without having to go back through the incorporation process. Shelf companies are less common nowadays as the Companies Registry in many more offshore jurisdictions offer a fast-track incorporation service enabling companies to form in a matter of hours.

6.1 Liechtenstein

Heinrich Keiber was an employee of Liechtenstein Global Trust Bank, a bank owned by the ruling family of Liechtenstein. Keiber was a disgruntled employee who left the bank in 2002 with the details of around 1,400 clients, including 600 German nationals. In 2006, he sold the data to the German authorities who suspected that Liechtenstein vehicles were being used by German nationals to evade tax. The German authorities decided to go public and Keiber handed over data to other jurisdictions including the US and the UK, fueling anti-offshore financial centre sentiment.

6.2 Cayman and Jersey

Case law: Weavering

In *Re Weavering Capital (UK) Limited* [2012], Weavering Capital (UK) Limited and its liquidators sought relief under the Insolvency Act 1986. The judgment of the Weavering Case of 30 May 2012 refers to proceedings against two directors of a Cayman Islands hedge fund, the Weavering Macro Fixed Income Fund (the "**Macro Fund**"), which was managed by Weavering Capital (UK) Limited.

The 2011 Cayman judgment on Weavering – *Weavering Macro Fixed Income Fund Limited (In Liquidation) v. Stefan Peterson and Hans Ekstrom [Grand Court of the Cayman Islands]* – found the two directors, both based in Sweden and one of whom was in his 80s, guilty of wilful neglect or default of their duties as directors of the Macro fund. The Cayman judgment found they had failed to detect that Mr Magnus Peterson of Weavering Capital (UK) Limited had "dishonestly manipulated the Macro Fund's income statement and defrauded its investors". Mr Peterson had failed to disclose the existence of risky over the counter (OTC) swap transactions which accounted for the majority of the value of the Macro Fund, despite it supposedly having a low-risk strategy "to ensure a balanced and diversified risk profile". If fact, reports sent to investors stated that the fund "traded very little in OTC instruments" and failed to notify them that the swaps were with a related party. This allowed Mr Peterson to misuse his position and overstate the value of the investments.

The financial implications of the judgment against the negligent directors of the Cayman hedge fund amounted to US$111m each. This was the first time the Cayman Islands took action against directors and, in this case, neither were based in the Cayman Islands.

In the UK, on 30 May 2012, the High Court of Justice awarded payables of Weavering Capital (UK) Limited more than $450m in civil damages. The judgment states that "Mr Peterson admittedly owed Weavering Capital (UK) Limited fiduciary duties as a director.

For example, to act at all times in good faith and in Weavering Capital (UK) Limited's best interests, not to put himself in a position where his interests and duties conflicted, to act in accordance with Weavering Capital (UK) Limited's constitution, statutory duties under s.171–177 of the 2006 Act and duties to exercise reasonable care, skill and diligence in performing his duties as a director."

The Serious Fraud Office is now under mounting pressure to re-open its criminal investigations into Weavering Capital (UK) Limited. A number of offshore jurisdictions and vehicles were used by Peterson, including the Cayman Islands, the Bahamas, the British Virgin Islands and Isle of Man. Investors suffering heavy losses included a Jersey-based fund of funds.

Company secretaries can learn from the 2011 Weavering judgment in the Cayman Islands which highlighted the importance of directors' supervisory duties and the need to monitor service providers to whom functions have been delegated. It also emphasised the need to maintain accurate board minutes, ensuring they fully reflect the substance of discussions that are held. Directors should be careful not to simply sign pre-prepared minutes which do not fully and accurately reflect the debates that have taken place.

There have been calls for greater regulation of mutual funds in the Cayman Islands following the Grand Court judgment on Weavering. Measures to strengthen regulation could, for instance, include a tighter span of control policy and a requirement for at least two directors of a Cayman fund to be resident in Cayman and suitably independent, competent and experienced for the nature of the business.

In Jersey, for example, it is regulatory requirement for collective investment funds to have at least two resident directors and the span of control requirements in the Codes of Practice for Certified Funds specifically refer to the requirements for the Investment Manager of a fund, the principals of whom 'must be able to demonstrate independence, competence, experience and integrity and be able to effectively exercise management control over the Investment Manager. Together, the persons providing the "four or six eyes" should be able to demonstrate a balance of appropriate qualifications, skills and experience. As part of the independence requirement care must be taken where members of the same family form principal persons of the Investment Manager.'

In the Weavering case the two directors (Stefan Peterson and Hans Ekstrom) were the brother and stepfather of Magnus Peterson, who was the founder and driving force behind the investment manager and the fund.

Case law: Nicholas Bell and Caversham Fiduciary Services Ltd and Caversham Trustees Ltd v. The Attorney General [Court of Appeal, Jersey, 2006 JCA014 JLR61]

In the *Caversham* case, Mr Bell, who was a director of both Caversham Fiduciary Service Ltd and Caversham Trustees Ltd in Jersey, was found guilty of failing to verify the identity of a client prior to entering into a business relationship. In 2002, Mr Bell was contacted by a solicitor in England, Mr Timothy Clarke, introducing a Mr Stevens. Mr Stevens, as attorney for a certain Mr Lee, had purportedly received monies from the proceeds of the sale of a sauna in London. It was claimed that Mr Lee was a non-resident who wished for the monies to be kept offshore and for a trust to be established to hold the proceeds of the sale. Mr Stevens was to be the sole beneficiary of the discretionary trust.

£850,000 was received in the Caversham client account on 10 December 2002. Just two days later, Mr Clarke requested that £825,000 be transferred to four separate accounts in the UK from the funds held for Mr Stevens. The Advent Trust was created the very next day under the common seal of Caversham Trustees Ltd and had the £850,000 as initial trust property. There was no named settlor and no mention of Mr Lee. On the same day, the sum of £825,000 was paid out as requested by Mr Clarke. Insufficient due diligence had been undertaken and funds should not have been paid out until verification of identity had taken place. There were anomalies in respect of the verification documents for Mr Stevens and no due diligence carried out on Mr Lee or the UK entities to which the payments were made. There appeared to be no commercial reason for the transaction.

Mr Bell and Caversham were charged and convicted for failing to maintain proper client verification procedures and comply with certain requirements of the Money Laundering (Jersey) Order and the Proceeds of Crime (Jersey) Law.

The Court of Appeal case highlighted that client verification procedures are supposed to prevent money entering the Jersey financial system in the first place and that a single failure to "maintain" appropriate internal controls and procedures is sufficient to commit an offence under Article 37 of the Proceeds of Crime (Jersey) Law.

Offshore jurisdictions are also sometimes used by fraudsters who set up **boiler room scams** onshore and transfer the proceeds of their crime to offshore accounts. Whilst the initial crime may take place onshore, offshore jurisdictions are often favoured by criminals to conceal the proceeds of crime. For example, a Mr Michael McInerney was found guilty by Southwark Crown Court in April 2012 for defrauding investors out of £27.5m in 2006 and 2007. The proceeds of the share scams had been transferred by McInerney to bank accounts in Jersey and Malta.

boiler room scams are share scams which are so called because the fraudsters use unethical sales tactics to "pressurise" investors into parting with their cash in exchange for shares which either do not exist or are overpriced and illiquid.

Jersey deals firmly with money laundering offences and, in 2010, the Royal Court of Jersey convicted Raj Bhojwani of India on three counts of money laundering contrary to the Proceeds of Crime (Jersey) Law. Bhojwani laundered some £28m through the Jersey branch of Bank of India and was sentenced to 8 years imprisonment (later reduced to six years for good character). Bhojwani's business activities were linked with former Nigerian President, General Abacha, and the £28m stemmed from a deal with Abacha to sell overpriced military vehicles to the Nigerian government. In 2011, Bhojwani's appeal was unsuccessful and the Royal Court made a Confiscation Order of over £26.5m. Bhojwani was also ordered to make a significant contribution towards the prosecution's costs.

7. Tax jurisdictions

High net worth individuals and multinational companies often use low-tax jurisdictions and international finance centres to base their business activities and benefit from the reduced taxation charges which can be as low as zero per cent for corporate income tax.

In the UK, HM Revenue and Customs (HMRC) is currently trying to narrow down the window of opportunity for tax avoidance schemes which are growing in number and complexity. In determining whether an individual has a liability to tax, HMRC will look at jurisdiction of residence, ordinary residence and domicile of the individual. The concept of ordinary residence is being abolished in the UK from 6 April 2013 but the concepts of residence and domicile still remain.

The tax authorities around the world use a number of connecting factors to determine an individual's liability to tax. In the case of offshore trusts, for example, the authorities are concerned with where the settlor is resident for tax purposes. In the UK, HMRC applies a residency test whereby an individual, who spends more than 183 days per year in the UK, or more than 90 days on a four-year average, is deemed to resident in the UK for income tax purposes. The onus is usually on the individual to prove he was not resident in the UK, rather than HMRC proving he was resident in the UK.

tax nomads are high net worth individuals who keep on the move to avoid spending 91 days or more in the UK on average over a four-year rolling cycle, thereby ensuring they are neither resident nor deemed ordinarily resident in the UK.

The significance of the residency rule is that individuals using offshore structures to mitigate tax, such as **tax nomads**, may find themselves classified as UK resident and liable to UK tax on their worldwide income and gains rather than just on income and gains arising or remitted to the UK.

As part of the UK government's new strategic approach, there will also be closer scrutiny on offshore property holding companies used for tax avoidance schemes and an extension of the capital gains tax regime to gains on the disposal of UK property and interests in such property by non-resident offshore structures. Offshore holding companies are currently used by some individuals to keep gains on the sale or transfer of property at the offshore company level so that the individual occupier or beneficiary of the property avoids a tax liability. The UK is likely to introduce a withholding tax on UK property transactions with foreign ownership to help capture such tax avoidance schemes. Elsewhere in Europe, offshore property holding structures are also used in some jurisdictions, such as Malta and Cyprus, in order to benefit from any **double tax treaties** that may exist.

A key factor in determining whether an offshore structure is legitimate for tax purposes, is whether management and control is firmly offshore or whether it remains in the UK. The proceeds of offshore structures must be lawfully distributed and the appropriate taxes (if any) paid. The House of Lords rulings on the *Dimsey* and *Allen* appeal judgments highlight the importance of operating offshore vehicles in an appropriate manner. The *Dimsey* appeal judgment is summarised below.

double tax treaty
is an agreement between two jurisdictions, under which individuals who find themselves subject to tax in the two jurisdictions are able to claim under the relevant agreement to avoid a double taxation charge.

Case Law: Regina v. Dimsey – Appeal Judgment [2001]

The appellant, Dermot Jeremy Dimsey, was a Jersey resident financial services provider whose services included the establishment and administration of offshore companies for persons resident in the United Kingdom. One of Dimsey's clients was a Mr Chipping, a UK resident. Mr Chipping became involved as an intermediary in the supply of avionic equipment to South Africa. On Mr Chipping's instructions Dimsey formed two offshore companies to deal with the South African contracts that Mr Chipping had obtained. Mr Chipping was the beneficial owner of the shares in and was in control of the two companies.

The South African contracts were signed by Dimsey in Jersey on behalf of the companies. The profits made by the two offshore companies were £664,057 and £582,000 respectively. Dimsey then arranged for credit cards to be issued in the names of the two companies but for the personal use of Mr Chipping (thereby giving him the power to enjoy the assets of the offshore structure). Dimsey arranged for the payment by the companies of liabilities incurred through Mr Chipping's use of these cards for personal expenditure.

Dimsey set up a third offshore company for Mr Chipping to receive some of the profits derived from the South African contracts. The offshore company was also used to purchase a flat for a member of Mr Chipping's family.

In 1993 the UK's Inland Revenue (now known as HMRC) began an investigation into Mr Chipping's tax affairs. Dimsey assisted Mr Chipping in providing false and misleading information to the revenue regarding the offshore companies, the South African contracts and certain bank accounts that Mr Chipping held in Jersey. Mr Chipping employed the services of a solicitor in England, Mr Da Costa, to act for him in the Inland Revenue investigation. Mr Da Costa also played a part in the provision of false and misleading information. Criminal proceedings followed.

The offshore companies were liable to corporation tax because they were resident in the United Kingdom by virtue of the fact that the management and control of their respective businesses took place in the United Kingdom.

Mr Chipping was sentenced to three years' imprisonment. He did not appeal. Mr Da Costa was sentenced to 12 months' imprisonment. He, too, did not appeal. Dimsey was sentenced to 18 months' imprisonment. He appealed but had served the sentence before his appeal came to be heard in the Court of Appeal.

In the House of Lords, Lord Scott of Foscote said, "For the reasons I have given [UK management and control] the three offshore companies, resident in the United Kingdom through Mr Chipping's activities as the jury must have found, were in law liable to corporation tax. It follows that there was no legal impediment standing in the way of a conviction of the appellant [Dimsey], and the others, of the offence of conspiring to cheat the revenue of corporation tax payable by the three companies."

Where management and control remains firmly in the offshore jurisdiction then it is possible for individuals to benefit from the non-resident status of the offshore vehicle, so long as the **anti-avoidance rules** are not broken.

With regard to transparency, exchange of information and fair tax competition, the Crown Dependencies of Jersey, Guernsey and the Isle of Man, have in pursuance of good corporate governance and tax transparency, voluntarily implemented the **European Savings Directive (ESD)** measures in line with those measures in place between EU member states. Other low-tax jurisdictions which have also agreed to apply the ESD measures include Andorra, Liechtenstein, Monaco and San Marino. Where an offshore jurisdiction has agreed to implement the withholding tax option (or "retention tax" as it is known in Jersey, Guernsey and Isle of Man), EU residents earning savings income in that jurisdiction may still be able opt for exchange of information (if their financial institution offers this choice) instead of paying a retention tax on the income arising. Low-tax jurisdictions are also signing an ever-increasing number of Memoranda of Understandings with other jurisdictions to facilitate the sharing of information.

anti-avoidance rules
are measures introduced to reduce the number of cases of tax avoidance in relation to offshore schemes that have no other purpose than to avoid tax. For example, in the UK, anti-avoidance legislation has helped prevent UK investors avoiding a higher rate of tax by accumulating income in an investment offshore and only being taxed on capital gains when the investment was eventually realised.

European Savings Directive (ESD)
is an agreement between EU member states to automatically exchange information with one another about clients who earn savings income in one EU member state but reside in another.

Making it work – The Liechtenstein Disclosure Facility (LDF)

A Memorandum of Understanding was signed in August 2009 between the Principality of Liechtenstein and HMRC concerning tax cooperation matters. Resulting from this, the Liechtenstein Disclosure Facility enables UK individuals with unpaid tax linked to investments or assets in Liechtenstein to settle their tax liability under a special arrangement which runs until 31 March 2015. The facility's terms include:

- 10% fixed penalty on the underpaid liabilities;
- no penalty where an innocent error has been made;
- assessment period limited to periods commencing on or after 1 April 1999;
- ability to elect whether to use a single composite rate of 40% or to calculate actual liability on an annual basis;
- assurance about criminal prosecution; and
- a single point of contact for disclosures.

8. Partnerships

8.1 Limited partnerships

general partner (GP) is the person who assumes the management responsibility for the limited partnership. The general partner has unlimited liability for the debts and obligations of the partnership and, therefore, is typically a limited company.

A limited partnership (LP) comprises limited partners, who invest in the partnership, and one or more **general partners** (GPs), who manage the partnership. Generally speaking, LPs do not have their own separate legal personality and each partner is jointly and severally liable for losses and debts incurred by the LP to the extent of the amount of capital committed less the amount already contributed. General partners also have unlimited liability for the debts of the partnership and, therefore, tend to be formed as limited liability companies in order to limit their liability.

A number of offshore jurisdictions allow LPs to have their own separate legal identity and this type of partnership is favoured by promoters of private equity funds who, *inter alia*, prefer the LP's assets to be recorded in its own name. In Guernsey, the Limited Partnerships (Guernsey) Law 1995 allows LPs to elect to have a separate legal personality upon initial registration, meaning they are treated as body corporate in certain circumstances. In Jersey, the introduction of new LP legislation in 2011 allowed for the formation of Separate Limited Partnerships (SLPs), which are not body corporates, and Incorporated Limited Partnerships (ILPs), which are body corporates. SLPs are governed by the Separate Limited Partnerships (Jersey) Law 2011 and ILPs are governed by the Incorporated Limited Partnerships (Jersey) Law 2011.

As mentioned above, and LPs are used in fund structures (as an alternative investment vehicle to a company or unit trust), whereby limited partners invest through the LP and the GP, a limited company, undertakes the management function. LPs used as vehicles for collective investment schemes and undertaking regulated activities in the Channel Islands are required to be regulated under the relevant supervisory law(s), namely the Protection of Investors (Bailiwick of Guernsey) Law, 1987 (if in Guernsey) and the Collective Investment Funds (Jersey) Law 1988 (if in Jersey). In Jersey, the LPs which are structured as collective investment schemes, are typically registered under the Limited Partnerships (Jersey) Law 1994 and have no separate legal personality. The limited partners have limited liability providing they remain passive investors and, subject to certain exceptions (e.g. a limited partner may act as a director of a corporate GP or may advise the GP in respect of the activities of the LP), do not participate in the management of the LP. The GP performs the management function and has unlimited liability. The GP is, therefore, usually formed as a Jersey limited company in which its shareholders have limited liability. The relationship between the limited partners and the GP is set out in the **Limited Partnership Agreement (or LPA)**.

8.2 Limited liability partnerships

Limited liability partnerships (LLPs) are a type of limited partnership which offers its partners limited liability. These vehicles are often used by accountancy and law firms and other employee owned businesses where it is not always appropriate or desired to separate ownership and management. In some jurisdictions, such as the UK, LLPs are required to file accounts whereas limited partnerships may keep their financial statements private. In offshore finance centres, the filing requirements for LLPs tend to be less onerous. For example, in Jersey, an LLP is not required to have its financial statements audited, unless required by the partnership agreement. However, various safeguards are set out in statute, namely the Limited Liability Partnerships (Jersey) Law 1997. The LLP must maintain sufficient accounting records (and keep them for at least 10 years) in order to be able to disclose its financial position, with reasonable accuracy, at any time. A Jersey LLP is also required have in place a £5m financial provision by a bank or insurance company for the benefit of creditors on winding up.

limited partnership agreement (LPA) is a written document setting out the powers and obligations of the limited partners and of the GP. It will include the name of the LP and GP, will state the purpose for which the LP was formed, will set out how income and capital should be allocated, how distributions should be made, the various rights and obligations of both parties (e.g. the obligation of the GP to contribute to the debts of the LP) and the administrative arrangements.

The similarities and differences between Jersey limited partnerships and limited liability partnerships can be summarised as follows:

Limited Partnership (LP)	Limited Liability Partnership (LLP)
Governed by Limited Partnerships (Jersey) Law 1994.	Governed by Limited Liability Partnerships (Jersey) Law 1997.
LP's name must use the suffix "Limited Partnership" or the abbreviation "L.P." or "LP".	LLP's name must use the suffix "Limited Liability Partnership" or the abbreviation "L.L.P." or "LLP".
Each partner is jointly and severally liable for losses and debts incurred by the LP to the extent of the amount of capital committed less the amount already contributed. The LP cannot sue and be sued in its own name.	Separate legal personality (but not a body corporate), which means that the LLP is liable for any debt or loss and can sue or be sued in its own name.

Limited Partnership (LP)	Limited Liability Partnership (LLP)
Two partners minimum, of which at least one must be a GP.	Two partners minimum, of which at least one must be a designated partner.
No limit on number of limited partners.	No limit on number of limited partners
Capital contributions are permitted to be recognised from a variety of different sources, e.g. cash, provision of services, transfer of property.	Capital contributions are permitted to be recognised from a variety of different sources, e.g. cash, provision of services, transfer of property.
The partners are entitled to the profits and an interest in the property of the LP as set out in the LPA and so long as the LP remains solvent.	The partners are entitled to the profits and an interest in the property of the LLP as set out in the partnership agreement and so long as the LLP remains solvent.
Assets are typically held in the GP's name.	Assets may be held in own name.
Must maintain accounting records and may choose reporting currency.	Must maintain accounting records and may choose reporting currency.
No requirement to file accounts.	No requirement to file accounts.
No statutory audit requirement.	No statutory audit requirement.
No financial provision requirement.	Must maintain a £5m financial provision as a creditor safeguard.
Registered office must be in Jersey.	Registered office must be in Jersey.
No annual return, no annual fee and no requirement to name the limited partners.	Annual declaration to be filed with Companies Registry with the £500 annual declaration fee before the last day in February stating the names and addresses of every person who was a partner on 1 January of that year.
The partnership agreement is not a matter for public record.	The partnership agreement is not a matter for public record.
Fiscally transparent – profits of the business are taxed on the limited partners. The fiscal transparency enables investors to benefit from any relevant double tax treaty that may exist between their country of residence and the country in which the investment is made.	Fiscally transparent – profits of the business are taxed on the limited partners. The fiscal transparency enables investors to benefit from any relevant double tax treaty that may exist between their country of residence and the country in which the investment is made.

Chapter summary

◆ Companies have their own legal personality which is separate from the legal personalities of the individuals who own and manage the company. Limited companies, therefore, offer protection to the owners of the business and this is why sole traders often form companies to limit their liability for debts. A company contracts in its own name.

◆ In the UK, the Companies Act 2006 sets out the requirements of limited companies. Limited companies are either public or private and may be limited by shares or by guarantee.

◆ A private company may re-register as a public company and a public company may re-register as a private company provided certain conditions are met. The company must also make the necessary changes to its Articles of Association.

◆ A Jersey public company is a company with more than thirty members or which has at least two members and states in the Memorandum of Association that it is a public company.

◆ An important distinction between Companies (Jersey) Law 1991 and the Companies Act 2006 in the UK is that the minimum age requirement for a director in Jersey is 18, whereas it is only 16 in the UK.

◆ A Jersey public company may issue an offering document (or prospectus) in respect of offering its shares for subscription to the general public.

◆ A Jersey public company is required to file audited financial statements with the Registrar of Companies within seven months of the financial period end.

◆ A Jersey private company is a company that is not a public company and whose Memorandum of Association states that it is a private company.

◆ There is no requirement for Jersey private companies to file audited financial statements with the Registrar of Companies but accounting records do need to be maintained and accounts prepared to enable the company to establish its financial position at any point in time. Unaudited financial statements may also need to be filed with the tax authorities.

◆ The Companies (Guernsey) Law, 2008, does not distinguish between public and private companies.

◆ As well as limited liability companies, it is possible to have a mixed liability company in Guernsey which can be a hybrid of guarantee members and shareholders.

◆ The accounts of a Guernsey company must be audited unless the company is exempt under s.256 of Companies (Guernsey) Law, 2008. The company is exempt if the members pass a waiver resolution in the financial year before the financial year to which it relates, or if it is in respect of the company's first financial year, in that financial year.

- Companies in the BVI are governed by the British Virgin Islands Business Companies Act 2004.

- A key feature of BVI companies is that, with the exception of restricted purpose companies, they are not required to state their objects. This gives corporate capacity and flexibility and effectively removes the ultra vires doctrine.

- Long-term financing is achieved by either issuing equity shares (to shareholders as members of the company) or issuing debt such as loan stock (to the lenders as creditors of the company).

- Share capital represents the amount of cash and non-cash considerations raised by a company in return for issuing shares. Share capital is the investment in the company by its shareholders.

- Authorised share capital represents the amount of share capital that a firm is allowed to issue.

- The issued share capital is the nominal value of all shares which have been issued and taken up by the members.

- Called up share capital is the amount that has been requested for payment in exchange for the shares that have been issued.

- Paid up share capital is the amount of called up share capital that has been paid.

- Loan capital is often preferred to equity because issuing debt does not affect ownership and control of the company.

- Debentures are secured loans which rank ahead of shareholders and trade payables in the event the company enters into liquidation.

- The interest element on debt is usually deductible for corporation tax purposes, which reduces the net rate of taxation and thereby the company's cost of capital.

- Increasing debt to equity has a direct impact on gearing.

- Companies which are highly geared are at risk of not being able to pay their debts as they fall due and banks may impose loan covenants restricting the activities of the company if gearing exceeds a pre-determined limit.

- A cell company is a private or public company which is able to segregate its assets and liabilities between different cells. Each cell may be used to carry out distinct and independent businesses.

- Protected cells have no separate legal personality and therefore transact through the overarching cell company.

- With incorporated cells (ICs) of an incorporated cell company, each cell has its own separate legal personality.

- Having separate legal personality is an important factor for stakeholders to consider because an ICC/IC structure is less likely to face challenges from creditors than a PCC/PC structure whose ring-fencing capability is less substantive and might not be recognised by foreign court.

◆ Foundations are an alternative vehicle to a trust or a company. A foundation is a legal entity which can own assets and contract in its own name.

◆ Whilst in the large majority of cases, international finance centres in offshore jurisdictions are used for legitimate reasons by multinational organisations, families and private individuals (for tax and estate planning, wealth management, financial expertise, etc.), offshore jurisdictions are also, on occasions, used for tax evasion and other illegitimate purposes.

◆ High net worth individuals and multinational companies often use low-tax jurisdictions and international finance centres to base their business activities and benefit from the reduced taxation charges which can be as low as zero per cent for corporate income tax.

◆ In the UK, HM Revenue and Customs (HMRC) is currently trying to narrow down the window of opportunity for tax avoidance schemes which are growing in number and complexity.

◆ A key factor in determining whether an offshore structure is legitimate for tax purposes, is whether management and control is firmly offshore or whether it remains in the UK. The proceeds of offshore structures must be lawfully distributed and the appropriate taxes (if any) paid.

◆ A limited partnership (LP) comprises limited partners, who invest in the partnership, and one or more general partners (GPs), who manage the partnership. Generally speaking, LPs do not have their own separate legal personality and each partner is jointly and severally liable for losses and debts incurred by the LP to the extent of the amount of capital committed less the amount already contributed. General partners also have unlimited liability for the debts of the partnership and, therefore, tend to be formed as limited liability companies in order to limit their liability.

◆ Limited liability partnerships (LLPs) are a type of limited partnership which offers its partners limited liability. These vehicles are often used by accountancy and law firms and other employee-owned businesses where it is not always appropriate or desired to separate ownership and management.

Part Five

**Chapter 10
Financial sector
regulation**

**Chapter 11
Frameworks and
governance**

corporate governance
is a set of policies
and procedures, laws,
frameworks and practices
under which companies
are administered, governed
and controlled in order
to ensure accountability
and the protection of the
interests of shareholders.

In Part Five of this study text, students will be given a brief introduction to banking regulation. Students will learn about the entry criteria that the regulator might expect the bank to meet before a banking licence is issued. Students will also learn about some of the main supervisory functions of the regulator, the importance of licensed banks to be able to demonstrate adequate systems and controls and to follow the necessary legislative and regulatory requirements.

Students will learn about what is meant by the term **corporate governance** and the issues that underpin the key corporate governance codes and reports. Part Five also explains a number of key corporate governance failings which have led to the demise of public companies and accounting firms. These, in turn, have resulted in a number of reviews and reports on the conduct and composition of boards, board remuneration, the role of the audit committee, internal controls and the overall system of corporate governance within organisations. The development of legislative and regulatory frameworks in response to high-profile corporate scandals and recent bank failings is also discussed, as are the corporate governance requirements which have been introduced to address new statutory measures.

Learning outcomes

At the end of this part, students should be able to:

◆ explain recent corporate governance failings of banks;

◆ understand what is meant by the term "shadow banking";

◆ summarise the various regulatory criteria in respect of a banking licence application;

◆ discuss the ways in which supervisory oversight might be carried out by financial sector regulators;

◆ discuss the role of a central bank;

◆ explain what is meant by probity and ethical standards in corporate governance;

◆ explain the development of corporate governance and business;

◆ understand the concept of agency theory and conflicts of interest;

◆ discuss the impact of corporate governance on the company secretary, compliance officer and auditor of a business;

◆ discuss the main points arising out of the Cadbury, Greenbury and Hampel reports;

◆ summarise the disclosure requirements required by the UK Corporate Governance Code;

◆ explain the key principles and issues arising from the Higgs report, Smith report, Turnbull report, Myners report, UK Stewardship Code, Larosière report and the various corporate governance frameworks;

◆ understand and explain what is meant by the term corporate social responsibility;

◆ understand and advise on the key points pertaining to the Walker review;

◆ explain the requirements of Basel II and Basel III in relation to banking regulation;

◆ outline the key provisions of the Sarbanes-Oxley Act 2002 and the implications for US, UK and offshore companies and their senior executives;

- summarise the Dodd-Frank Wall Street Reform and Consumer Protection Act and understand the reasons for recent US regulatory reform;
- explain the key areas and themes of the Dodd-Frank Act;
- define the Volcker Rule on proprietary trading; and
- discuss the events leading up to the collapse of Lehman Brothers and state a number of key failings which contributed to the demise of this global investment bank.

Chapter ten
Financial sector regulation

List of topics

Introduction

In this chapter, students will learn about banking in the context of financial sector regulation. The chapter discusses the policies that may be applied by banking supervisors in international finance centres and the requirements that may be set by the regulator before granting a banking licence.

The chapter also explains the need for on-going supervision of a licensed bank. Banking supervisors tend to have specific rules for regulated banks which vary from jurisdiction to jurisdiction but the principles that banks are required to follow are largely the same.

Finally, students will learn about the role carried out by central banks with regard to ensuring financial stability and regulation.

1. Banking

The banking sector has recently been under close scrutiny by the general public due to corporate governance failings. These include failings in risk management and internal control systems, tone at the top and financial reporting weaknesses.

Sir David Walker was commissioned by the UK government in February 2009 to review corporate governance in UK banks and to make recommendations (see Chapter 11). In his review, Sir David Walker commented that, "Institutional investors should be less passive and prepared to engage earlier if they suspect weaknesses in governance. They enjoy the privilege of limited liability whereas taxpayers have ended up assuming unlimited liability in respect of the big banks. Early preventive medicine through shareholder engagement can save everyone substantial time and money later on."

Walker also said that "Improved governance can play an important complementary role by instilling greater confidence in the way banks are being run by their boards and overseen by their owners. This should help regulators to strike the right balance."

Shadow banking activities have also been criticised and are now an additional area of focus within Europe. Shadow banking activities are likely to fall within the scope of regulation in due course. Shadow banking is effectively the supply of credit by entities and through activities that fall outside the regular banking system.

Possible shadow banking entities and activities include:

◆ money market funds (low risk, liquid investment vehicles);

◆ exchange-traded funds that provide credit or are leveraged;

◆ finance companies that provide credit;

◆ insurance and reinsurance undertakings which issue or guarantee credit products; and

◆ securitisations such as mortgage-backed securities and other financial instruments that are packaged together and then divided up into tranches for resale.

2. Banking licences

2.1 Applying for a banking licence

Banks are required to apply for a banking licence before undertaking regulated activities in offshore financial centres. The requirements differ from jurisdiction to jurisdiction and will depend on the specific licensing policy of the offshore regulator. Jersey, for example, has a higher level of entry than most other offshore international finance centres, and indeed many onshore jurisdictions, as it requires deposit-taking businesses to be in the top 500 banking groups worldwide, measured by **Tier 1 capital**.

Before issuing a license, the relevant supervisory authority is likely to consider:

◆ Ownership and control. Reputable offshore international finance centres will wish to identify the significant ultimate owners and controllers and ensure they are fit and proper. Publicly quoted banks are generally preferred to the small private banks as it is unusual for publicly quoted "top 500" banks to have dominant controller shareholders.

◆ Real presence of the bank as many offshore supervisory authorities will not licence shell banks which have no management and control in the offshore jurisdiction.

◆ Integrity, competence, knowledge and experience of the principal persons.

◆ Track record, including an audit history and stable management team.

◆ Stature of the applicant including its financial strength, risk profile, capital resources and liquidity levels.

◆ Internal controls and risk management systems to ensure they are taking adequate account of the nature and scope of the activities undertaken.

Tier 1 capital
is capital which is considered to be a safer form of capital than Tier 2 capital (supplementary capital such as undisclosed reserves, revaluation reserves and subordinated debt) and Tier 3 capital (such as short-term subordinated debt) and comprises largely equity and retained profits.

◆   Systemic importance of the bank's home jurisdiction such that the home jurisdiction is capable of providing support if required.

Once the regulator is (i) satisfied with the completeness and suitability of the application; and (ii) has carried out its due diligence and regulatory checks on the bank, the principal persons and other connected parties, then a licence is likely to be granted subject to general conditions of registration. Some banks may find themselves subject to additional special conditions which are deemed necessary to a bank's registration to enable the regulator to carry out its functions and fulfil its responsibilities under the relevant legislation. Failure to comply with a registration condition would be an offence under the relevant legislative framework and the offending bank would most likely find itself under heightened regulatory supervision.

2.2 On-going supervision

After a bank has received its licence for deposit taking, it becomes subject to ongoing **prudential regulation** by the banking division of the relevant supervisory authority, e.g.:

prudential regulation is the term given to the regulatory framework surrounding capital adequacy and liquidity requirements of financial institutions such as banks and deposit takers.

Jurisdiction	Supervisory body
UK	From 2013: The Prudential Regulation Authority (subsidiary of the Bank of England)
Jersey	Jersey Financial Services Commission
Guernsey	Guernsey Financial Services Commission
IOM	Financial Supervision Commission
Bermuda	Bermuda Monetary Authority
Cayman	Cayman Islands Monetary Authority
BVI	British Virgin Islands Financial Services Commission

Regulation may take the form of both off- and onsite supervision.

offsite supervision describes the desk-based supervisory activities undertaken by the regulator at its own offices such as the review of financial statements and prudential returns.

Offsite supervision describes the desk-based supervisory activities undertaken by the regulator at its own offices. It includes the following activities:

◆   Review of financial statements.

◆   Review of reports, declarations and other documentation received.

◆   Analysis of prudential and statistical returns.

◆   Monitoring capital levels and ensuring requirements are maintained.

◆   Processing of data and systems changes to reflect changes in connection with a regulated activity or the notification of significant events.

◆   Assessing the "fit and proper" status of firms and individuals, e.g. directors, controlling shareholders, compliance officers, money laundering reporting officers, money laundering compliance officers.

◆   Participation in matters of international financial and banking policy, thematic studies and attendance at user group meetings.

Onsite supervision is the term given to examinations undertaken by the regulator at the licensee's place of business and this might be at one or more of its offices. The examination programmes are designed to enable the regulator to determine whether the bank has the necessary processes, procedures, systems and controls in place to mitigate risks within the bank and to enable it to comply with relevant legislation and regulations such as regulatory guidelines and codes of best practice.

Onsite examinations vary in nature and scope and depend on the activities performed by the bank. Broadly speaking, there are three types of supervisory examinations:

1   themed examinations;
2   focused examinations; and
3   discovery examinations.

A **themed examination** is an examination on a specific theme, e.g. wire transfers, corporate governance, anti-money laundering/countering of financing of terrorism. The theme is derived from an analysis of recent data or significant changes to legislation such as the implementation of the Dodd-Frank Act (see Chapter 11). A number of regulated entities will be subject to the same themed examination to enable the supervisory body to analyse trends and draw comparisons between regulated entities.

A **focused examination** is targeted at specific matters related to the regulated entity, be it to do with risk management staff structure and responsibilities, internal systems and controls, conduct of business, transaction monitoring, business continuity planning, financial standing, corporate governance or any other matter, and includes monitoring corrective action taken following an earlier examination of that bank.

A **discovery examination** describes the type of examination which may be wide in scope and might include a review of a wide range of activities as well as a bank's risk management systems and internal controls, policies and procedures, processes, conduct of business, financial standing and corporate governance. The regulator's examination team typically review files, minute books, breach logs, complaints files and other relevant documentation. The regulator also conducts interviews with bank executives and staff involved with the day to day running of the banking operations, with a view to discovering material weaknesses, if any.

2.3 Key themes

Corporate governance
Corporate governance is of particular interest to banking supervisors particularly in light of recent banking failures which have highlighted that banks with robust risk management systems and internal controls, which are well managed, are less likely to fail. A bank with high standards of corporate governance installs confidence in the regulator, the market and depositors.

onsite supervision
is the term given to examinations undertaken by the regulator at the licensee's place of business in order to monitor compliance with relevant legislation and regulations and to determine whether the bank has the necessary processes, procedures, systems and controls in place to mitigate risks.

themed examination
is an examination on a specific theme, e.g. wire transfers, corporate governance, anti-money laundering/countering of financing of terrorism. The theme is derived from an analysis of recent data or significant changes to legislation such as the implementation of the Dodd-Frank Act. A number of regulated entities will be subject to the same themed examination to enable the supervisory body to analyse trends and draw comparisons between regulated entities.

focused examination
is targeted at specific matters related to the regulated entity, be it to do with risk management, internal systems and controls, conduct of business, financial standing, corporate governance or any other matter, and includes monitoring corrective action taken following an earlier examination of that bank.

discovery examination
describes the type of examination which may be wide in scope and might include a review of a wide range of activities as well as a bank's risk management systems and internal controls, policies and procedures, processes, conduct of business, financial standing and corporate governance.

There are a number of key corporate governance processes which are of interest to banking supervisors and these include:

◆ Business strategy – understanding the goals and objectives of the bank and the strategy-setting process in order to assess related business risks and likelihood of success or failure.

◆ Organisational structure – understanding the senior management team and its committees in order to assess the level of effectiveness of corporate governance within the bank.

◆ Change management – understanding the key projects being undertaken, if any, in order to assess the impact of these changes on the business and how they are managed and controlled.

◆ Staff training – understanding whether staff have received relevant training commensurate with their level of seniority and the business activities being undertaken.

◆ Bank group activities – understanding the group structure and inter-relationships of group entities which may affect the risk profile of the regulated entity and its level of capital.

Systems and controls

A bank requires robust systems and controls to ensure that transactions are properly authorised and carried out, are lawful, correctly recorded and that management is aware of the type and level of business being conducted. This requires a reliable and secure ICT (Information Communication Technology) infrastructure and strategy linked to business needs and business continuity. Having adequate controls includes the provision of an internal audit function which has clear terms of reference, unrestricted access to the business and independent escalation and reporting lines.

A well managed bank should implement recommendations of its banking supervisor in a timely manner and should be prepared to adapt quickly to changes that may be required to comply with new legislation and regulatory measures.

The supervisory oversight of banks includes prudential risk control to ensure capital requirements are met on an on-going basis. The relevant banking authority will also monitor asset and gearing ratios.

Making it work 10.1

Business continuity is an important aspect of systems and controls. The FSA and Bank of England are keen to avoid other UK lenders suffering systems failures like those suffered by RBS in June 2012. Millions of bank customers suffered the effects of a payments system failure following a systems upgrade by the bank. The inability to make payments lasted a fortnight and up to a month for its Ulster Bank account holders. The FSA is, consequently, expected to levy a significant fine on the bank for its ICT failure. RBS is expected to have to pay out millions in compensation. From 2013, the regulatory body responsible for monitoring conduct in retail and wholesale financial markets, as well as consumer products, will pass to the Financial Conduct Authority. The new regulatory body will be keen to ensure banks have robust systems and controls. It is important that banks consider not only the impact of failure of their own ICT system but also the impact on their operations resulting from failures of other banks.

2.4 Guidance

Guidance sets out best practice and reflects what is expected of a regulated entity. In most offshore jurisdictions, as with the UK's Financial Services Authority (FSA), there is usually no firm requirement to follow guidance. Guidance provides clarification on regulatory matters and therefore it is in a bank's best interests to understand the key issues covered in guidance notes and to adhere to the guidance, where applicable. Failure of a bank's compliance function to keep abreast of the latest guidance could ultimately result in the bank being accused of a breach of a regulatory requirement which might include a breach of the relevant Codes of Practice or licensing condition.

2.5 Codes of practice

Banking supervisors often issue codes of best practice which form part of the supervisor's regulatory requirements. Key requirements set out in codes of practice may include the following principles:

◆ The licensee must conduct its business with integrity.

◆ The licensee must have due regard for the interests of its customers.

◆ The licensee must organise its affairs effectively for the proper performance of its business activities and be able to demonstrate the existence of adequate risk management systems.

◆ The licensee must be transparent in its business arrangements.

◆ The licensee must maintain, and be able to demonstrate, the existence of adequate capital resources.

◆ The licensee must deal with the regulator and other authorities in the jurisdiction in an open and co-operative manner.

◆ The licensee must not make statements that are misleading, false or deceptive.

2.6 Regulator to regulator correspondence

The offshore banking regulator may write to the home regulator of the offshore deposit-taker to provide it with a summary of the regulator's current view of the bank. This may include an assessment of the bank's systems and controls as well as its exposure to risk.

The offshore regulator may also seek information from the home regulator, which may include:

◆ Confirmation that the home regulator undertakes consolidated supervision to include the offshore bank.

◆ Confirmation that the banking group is in compliance with the home regulator's regulatory requirements and that the home regulator is satisfied with the financial soundness of the bank.

◆ Details of any special conditions that the home regulator may have imposed on the bank.

◆ Material facts or issues that may have a bearing on the supervision of the regulated bank.

2.7 Risk-based approach

Banking supervisors often adopt a risk-based approach to the supervision of their respective banks. In doing so, the supervisor will consider factors such as the bank's financial standing, the integrity of its principal persons and controlling parties, the competence of staff undertaking regulated activities, the corporate governance regime and internal controls.

Banking supervisors maintain risk models for the banks they regulate. The models are typically based on a combination of impact and probability scores. All relevant supervisory findings following an onsite examination of a bank, or arising from desk-based supervision, are fed into the model so that, at any point in time, the bank's exposure to risk may be assessed and compared to other banking businesses.

3. The role of central banks

Central banks play a number of key roles including managing a nation's currency, managing the supply of money and either setting interest rates or recommending interest rate changes to government. Central banks are also concerned with financial stability and financial regulation. In carrying out their functions, central banks seek to reduce systemic risk through monetary policy, the provision of liquidity in money markets, lending (as a lender of last resort) and through the oversight of clearing and settlement systems.

Examples of central banks based in the UK, Europe, China, USA and International Finance Centres are:

◆ Bank of England (UK)

◆ Banque de France (France)

◆ Deutsche Bundesbank (Germany)

◆ People's Bank of China (China)

◆ Federal Reserve System (USA)

◆ European Central Bank (European Union)

◆ The Central Bank of the Bahamas (The Bahamas)

◆ Bermuda Monetary Authority (Bermuda)

◆ Cayman Islands Monetary Authority (Cayman Islands)

◆ Hong Kong Monetary Authority (Hong Kong)

◆ Central Bank of Luxembourg (Luxembourg)

◆ Bank of Mauritius (Mauritius)

The Larosière report of the High-Level Group of Financial Supervision in the EU refers to the many roles that are performed by central banks to manage the economy and deal with the systemic risks:

> 'Governments and Central Banks across the world have taken many measures to try to improve the economic situation and reduce the systemic dangers: economic stimulus packages of various forms; huge injections of Central Bank liquidity; recapitalising financial institutions; providing guarantees for certain types of financial activity and in particular inter-bank lending; or through direct asset purchases, and *Bad Bank* solutions are being contemplated by some governments. So far there has been limited success.'

3.1 Supply of currency

Central banks help set monetary policy and can influence currency supply by buying or selling currency directly on the global currency market. A central bank can increase the value of the country's currency, by purchasing its currency and accumulating currency reserves. This cuts the supply of the currency that is available to others on the foreign exchange market. Reduced supply leads to an increase in demand which, in turn, leads to a strengthening of the currency. A central bank can also influence a downward movement in the currency's exchange rate by selling its currency reserves into the foreign exchange market and boosting supply. A central bank might devalue its currency in an attempt to increase exports. Central banks can also adjust the level of cash reserves that they require commercial banks to maintain and thereby influence the supply of money.

3.2 Interest rate policy

Central banks lend capital to commercial banks to provide them with liquidity to cover day-to-day operations and transactions. The interest rate charged to the banks affects the interest rates charged to consumers for mortgages and loans. The central bank can manipulate interest rates to stimulate or slow down the economy. It can stimulate the economy by lowering interest rates and can curb inflation by increasing interest rates.

3.3 Provision of liquidity

Central banks also play a key role in providing liquidity to the market and by facilitating and regulating interbank lending. They play the part of "market maker of last resort", intervening with interbank lending when banks are reluctant to lend to one another.

3.4 Lender of last resort

A country's central bank is commonly referred to as the "lender of last resort", meaning it provides emergency funds to systemically important banks and other financial institutions when there is a money supply shortage and credit lines have dried up. In other words, it is the central bank that will, in certain situations, provide liquidity assistance to stricken financial institutions such as banks and insurance companies whose failure could prove extremely disruptive to the wider economy and financial community.

Examples of recent "bail outs" include the Bank of England providing emergency funding to the UK deposit taker, Northern Rock, in 2007 and the Federal Reserve in the US propping up Bear Stearns and AIG, in 2008, by providing lines of credit and acting as a bridge bank (ensuring the continuation of operations) whilst a more permanent solution was being sought. Banks and non-bank financial institutions, which are systemically important, often have significant assets which are interconnected with lots of other financial products, such that the failure of the institution would start a domino effect of other failures. In the case of Northern Rock, when credit lines were no longer available on the open market, due to uncertainty over the future viability of the stricken bank, the Bank of England provided emergency liquidity support rather than risking the impact of allowing the bank to fail.

The difficulty central banks face is that some financial institutions believe they are "too big to fail" and expect to receive emergency financial assistance should they run into difficulties. Central banks have to be careful not to risk reputational damage by bailing out poorly governed institutions unless there are compelling reasons. They usually take a keen interest, therefore, in prudential regulation to ensure there is effective oversight of capital adequacy rules and liquidity requirements and that banks are subject to effective supervision.

3.5 Oversight of payment and settlement systems

Central banks oversee payment and settlement systems and play a role in reducing counterparty credit risk, although there are still significant challenges facing central banks in connection with the oversight of over-the-counter derivative payment and settlement systems.

Chapter summary

◆ The banking sector has recently been under close scrutiny by the general public due to corporate governance failings. These include failings in risk management and internal control systems, tone at the top and financial reporting weaknesses.

◆ Shadow banking activities have also been criticised and are now an additional area of focus within Europe. Shadow banking is effectively the supply of credit by entities and through activities that fall outside the regular banking system.

◆ Banks are required to apply for a banking licence before undertaking regulated activities in offshore financial centres. The requirements differ from jurisdiction to jurisdiction and will depend on the specific licensing policy of the offshore regulator.

◆ Before issuing a banking licence, the regulator is likely to consider: ownership and control; real presence; integrity, competence, knowledge and experience of principal persons; track record; stature; internal controls and risk management systems; home jurisdiction.

◆ Regulation may take the form of both off- and onsite supervision.

◆ Offsite supervision describes the desk-based supervisory activities undertaken by the regulator at its own offices such as the review of financial statements and prudential returns.

◆ Onsite supervision is the term given to examinations undertaken by the regulator at the licensee's place of business and this might be at one or more of its offices. The examination programmes are designed to enable the regulator to determine whether the bank has the necessary processes, procedures, systems and controls in place to mitigate risks within the bank and to enable it to comply with relevant legislation and regulations such as regulatory guidelines and codes of best practice.

◆ Central banks play a number of key roles including managing a nation's currency, managing the supply of money and either setting interest rates or recommending interest rate changes to government. Central banks are also concerned with financial stability and financial regulation.

Chapter eleven
Frameworks and governance

List of topics

1   Agency theory
2   Corporate govenance – codes and reports
3   Corporate social responsibility
4   The Walker Review
5   Basel II and III
6   Sarbanes–Oxley Act (2002)
7   Dodd–Frank Act (2010)

Introduction

A country needs to have a good corporate governance framework in place to install investor confidence. If investors lose confidence in the level of governance and disclosure, capital will flow elsewhere.

This chapter discusses the need for companies to have a sound system of corporate governance in place underpinned by regulatory and legislative frameworks. Students will learn about the conflicts arising between agents (who manage and control companies) and shareholders (who own companies).

Students will also learn what is meant by corporate social responsibility and will gain an insight into a number of important corporate governance codes and the recommendations arising from corporate governance reports from Cadbury, Greenbury and Hampel to the more recent UK Corporate Governance Code and the Larosière report of the High-Level Group of Financial Supervision in the EU.

The chapter also discusses offshore developments including the Guernsey Finance Sector Code of Corporate Governance.

In the wake of a number of recent corporate scandals and the ensuing global financial crisis, a number of other reports and reviews were commissioned and significant regulatory and legislative changes were introduced on the back of these reviews. Students will learn about the Walker Review on corporate governance in UK banks and the action taken by the Basel Committee on Banking Supervision to strengthen the soundness and stability of the international banking system. Students will also learn about two significant and wide-reaching pieces of US legislation, namely the Sarbanes-Oxley Act and the Dodd-Frank Act.

1. Agency theory

Agency theory is based on the belief that the managers of a company are appointed to act as agents of the owners of the company and that there is an inherent conflict of interest between the managers (who control the company) and the shareholders (who own the company). Agency theory is concerned with aligning the interests of the owners and agents.

1.1 Ownership versus control

A problem arises when the directors, who manage and control the company, make decisions which are not consistent with the objective of maximising owner wealth. For example, directors may aim to please the market and influence the company's share price in order to influence their bonuses. Shareholders, the owners, will welcome an increase in value of their company provided this is not short-termism and artificially inflating profits at the expense of longer term gains.

1.2 Goal congruence

Aligning the goals of owners and managers is an important means of helping overcome the agency problem and ensuring managers act in the best interests of the shareholders. If managers are to act in the best interests of the owners then they should have the appropriate incentives such as performance-related pay. Performance-related benefits need to be carefully structured to ensure a manager does not put his own personal gain ahead of the objective of maximising shareholder wealth. This can be achieved by a good framework of corporate governance which might ensure bonuses do not focus fully on short-term gains at the expense of the company in the long term. Good corporate governance seeks to address conflicts between managers and owners by the achievement of **goal congruence**. In other words, the company directors and other members of senior management need to be motivated to align their goals with the objectives of the company so that their behaviours and actions result in mutually beneficial outcomes.

1.3 Asymmetry of information

Agency theory is based on the belief that owners are not in a position to fully monitor the managers of the company as they do not have full knowledge of the business and access to all information. For example, the shareholders will see the annual report but may not be privileged to the management accounts and underlying information. This asymmetry of information puts managers in a position where they can, if they lack integrity and high moral standards, focus on their own wealth maximisation to the detriment of shareholder wealth maximisation without always being challenged. Managers may pursue their

agency theory
is based on the belief that the managers of a company are appointed to act as agents of the owners of the company and that there is an inherent conflict of interest between the managers (who control the company) and the shareholders (who own the company).

goal congruence
describes the alignment and harmonization of goals and objectives. In the context of agency theory, this means matching the interests of the directors with the interests of shareholders so that directors are incentivised to act in the best interests of the company.

own goals of increasing their own rewards and bonuses, introducing rewards for failure such as **golden handshakes**, growing the company or even following their own agendas. Shareholders, who may lack knowledge of the running of the business, may remain passive and unengaged in the business in which they invest.

There has been a move in recent years, however, to encourage greater shareholder engagement especially in wake of a number of financial scandals. Institutional shareholders, such as large pension funds, which typically hold large volumes of shares, can have a significant influence on how companies are run by challenging the board's decisions and aligning the objectives of the directors with their own objective of wealth maximisation.

share option scheme
is a management incentive scheme which gives participants the right to buy a set number of shares at a set price at a specified time in the future. A share option scheme is designed to help achieve goal congruence between managers and owners by rewarding managers for maximising shareholders' wealth.

A **share option scheme** is one type of incentive scheme which has become more common in an attempt to encourage goal congruence between the owners of a company and its managers. By giving the managers the right to purchase a set number of shares at a set price at a set point in time in the future, they are incentivised to maximise the share price and exercise their share options. If the market price of shares is above the option price at the specified time the option may be exercised, then managers will be rewarded by being able to purchase a set number of shares at the option price, i.e. below market value. If the market price of the shares is below the option price, however, then the managers will not be able to benefit from the option. The difficulty with share option schemes is ensuring the option price is set at a realistic level to keep managers motivated to achieve shareholder wealth maximisation.

satisficing
describes the behaviour of managers to do just enough to satisfy shareholders and achieve an adequate return on their investment rather than maximising the return for shareholders.

Managers will lose motivation if the required increase in share price looks unachievable. They may also lack drive to maximise the share price if they have already been rewarded for achieving a satisfactory return. Such behaviour is known as **satisficing**. Profit-related incentives and share option schemes therefore need to be properly structured and regularly reviewed to ensure ongoing goal congruence of the interests of managers and the shareholders.

In respect of the annual report and financial statements, the audit function acts as a safeguard for shareholders who may be concerned managers are achieving their goals with the help of aggressive accounting practice. The auditor is required to give an independent opinion on whether the financial statements give a "true and fair" view of the state of affairs of the company and the financial position as at the income statement date. If accounting standards have not been strictly applied, this will be highlighted in the audit report. The audit report should also confirm if relevant laws and codes of practice have been complied with, which for listed companies in the UK might include certain aspects of the UK Corporate Governance Code.

High standards of reporting and corporate governance provide comfort that managers are acting appropriately and with integrity and helps reduce the agency problem. Institutional investors have helped minimise the agency problem in recent years by challenging board decisions and taking an increased interest in corporate governance measures employed by the companies in which they invest. A company can ill afford to ignore institutional investors who are highly influential due to the voting rights that come with large number of shares they own.

As well as challenging corporate governance standards and how well a company is run, institutional shareholders are well placed to challenge investment decisions and financing decisions, especially where it is believed that directors may not be motivated to align their goals with the interests of the shareholders. For example, if directors have already hit their targets, they might no longer be incentivised to take on investment decisions other than low-risk investments which offer lower returns. Likewise, if directors have poorly structured performance-related pay, they may become overly focused on high-risk investments which might achieve greater returns, but at significant risk to the company. The directors may become so focused on their performance-related pay that they lose sight of the risks they are taking with the shareholders' funds.

With regard to financing decisions, the company's management might favour equity over debt in order to reduce the company's gearing and exposure to loan interest payments. **Equity finance** might prove more expensive, however, especially if there is a public offering. If existing owners do not take up the offer for shares, their shareholding will be diluted because there will be more shares in issue. If **debt financing** is undertaken, however, there may be an agency conflict between the debt holders (who provide the loans in exchange for bonds) and the equity holders (who have purchased shares) because debt holders, unlike the shareholders, do not benefit from the profits of the company. The equity holders will want to achieve maximisation of value, which might mean higher risk investments, whilst the debt holders will simply want to receive the regular bond fixed-interest payments on the **principal** which has been borrowed by the company.

equity finance
is capital raised by selling shares in the company, typically by public offering.

debt financing
occurs when a company raises finance by issuing bonds, bills or notes and, in exchange, promises to repay the lender the interest and capital on the loan.

principal
describes the capital element of the loan which is the amount outstanding less the interest.

2. Corporate governance – codes and reports

Corporate governance is the process by which organisations are directed and controlled. It is through good corporate governance that the interests of investors and other stakeholders are safeguarded and, in so far as possible, aligned. Displaying sound governance is good for companies as it helps with their smooth running, attracts inward investment and helps raise finance.

Corporate governance encompasses the following areas:

◆ Effective risk management systems and internal controls.

◆ Timely financial reporting and annual audit confirming that the financial statements give a true and fair view of the state of affairs and performance of the company.

◆ Good communication, disseminating accurate and relevant information and dealing with shareholders in an open and honest manner to enable them to make informed decisions.

◆ Transparency and disclosure, particularly in respect of directors' remuneration and the appointment of the remuneration committee.

- ◆ Accountability.
- ◆ Integrity.
- ◆ Ethical behaviour and a culture that delivers the right outcomes.
- ◆ Adequate span of control appropriate to the nature of the business.
- ◆ Balance on the board with a diverse mix of individuals possessing the relevant skills, knowledge and experience and who have clear lines of responsibility and who can exercise independence of judgement.
- ◆ Fitness and propriety of directors.
- ◆ Effective oversight by senior management and the board of directors.
- ◆ Compliance with regulatory standards and legislation.

2.1 Cadbury report (1992)

In 1991, in response to financial scandals (including the Bank of Credit and Commerce International, Maxwell Communications Corporation, the Mirror Group, Polly Peck and Guinness) and the resultant growing public concern over the management of large companies, the quality of their financial reporting, the apparent lack of accountability and the high levels of executive remuneration, Sir Adrian Cadbury was charged with conducting a review on the Financial Aspects of Corporate Governance. The Cadbury Committee, which was appointed by the Financial Reporting Council and the London Stock Exchange in conjunction with the accounting profession, issued its report and Codes of Best Practice on corporate governance in December 1992.

In its report, the Cadbury Committee defines corporate governance as "the system by which companies are directed and controlled" and discusses the need for separating the role of management, which is about running the business, from the role of governance, which is about making sure the business is run properly. The Cadbury Code is based on the principles of openness, integrity and accountability.

The Cadbury Code was introduced on a voluntary basis and was designed "to achieve the necessary high standards of corporate behaviour". However, shortly after its publication, the London Stock Exchange included in the Listing Rules the requirement for all listed companies to either comply with the Code or explain in their annual report why they had not applied the Code and to disclose the areas of non-compliance.

unitary board structure
is a form of board structure, common in the UK, in which executive and non-executive directors combine on the same board pooling their skills, knowledge and experience.

The report found the **unitary board structure** needed to be strengthened and made more effective but did not need replacing. It highlighted the need for all directors to have oversight of their company's activities and to take responsibility to ensure control mechanisms are in place and working effectively.

Principal recommendations of the Cadbury Code:

Board of directors
The board should meet on a regular basis, monitoring the performance of the executive management.

◆ The roles and responsibilities of the Chief Executive Officer and Chairman should be clearly separated to avoid domination by any one individual. If the same person occupies the position of CEO and Chairman then there should be a senior independent director on the board.

◆ There should be a sufficient number of appropriately qualified non-executive directors.

◆ There should be a formal schedule of matters exclusively reserved for the board's decision so as to ensure control of the company remains a matter for the board.

◆ There should be an agreed procedure for directors to seek professional advice should they need to and this should be at the company's expense.

◆ All members of the board should have access to the services of the company secretary and the company secretary should not be removed without collective consent.

Non-executive directors (NEDs)

NEDs should be able to bring independent judgement to the deliberations of the board.

non-executive directors (NEDs) are directors, who are not employees of the company, and who are not involved in the day-to-day management responsibilities. They, therefore, have no executive responsibilities.

◆ The majority of NEDs should be independent of management and free from conflicts of interest.

◆ NEDs should be appointed for a fixed term and reappointment should not be automatic.

◆ There should be a formal process for the selection and appointment of NEDs.

Executive directors

The service contracts of directors should not exceed three years (subsequently reduced to 1 year) meaning that the notice period given to directors upon termination of a contract (e.g. for poor performance) cannot exceed this amount.

◆ Directors' remuneration should be fully disclosed including non-cash and performance-related elements such as share options.

◆ There should be a remuneration committee to determine the pay for executive directors, comprising entirely, or principally, of non-executive directors.

Financial reporting

The board ensure the financial statements are presented in a balanced manner and are understandable.

◆ There should be an audit committee, established by the board, which comprises at least three NEDs and which has clearly defined duties set out in the terms of reference.

◆ The audit committee should review the financial statements prior to their consideration by the board and maintain a professional relationship with the auditors.

◆ In the financial statements, the directors should set out their responsibilities for preparing accounts, report on the effectiveness of the company's internal controls and include a statement on the company's ability to continue as a going concern.

2.2 Greenbury report

The Greenbury report on directors' remuneration was published in 1995. The report addresses the public concern over the directors of recently privatised companies who engineered significant salaries for themselves irrespective of their performance.

The recommendations of the report cover four key themes:

◆ Remuneration committee.

◆ Disclosure and approval provisions.

◆ Remuneration policy.

◆ Service contracts and compensation.

2.2.1 Remuneration committee

The Greenbury committee recommended that a remuneration committee consisting entirely of NEDs, who should be named as members of the committee in the annual report, be responsible for setting remuneration policy and deciding executive remuneration packages. The Greenbury report also stated that the determination of non-executive pay should be a matter for the board. The remuneration committee should consult with the Chairman and/or CEO about their proposals and have access to professional advice from both inside the company and from external professionals, if required. The remuneration committee should also be present at the AGM to answer shareholder questions on directors' remuneration and the committee's annual report to shareholders should be a standard agenda item for the AGM.

2.2.2 Disclosure and approval provisions

The remuneration committee should report annually to shareholders setting out the company's policy on executive pay and providing a comparative analysis of executive remuneration in similar companies, disclosing full details of all elements of the remuneration package of each and every director including basic salary, benefits in kind, bonuses, long-term incentive schemes and share options. An explanation should be given where any element of pay, other than basic salary, is pensionable. Where share options are granted, these should either be granted in a phased manner, or justification given as to why a large block is granted in one go.

2.2.3 Remuneration policy

The remuneration committee should ensure that executive pay is not excessive but, at the same time, executive remuneration packages need to be sufficient to attract, retain and motivate individuals of the right calibre. In setting pay, the remuneration committee should ensure any performance-related element aligns the interests of directors and shareholders and that consideration is given to capping the pay at a certain level and rewarding directors with shares, rather than completely in cash, with a proviso that the shares must not be sold for a set period of time.

2.2.4 *Service contracts and compensation*

Remuneration committees should give strong consideration to setting contracts and notice periods at no more than one year so that directors who are dismissed for poor performance are not compensated for an undue length of time. Where longer term contracts, of say three years are given, to attract new directors to the board, consideration should be given to reducing the notice period in the contracts after a period of time so that, in the event the director fails to deliver, he/she is not rewarded for failure. It might also be appropriate to structure termination clauses in contracts of service so that an individual director's compensation is reduced if the reason for departure is poor performance. The Greenbury report specifically states that the aim of the remuneration committee should be to avoid rewarding for unsatisfactory performance whilst dealing fairly with directors whose departure is for reasons other than poor performance.

2.3 Hampel report

The Hampel committee was established in 1995 charged with reviewing the implementation of the findings of the Cadbury and Greenbury committees. The Hampel committee's final report was issued in 1998. The Committee drew up a list of corporate governance principles covering also the role of directors, directors' remuneration, the role of shareholders and accountability and audit, built on the findings of Cadbury and Greenbury.

Key principles:

Directors

In respect of the board of directors, there should be effective leadership and control of every listed company.

- There are two distinct roles at the head of every company, the role of the Chairman, who runs the board, and that of the CEO who is responsible for executive management and the day-to-day running of the business. Any decision to have both roles carried out by one person should be publicly explained.
- There should be a balance on the board with the right mix of executive and non-executive directors. No one director or group of directors should be able to dominate board proceedings.
- Accurate and relevant information should be supplied to the board in a timely manner to enable it to carry out its functions.
- A nomination committee should make recommendations to the board in respect of board appointments and should follow a formal and transparent procedure.
- All directors should stand for re-election at least every three years in order to promote boardroom effectiveness and recognise the inherent rights of shareholders, as owners of the company.

Remuneration

Directors' pay packages should be sufficient to attract and retain individuals of the required calibre and should include a performance related element.

- ◆ Companies should have a formal and transparent procedure for setting remuneration policy on executive pay.
- ◆ The Hampel report backs the recommendations of Cadbury and Greenbury in respect of the appointment of remuneration committees but states that directors should not have any involvement in decisions over their own individual pay packages.
- ◆ The annual report should disclose the pay of board members and include a statement on remuneration policy.

Shareholders

The Hampel committee concluded that institutional investors should make it their responsibility to vote and to use their vote in a responsible manner.

- ◆ Shareholders and companies should be prepared to enter into dialogue on matters based on the mutual understanding of objectives.
- ◆ Institutional investors should consider all relevant issues brought to their attention in their evaluation of governance disclosures.
- ◆ The AGM should be used to engage with private investors who, on average, hold around 20% of shares in listed companies. Participation of smaller shareholders is encouraged.

Accountability and audit

The board should present a balanced and understandable picture of the financial position of the company in its financial statements.

- ◆ The board should maintain a sound internal control and risk management system to safeguard the interests of shareholders and the assets of the company.
- ◆ The Cadbury recommendations for all listed companies to have an audit committee, made up exclusively of non-executive directors and that reports to the board, are upheld by the Hampel committee.
- ◆ The role of the audit committee should be to monitor the scope and results of the audit, review cost-effectiveness and ensure the independence and objectivity of the auditors.
- ◆ The auditors should report, not only to shareholders on the financial statements, but also to the directors on operational and other matters.

The Hampel committee recommended that its principles be combined with the Cadbury and Greenbury recommendations and published in one consolidated code – the Combined Code (now known as the UK Corporate Governance Code).

2.4 UK Corporate Governance Code

In June 1998, the Combined Code on Corporate Governance was published. It was later revised in 2003 following a review of the role and effectiveness of non-executive directors by Derek Higgs and a review of audit committees by a group led by Sir Robert Smith. Further reviews were undertaken in 2006 and in 2009, the latter triggered by the financial crisis and to consider the recommendations of the Walker Review. The revised code was renamed in 2010 as the UK Corporate Governance Code and assumes a "comply or explain" approach to corporate governance, whereby the boards of companies should either comply with the principles of the Code or explain the areas of non-compliance to their shareholders.

The Code combines and consolidates the recommendations of Cadbury, Greenbury and Hampel to establish best practice principles and more detailed requirements in respect of board leadership and effectiveness, accountability, remuneration and shareholder relations. The Code is designed to help directors discharge their duties to shareholders by acting in their best interests. The Code recommends that the Chairman of a company reports personally to shareholders on board effectiveness and the application of the Code's principles in this respect. The application of the principles by UK listed companies is on a mandatory "comply or explain" basis.

The Code also recommends that companies consider their policies in respect of the re-election of directors and that FTSE 350 company board members should stand for election on an annual basis, effectively making them more accountable for their past actions. Whilst the Code encourages shareholder engagement and directors to report to shareholders on a "comply or explain" basis, departures from the Code should not automatically be treated as a breach, as it may be appropriate for certain complex companies to depart from the requirements of the Code in certain circumstances. Shareholders should consider the explanations given and engage with the board if they remain unconvinced about the reasons for departure from the requirements of the Code.

In addition to the "comply or explain" approach required by the UK Listing Rules, the Code lays down certain disclosure requirements in respect of information which should be included in the annual report, made available on the company's website, or included in shareholder communications.

UK Corporate Governance Code disclosure requirements:

A company's annual report should contain the following information disclosures:

◆ a statement of how the board operates and delegated authorities;
◆ the names of the Chairman, Deputy Chairman, CEO, the senior independent director and the names of the Chairmen and members of each of the board committees;
◆ the names of the independent non-executive directors;
◆ board and committee meeting attendance records;
◆ where the CEO also fulfils the role of Chairman, the reasons should be explained;

- particulars of the nomination committee, the work it has undertaken and processes it follows in relation to new board appointments;
- an explanation of the work of the audit committee;
- an explanation of the work of the remuneration committee;
- details of the Chairman's commitments;
- a statement on board evaluation;
- an explanation in the directors' report of their responsibility for preparing accounts;
- a statement by the auditors in respect of their duties and responsibilities;
- a explanation of the business model and long-term strategy of the company;
- a confirmation from the directors that the business is a going concern (i.e. is expected to be able to continue to operate for the foreseeable future);
- a report confirming that a review has been undertaken on the effectiveness of internal controls and risk management systems and an explanation given if the company has no internal audit function;
- explanations where the board does not follow the recommendations of the audit committee, e.g. regarding the appointment or removal of auditor;
- details of measures in place to safeguard auditor objectivity and independence where the auditor provides additional services, e.g. non-audit consultancy; and
- a description of the steps taken by the directors to engage with major shareholders and understand their views in respect of the company.

A company's website should disclose the following information:

- the terms of reference of the main board committees (remuneration committee, nomination committee and audit committee);
- the terms and conditions in connection with the appointment of non-executive directors; and
- where an external valuation of board effectiveness has been carried out, or remuneration consultants have been employed by the company, a statement must be given confirming whether the parties have any other connection with the business.

Shareholder communications are also subject to specific requirements to enable shareholders to make an informed decision when electing or re-electing directors to the board.

The UK Corporate Governance Code was updated again in 2012 to incorporate changes in relation to gender diversity on boards and to make possible changes in respect of audit committees and audit retendering. These changes took effect from 1 October 2012.

2.5 Higgs report

The Higgs report on the role and effectiveness of non-executive directors was commissioned following a number of corporate scandals in the US which emerged in 2001 and 2002, including the scandals and accounting frauds of WorldCom, Tyco, Enron and Global Crossing.

The report augments the responsibilities of non-executive directors who must be influential members of the board who do not just make up the numbers but constructively challenge the decisions and the development of strategy. The Higgs recommendations were incorporated into the Combined Code (now known as the UK Corporate Governance Code) in 2003. Higgs believed that codifying the recommendations, rather than prescribing them in legislation, would permit continued flexibility whereby companies would be able to report on a "comply or explain" basis and tailor the recommendations to their specific business model.

The main changes brought about by the Higgs recommendations were in relation to board structure and composition, with the balance of power shifting towards independent non-executive directors. The requirement to strike a better balance on the board also led to a widening of the "talent pool" of available non-executive directors. This means that many companies are now selecting non-executive directors from a broader range of backgrounds with complementary skills.

The key recommendations in respect of non-executive directors were that they should:

◆ challenge and scrutinise management performance;
◆ contribute towards company strategy;
◆ satisfy themselves with the quality of financial reporting;
◆ ensure that the company's systems of internal control and risk management are both robust and are commensurate with the activities and complexity of the company;
◆ determine appropriate levels of remuneration for the executive directors and be actively involved in succession planning;
◆ attend the AGM;
◆ meet at least annually without the Chairman and executive directors and confirm in the annual report that these non-executive meetings have taken place; and
◆ engage more with major shareholders.

Non-executives are expected to be independent in judgement and have an enquiring mind. In this respect, the Higgs report resulted in more guidance being issued on how to assess independence and determine whether or not a director is truly independent.

2.6 Smith report

In 2002, the Financial Reporting Council appointed Sir Robert Smith to chair an independent group charged with the task of clarifying the role and responsibilities of audit committees and to develop the guidance of the Combined Code on Corporate Governance. The Smith report was published in January 2003 and provided additional guidance on the following areas:

Composition of the audit committee

◆ The audit committee should include at least three members, none of whom should be the company chairman and all of whom should be independent non-executive directors.

◆ At least one member of the audit committee must have considerable financial experience, which is recent and relevant.

◆ Proper induction and relevant financial training should be provided to all members of the audit committee.

Role of the audit committee

◆ To ensure the company's financial statements present a true and fair view of the state of affairs and performance of the company for the reporting period.

◆ To monitor the company's financial control and risk management systems where alternative arrangements are not in place (e.g. risk management committee).

◆ To make recommendations to the board in respect of the appointment of the **internal auditor** and regularly review the effectiveness of the internal audit function.

◆ To make recommendations to the board in relation to the appointment of the external auditor and ensure that any recommendations that are not followed by the board are justified by the board and explained to shareholders in the company's annual report.

◆ To regularly review the external auditor's terms of appointment, independence, objectivity and effectiveness and make recommendations to the board in respect of the re-appointment or dismissal of the external auditor.

◆ To set policy on the provision of non-audit services (e.g. consultancy services) provided by the external auditor that does not conflict with auditor independence.

◆ To report on its activities in the annual report.

◆ The chairman of the audit committee should attend the AGM and be available to answer questions.

internal auditor
is an employee of the company whose role it is to provide an independent confirmation that the company's systems of corporate governance, internal control and risk management are operating effectively.

2.7 Turnbull report

The Turnbull report, which was drafted by a committee chaired by Nigel Turnbull in 1999, provides guidance to directors of their obligations under the Combined Code (as it was then known). The guidance is about adding value to a company through good risk management and strong internal controls. It is about the adoption of a risk-based approach and testing the effectiveness of the internal controls.

2.8 Myners report

The 2001 Myners report entitled "Institutional Investment in the UK: A Review" on shareholder voting explains the reasons why many shareholders, particularly institutional investors, such as pension funds, fail to exercise their votes at general meetings of UK companies. The Shareholder Voting Working Group which was chaired by Paul Myners, recommended that, in order to facilitate voting, electronic proxy voting should be encouraged, institutional investors should disclose their voting policies and practices to the beneficial owners of the shares and the beneficial owners should ensure they voice their opinions and give clear voting instructions in a timely manner.

The report raises a number of other points that were pertinent at the time of the review, particularly in connection with incentives and behaviours of pension fund trustees and fund managers. They are summarised as follows:

◆ unrealistic demands are placed on pension fund trustees who need to take important investment decisions but many of whom lack the necessary resources and expertise and instead rely on investment consultants for advice;

◆ insufficient focus on **asset allocation**;

asset allocation is an investment activity that relies on the selection of markets in which to invest rather than individual stock selection.

◆ the objectives of fund managers bear little relationship to the key objectives of the pension funds managed by them and results in fund managers benchmarking against each other rather than engaging in meaningful active fund management;

◆ lack of clarity of timeframes over which the performance of fund managers is assessed leading to short-term investment strategies at the expense of long-term returns;

◆ pension fees and broker commissions are significant and rarely questioned.

The report also sets out basic principles of an effective approach to investment decision making (Chapter 11 of Myners report), which if adhered to, would significantly change behaviours and the way decisions are made.

2.9 UK Stewardship Code

The UK Stewardship Code was born out of the Walker Review and published in 2010 establishing best practice in stewardship of UK listed companies. By encouraging best practice, it seeks to develop and improve engagement between institutional shareholders and the companies in which they invest. Compliance with the Code is not mandatory for everyone but all authorised asset managers and listed companies in the UK are required to either comply with the Code or explain any departures.

Stop and think 11.1

Why is it so important for an organisation to have a good system of corporate governance?

collateralised debt obligation (CDO)
is a security backed by bonds, mortgage loans and other assets. A CDO is typically packaged into different tranches each with varying maturity dates and risks associated with them. During the economic downturn of 2008, many mortgage-backed CDOs defaulted. These were typically the tranches backed entirely by poor-quality subprime loans. Some CDOs comprised layers of other repackaged CDOs with credit risks hidden within the complexity of the structures. Accordingly, the credit rating agencies were either unable or insufficiently experienced in the products to give an accurate credit rating. As home owners were unable to meet their mortgage repayments, so the subprime bonds, which acted as collateral for CDO investors, defaulted.

tail risk
is a term used to describe the risk of an investment moving more than three standard deviations from the mean price, i.e. the distribution of returns does not follow the normal expected pattern.

2.10 Larosière report

The Larosière report of the High-Level Group of Financial Supervision in the EU, chaired by Jacques de Larosière, was published in Brussels in February 2009 following the global economic downturn which commenced in 2007. The report links an overall lack of effective risk management systems with unwarranted risk-taking and highlights the fact that companies and supervisory authorities did not fully understand the risks, particularly in respect of complex structured and multi-layered products such as **collateralised debt obligations (CDOs)** and other credit derivatives. Exposure to **tail risks** was considered by the High-Level Group to be grossly underestimated and stress testing insufficient. There is also strong criticism in respect of the lack of transparency within the financial system, particularly in respect of credit risks, securitisation and the quality of credit counterparties. Instead of spreading risks across the financial system risks were often concentrated and concealed deep within financial complexity. Furthermore, liquidity risk was significantly underestimated by supervisory authorities and financial institutions.

The Larosière report also discusses the role of credit rating agencies which failed to give appropriate ratings to the senior tranches of CDOs. This was, *inter alia*, due to a lack of understanding of the structured products and the subprime mortgage market risk. There was a failure to grasp the likelihood of defaults that might occur in an economic downturn.

The High-Level Group concluded that the lack of regulation in the US mortgage market compounded the situation and led to an increase in defaults. The report also mentions regulatory, supervisory, crisis management and corporate governance failures, raising the question as to whether corporate governance measures are sufficiently effective or are simply poorly implemented.

The Larosière report recommended that the regulatory framework be enhanced to reduce the risk and impact of future financial crises. It recommended the creation of a European Systemic Risk Council and a European System of Financial Supervisors, made up of three European Supervisory Authorities, one for each of the following sectors:

◆ banking sector;

◆ securities sector; and

◆ insurance and occupational pensions sector.

In addition to an enhanced framework for both micro-prudential and macro-prudential supervision, to promote financial stability, and a recommendation to strengthen the IMF's role in macro-economic surveillance, a number of other recommendations come out of the Larosière report and may be summarised as follows:

2.10.1 The Basel II Framework
That the Basel Committee of Banking Supervisors review and amend the Basel II rules to increase minimum capital requirements, introduce provisioning on banks in "good times" to limit credit expansion and build up capital reserves,

tighten the rules on items off statement of financial position, improve liquidity management and tighten risk management and internal control systems.

◆ That a common definition for regulatory capital should be adopted in the EU.

2.10.2 Credit rating agencies

CESR (now ESMA) should be responsible for regulating credit rating agencies and the use of ratings in financial regulations should be gradually reduced. It is also recommended that new ratings are provided for structure products.

2.10.3 Accounting standards

Accounting standards should be reviewed particularly in respect of complex products and in respect of the valuation of illiquid assets. The IASB should involve regulatory and supervisory bodies more in its standard-setting process.

2.10.4 Insurance

The Solvency II directive should be adopted in order to help improve insurance regulation.

2.10.5 Supervisory and sanctioning powers

EU member states should have stronger supervisory and sanctioning powers.

2.10.6 The parallel banking system

Measures to address the vulnerability of the **parallel banking system** (e.g. to reduced credit lines and liquidity shortages as well as to leverage and non-payment by counterparties) by extending regulation and improving transparency in all financial markets. The recommendations extend to banks operating hedge funds or engaged in **proprietary trading** which should have appropriate capital requirements imposed to reflect the activities undertaken.

2.10.7 Securitised products and derivative markets

Measure to reduce risk in connection with derivatives and securitised products.

2.10.8 Investment funds

The development of common rules for investment funds in the EU including tighter supervision in respect of the independent role of depositories and custodians.

2.10.9 Regulatory inconsistencies

Harmonisation of rules within the EU.

2.10.10 Remuneration issues

Director remuneration should be more aligned with shareholder interests, with bonuses reflecting performance and being paid over a period of time rather than in one single lump sum.

2.10.11 Internal risk management

Internal risk management systems should be independently stress tested and, in respect of risk assessment, entities should not rely on external ratings at the expense of their own due diligence.

CESR
the Committee of European Securities Regulators which became the EMSA on 1 January 2011.

ESMA
the European Securities and Markets Authority which "contributes to safeguarding the stability of the EU financial system by ensuring the integrity, transparency, efficiency and orderly functioning of securities markets, as well as enhancing investor protection".

parallel banking system
describes the activities of institutions and financial intermediaries operating outside the regular banking system such as the activities of hedge funds, investment banks, finance companies, money market funds, structured investment vehicles, and mortgage brokers (in some jurisdictions) and whose activities could significantly impact the financial system due to inherent risks.

proprietary trading
describes the activities of banks which use deposits to trade in shares, bonds, commodities, private equity funds, hedge funds, derivatives and other types of financial instruments on a bank's own account for direct gain rather than on its customers' accounts for commission.

2.10.12 Crisis management

The Larosière High-Level Group calls for a coherent and workable regulatory framework for dealing with crisis management within the EU with the removal of cross-border legal obstacles and the financing of cross-border resolution efforts to be agreed between member states.

◆ Deposit Guarantee Schemes (DGS) should provide equal protection to all customers and should be implemented in the insurance and investment sectors.

2.11 European Commission and EU corporate governance framework

A current EU initiative of interest to Company Secretaries is the EU Corporate governance framework. In November 2011, the European Commission published a feedback paper following its consultation on corporate governance. The consultation paper covered key corporate governance issues including:

◆ Board composition, diversity (professional, international and gender diversity) and effectiveness;

◆ Improving shareholder engagement with greater focus on long-term benefits rather than short-termism; and

◆ How to apply the "comply or explain" approach.

Test yourself 11.1

In respect of the composition of a board of directors, give an example of three types of diversity?

Financial Reporting Council
is the UK's independent regulator responsible for promoting high quality corporate governance and reporting to foster investment.

The UK's **Financial Reporting Council** (FRC) also issues consultation papers, feedback statements and guidance on corporate governance issues. The areas of focus are often closely aligned to the issues of concern in the EU and, in 2011, included board effectiveness, gender diversity on boards and effective company stewardship.

Consultation papers, feedback statements and guidance in respect of corporate governance issues should be monitored by company secretaries on a continuing basis to ensure the implications on the compliance function are known and to enable relevant processes and procedures to be amended in a timely manner if necessary.

2.12 The AIC Code of Corporate Governance

The Association of Investment Companies Code of Corporate Governance (the "AIC Code") was published in 2003 with the objective of providing its members with best practice guidelines for the governance of investment companies, including guidance on the practical application of the UK Corporate Governance Code for investment companies. It provides directors of investment companies with a one-stop approach to corporate governance to ensure that they manage the issues pertinent to investment companies and meet the requirements of the UK Corporate Governance Code. It is a principles-based code and requires members to either comply with the principles or explain in their annual report why they do not. Alternatively, the directors of the investment company should set out the measures they intend to implement to ensure compliance with the principles going forward.

2.13 Guernsey Finance Sector Code of Corporate Governance

The Guernsey Finance Sector Code of Corporate Governance was issued by the Guernsey Financial Services Commission in September 2011 and took effect on 1 January 2012. It replaces the previous guidance on finance sector corporate governance issued in 2004 and applies to companies subject to the Guernsey regulatory framework. The Code establishes eight key principles underpinned by best practice guidelines.

The eight principles are stated in the Code as follows:

1 The board: Companies should be headed by an effective board of directors which is responsible for governance.

2 Directors: Directors should take collective responsibility for directing and supervising the affairs of the business.

3 Business conduct and ethics: All directors should maintain good standards of business conduct, integrity and ethical behaviour and should operate with due care and diligence and act honestly and openly at all times.

4 Accountability: The board should have formal and transparent arrangements in place for presenting a balanced and understandable assessment of the company's position and prospects and for considering how they apply financial reporting and internal control principles.

5 Risk management: The board should provide suitable oversight of risk management and maintain a sound system of risk measurement and control.

6 Disclosure and reporting: The board should ensure the timely and balanced disclosure to shareholders and/or to regulators of all material matters concerning the company.

7 Remuneration: The board should ensure remuneration arrangements are structured fairly and responsibly and that remuneration policies are consistent with effective risk management.

8 Shareholder relations: The board should ensure that satisfactory shareholder communication takes place based on the mutual understanding of needs, objectives and concerns.

Entities which comply with the UK Corporate Governance Code, the Guernsey Financial Services Commission's Licensed Insurers' Corporate Governance Code or the AIC Code of Corporate Governance are deemed by the Guernsey regulator to be in compliance with the Codes.

The principles-based approach, rather than the prescription of rigid and voluminous rules, enables companies to be flexible in their adoption of the

Code in order to reflect the nature, scale and complexity of their activities. In this respect, companies subject to the Code are required to submit an annual assurance statement to the Guernsey Financial Services Commission confirming that its directors have considered the effectiveness of their corporate governance practices and are satisfied that they have applied with the principles of the Code in a manner commensurate with the nature, scale and complexity of their business activities. The assurance statement is likely to form part of a Guernsey company's annual return submission from 2013 onwards.

Example pro-forma assurance statement to be submitted to the Guernsey regulator:

CORPORATE GOVERNANCE ASSURANCE STATEMENT

The Directors of [name of entity] have considered the effectiveness of the corporate governance practices of [name of entity]. In the context of the nature, scale and complexity of [name of entity], we are satisfied with the degree of compliance by [name of entity] since 1 January 2012 with the Principles set out in the Finance Sector Code of Corporate Governance issued by the Guernsey Financial Services Commission dated September 2011.

Signed ....

Full Name ....

On behalf of the Board ....

Date...

Stop and think 11.2

Why do you think it is important for owners of a company to monitor and challenge the investment decisions of the board and to question whether the strength of the company's internal control systems are commensurate with the risk profile of the investments?

Test yourself 11.2

What are the roles and responsibilities of non-executive directors?

What does Greenbury have to say on remuneration policy?

What are the disclosure requirements of the UK Corporate Governance Code?

Briefly describe some of the issues which contributed to the 2007–2012 economic downturn and triggered the review of the Larosière High-Level Group.

What are the eight principles of the Guernsey Finance Sector Code of Corporate Governance?

3. Corporate social responsibility

Corporate social responsibility (CSR) is a term used to describe the processes an organisation uses to produce a positive impact on society through its activities. It is about **corporate citizenship** and the ongoing commitment of businesses to behave ethically and responsibly towards its employees, its customers, its competitors, the environment and the community at large. CSR encompasses sustainable and responsible business decisions and development goals integrated with ethical values. Good CSR respects and embraces cultural differences and helps build the skills of the workforce.

The European Commission defines CSR as "the responsibility of enterprises for their impacts on society" and says that "it concerns actions by companies over and above their legal obligations towards society and the environment". The responsibility includes accountability through CSR reporting in the audited financial statements. The annual report should not just report on financial performance but on how the results are achieved. For example, has the increase in performance been achieved without compromising ethical values, human rights, and wellbeing of staff? If the company has a fair trade policy, has the board continued to uphold the policy? How has the company interacted with other companies, competitors and the community at large?

The corporate governance principles which underpin CSR – transparency, accountability, integrity, corporate ethics, trust and respect – are important for the proper running of a business and it is therefore important for companies to understand the potential benefits of adopting and investing in CSR because good CSR practice is likely to lead to a well run, successful, business. A business can build long-term trust amongst staff, customers and society at large as a basis for a sustainable business model, which will help to create the right environment in which it can innovate and grow. A company's board should therefore ensure that the values it has established and set for the company are upheld and adhered to throughout the company.

Corporate social responsibility
(CSR) is a term used to describe the processes an organisation uses to produce a positive impact on society through its activities. It is about ongoing commitment of businesses to behave ethically and responsibly towards its employees, its customers, the environment and the community at large. It is about doing business in a responsible and sustainable manner.

corporate citizenship
is another term used to describe the responsibilities of a business towards society and its role in the community. It is about sustainable strategy, promoting good governance and focus on social responsibilities, not just the statutory responsibilities. It is a term that is often associated with CSR.

Stop and think 11.3

What do you think are the key principles and themes that underpin good CSR?

Companies display both positive and negative CSR practice and bringing CSR on to the corporate agenda is about maximising positive CSR practices whilst minimising negative practices. It is also about embracing the benefits rather than viewing CSR merely as a compliance function. The company secretary has a key role in ensuring that the benefits of CSR are communicated to the board and that CSR considerations are a feature of boardroom discussions and decisions.

Negative CSR practice might include a company having a poor human rights record, a misleading advertising campaign, failing to have a policy to prevent pollution or to tackle claims of bribery and corruption, or disputing supplier invoices in order to delay payment. Poor practice might also include financial institutions allowing too much risk-taking with little regard for internal controls and the potential consequences of failure.

Positive CSR practice might be enhancing goods and services that are of benefit to society or investing money in the community by planting trees to offset a company's carbon footprint. Companies might also show good CSR by granting paid leave to employees for social involvement such as participation in environmental projects, or giving time to charitable organizations such as St John's Ambulance or the RNLI. Many firms contribute to society by providing financial support for humanitarian and charitable causes, perhaps by establishing a philanthropic foundation funded from a proportion of their profits. This model of positive CSR is not uncommon in offshore jurisdictions and other international finance centres. It enables financial service providers and other vehicles to give something back to society whilst preserving profitability for shareholders.

Test yourself 11.3

How can a company secretary elevate the importance of CSR within the company and ensure it receives support from the board?

Good CSR can have a positive impact on corporate competitiveness as the public like to see large multi-national companies giving something back to the community. People are also keen to do business with an organisation that supports and develops its staff and has a strong management team. A strong management team, supported by a happy and reliable workforce, is indicative of strong future financial performance.

A country should also advocate good corporate governance in order to develop a cohesive society, to instill stakeholder and market confidence and to attract inward investment. The thought of attracting investment through good CSR practice combined with the threat that customers might boycott products and services if poor CSR practice is displayed, encourages boards of directors to devote an appropriate amount of time to CSR. It has, therefore, developed into an important management concern.

As well as ensuring CSR features as a regular item on the board's agenda, the company secretary needs to ensure that the annual report contains the necessary CSR disclosure requirements. The company secretary should take care to ensure that any non-mandatory disclosures are relevant to the users of the accounts and that the CSR report gives a concise account of the business. There are currently calls to de-clutter the CSR report so that it is more relevant to users and CSR issues are only included where they can be demonstrated to have either (i) added value to the business; or (ii) because there is a CSR benefit which might enhance the reputation of the company.

Stop and think 11.4

As well as giving a company a good reputation, helping with social uplift can result in improved markets for a company's products and services. How can this ultimately help ensure a company's sustainability?

Following the recent economic crisis, the European Commission published a new policy on CSR in October 2011, in order to address some of the social and ethical issues which have been the focus of much attention. These include encouraging responsible business behaviour and the creation of favourable conditions for sustainable growth to help rebuild consumer confidence and levels of trust in business. The renewed EU strategy put forward by the European Commission is that "enterprises should have in place a process to integrate social, environmental, ethical, human rights and consumer concerns into their business operations and core strategy in close collaboration with their stakeholders, with the aim of:

◆ maximising the creation of shared value for their owners/shareholders and for their other stakeholders and society at large;

◆ identifying, preventing and mitigating their possible adverse impacts."

It has put forward an agenda for action for 2011–2014 covering the following areas:

◆ awareness-raising and best practice exchange;

◆ the improvement and tracking of levels of trust in business including addressing the issue of misleading commercial practices such as "**green-washing**", for example a car manufacturer promoting its motor vehicles as "green" when their use actually contributes to atmospheric and noise pollution. Just because the carbon footprint is relatively low for a motor vehicle, does not mean the car is "green". Another example is by prefixing bleaches and chemicals with the word "bio" and packaging them in such a way as to suggest they are good for the environment when, in fact, little or no investment has been made to mitigate damage to the environment;

◆ the improvement of self- and co-regulation processes involving sector-wide codes of conduct and the development of codes of good practice to improve the effectiveness of CSR;

◆ the enhancement of market reward for CSR in areas where the most socially responsible course of action is not the most financially beneficial

green-washing
describes the practice of misleading marketing concerning a company's products and their environmental impact in order to give the perception that the products are green.

course of action (one measure might be the requirement for all investment funds and financial institutions to inform their stakeholders about any ethical or responsible investment criteria they apply or any standards or codes to which they adhere);

◆ the improvement of non-financial disclosure (e.g. social and environmental information) to improve accountability and help build public trust in companies and large multi-national organisations;

◆ further integration of CSR into education, training and research and the improvement of consumer information and transparency;

◆ emphasis of the importance of national and sub-national CSR policies; and

◆ the global framework of CSR, including the better alignment of European and global approaches to CSR, ensuring that European policy is consistent with internationally recognised principles.

3.1 Internationally recognised principles and guidelines

For further information on CSR and its implementation within company policy, the company secretary can refer to various international standards and guidance, namely the:

◆ OECD Guidelines for Multinational Enterprises;

◆ Ten principles of the United Nations Global Compact;

◆ ISO 26000 Guidance Standard on Social Responsibility;

◆ ILO Tri-partite Declaration of Principles Concerning Multinational Enterprises and Social Policy; and

◆ United Nations Guiding Principles on Business and Human Rights.

Test yourself 11.4

Give two practical examples of CSR.

4. The Walker Review

Following a number of bank failings at the start of the global economic crisis, Sir David Walker was commissioned by the UK government in February 2009 to review corporate governance in UK banks and to make recommendations, including the following areas:

◆ the effectiveness of risk management at board level, including the incentives in remuneration policy to manage risk effectively;

◆ the balance of skills, experience and independence required on the boards of UK banking institutions;

◆ the effectiveness of board practices and the performance of audit, risk, remuneration and nomination committees;

◆ the role of institutional shareholders in engaging effectively with companies and monitoring of boards; and

◆ whether the UK's approach is consistent with international practice and how national and international best practice can be promulgated.

In April 2009, the terms of reference were extended to identify where the Walker Review recommendations are applicable to other financial institutions, for example non-bank companies such as insurance and life assurance companies.

Sir David Walker and his team found that banks operating in the same regulatory and financial environment were being run quite differently from one another and that there was a need to address certain issues in respect of board composition and performance, shareholder engagement, risk management and executive pay. Inevitably, the review recommends widespread reforms to enhance the governance of banks and other financial institutions. The findings focus on how financial institutions are directed and controlled and the final recommendations of the Walker Review, which were published in November 2009, cover the following five key themes:

1 Board size, composition and qualification.

2 Functioning of the board and evaluation of performance.

3 The role of institutional shareholders: communication and engagement.

4 Governance of risk.

5 Remuneration.

4.1 Board size, composition and qualification

The Walker Review has recommended overhauling the boards of banks and other major financial institutions. The review found that the UK **unitary board structure** (as opposed to a **two tier board system**) is still suitable and the report backs the Financial Reporting Council's UK Corporate Governance Code (formally known as the Combined Code on Corporate Governance). It states that the "comply or explain" approach combined with stricter liquidity and capital requirements and a firmer stance by the regulator provides the best platform for better corporate governance practice.

The key recommendations pertaining to board size, composition and qualification are summarised as follows:

◆ there must be improvements to director induction, training, development and their awareness of business issues;

◆ the board should be assured of dedicated support and/or there should be separate advice for non-executive directors (NEDs) in addition to that from normal board processes;

◆ there should be an increased time commitment from NEDs;

unitary board structure
is a form of board structure, common in the UK, in which executive and NEDs combine on the same board, pooling their skills, knowledge and experience.

two-tier board system:
In some countries, e.g. Germany, it is common to have a two-tier board structure comprising a separate board for the executive directors (who are involved in day-to-day management) and non-executive directors (who are independent of management).

◆   there is a need for enhanced supervisory oversight of the balance, experience and qualities of the board, and of board access to appropriate induction and development programmes; and

◆   the regulator's interview process for NEDs should be more robust.

4.2 Functioning of the board and evaluation of performance

One of the main findings in respect of the boards of banks and other financial institutions was that poor performance often relates to patterns of behaviour rather than to the institution itself – Walker refers to the executive's views being insufficiently challenged. The report states that the most critical need is for an environment in which effective challenge of the executive is expected and achieved in the boardroom before decisions are taken on major risk and strategic issues. This may be achieved by striking a good balance on the board by having the right mix of industry capability and high-level experience from other major business. It also requires NEDs to devote a significantly greater amount of time to their role. The review refers to the role of the Chairman being paramount and calls for both exceptional board leadership skills and the ability to get to grips with major strategic issues in a confident and competent manner. The Chairman of a major bank should be committed to the role such that he/she has little time for other business activity. Indeed, the review states that around two-thirds of the Chairman's time should be spent carrying out the role and that, in the event of need, the bank's requirements should take precedent over any other business activity in which the Chairman of the bank is involved.

The recommendations in relation to the functioning of the board and evaluation of performance are:

◆   ensuring NEDs have the capacity to challenge strategic proposals and access the necessary information to make informed decisions;

◆   ensuring the Chairman commits an appropriate amount of time to the role and this depends on the complexity of the business and whether there is a specific event "of need" which requires the Chairman to devote more time to the business;

◆   ensuring the Chairman is appropriately qualified for the role and possesses the relevant financial industry experience. The Chairman of a bank should have a good track record demonstrating leadership capability;

◆   ensuring the Chairman is responsible for the leadership of the board and the adequacy of information it receives;

◆   that the Chairman is subject to election on an annual basis;

◆   ensuring the senior independent director is responsible for supporting and evaluating the Chairman and serves as a trusted intermediary;

◆   the board should undertake a formal and rigorous evaluation of its performance with an external facilitation every two to three years; and

◆   enhanced reporting of the board evaluation, the process for identifying the board's skill requirements, and the Chairman's communication with shareholders.

4.3 The role of institutional shareholders: communication and engagement

The Walker Review stresses the importance of shareholder engagement especially by fund managers and other institutional investors, such as pension funds and insurance companies, who act on behalf of their clients, the beneficial owners. Institutional investors, as owners, should not only play a more active role and engage more effectively with the board of the company in which they are invested, particularly if they suspect weaknesses in governance, but they should also disclose to their clients how they have represented them and how they have exercised their voting rights.

Walker makes the following recommendations on shareholder communication and engagement:

◆ The board should be aware of, and respond to, material changes of ownership of the company's shares.

◆ The remit of the Financial Reporting Council should be extended to cover the development and encouragement of adherence by institutional investors and fund managers to best practice in stewardship of UK listed companies (Stewardship Code).

◆ There should be regulatory sponsorship of the Stewardship Code, as a code of best practice, akin to that of the Combined Code on Corporate Governance, with observance on a "comply or explain" basis.

◆ There should be regulatory oversight of the process for updating the Stewardship Code.

◆ All fund managers should sign up to the new independently monitored Stewardship Code.

◆ Ensuring a "comply or explain" reporting commitment to the Stewardship Code.

◆ Regulatory oversight is required to ensure the clarity of "comply or explain" reporting of commitment to the Stewardship Code.

◆ There should be sufficient guidance provided by the relevant regulatory bodies to ensure the requirements are adequately interpreted.

◆ The engagement of collective investors, such as institutional investors and fund managers, should be improved.

◆ That best practice in exercising voting powers and disclosure of voting should be improved. The voting policies of institutional investors and fund managers, should be described in statements on their websites or published by other means.

4.4 Governance of risk

The Walker Review states that board-level engagement in risk oversight should be materially increased and calls for NEDs to focus on high-level risk issues in addition to, and separately from, the executive risk committee process. The focus in the review is how risk management can be made more effective alongside enhanced regulation and supervisory oversight.

The recommendations in respect of risk governance are:

◆ The board of a FTSE 100-listed bank or life assurance company should establish a board risk committee separately from the audit committee. The risk committee should have responsibility for oversight and advice to the board on the current risk exposures of the entity and future risk strategy, including strategy for capital and liquidity management and the development of a culture that supports risk management.

◆ The role and independence of the chief risk officer should be strengthened.

◆ The board risk committee should have sufficient access to external risk information and should take full account of relevant experience elsewhere, challenging the analysis of information and assessment of risk, as appropriate.

◆ The board risk committee should ensure that appropriate due diligence is undertaken on significant acquisitions and disposals, taking into account risk appetite and tolerance and how this impacts the company.

◆ The annual reporting of risk management needs to be improved.

4.5 Remuneration

In recent years, it has emerged that a number of companies have paid excessive salaries and bonuses to directors irrespective of performance. There has been insufficient control of executive pay coupled with poor remuneration policies. The review recommends extensive reforms in respect of director and senior executive pay. It proposes new primary legislation requiring "mandatory disclosure of remuneration of senior employees on a banded basis".

The Walker Review recommends extending the role of the remuneration committee to cover firm-wide remuneration policy, as well as giving the committee direct responsibility for the pay of all highly-paid employees. At least half of variable pay or bonuses should be in the form of a long-term incentive scheme, with half vesting after three years and the rest after five years. Two-thirds of cash bonuses should also be deferred.

The review makes the following recommendations on remuneration:

◆ The board remuneration committee remit should be enhanced.

◆ The board remuneration committee should have oversight of the remuneration of senior staff.

◆ The external reporting of the process for setting the performance objectives for senior staff should be enhanced.

◆ The remuneration committee report within the set of financial statements should display greater transparency in respect of pay by disclosing the remuneration of "high end" employees (aggregated in bands), including executive board members, whose remuneration for the year is between £1m to £2.5m, £2.5m to £5m and in £5m bands thereafter. Within each band, a breakdown should be given of the main elements comprising the remuneration package, i.e. salary, cash bonus, deferred shares, performance-related long-term awards and pension contributions.

- There should be comparable disclosure of "high end" employees (aggregated in bands) by the UK subsidiaries of foreign companies.

- There should be changes to the structure of senior staff remuneration with at least half of variable pay and bonuses paid into a long-term incentive scheme subject to a performance condition. Furthermore, cash bonuses should be paid over a three-year period with no more than two-thirds paid in year one.

- Senior staff should maintain minimum shareholdings in the firm.

- The remuneration committee should seek advice from the risk committee on specific risk adjustments to be applied to performance objectives for incentive packages.

- The Chairman of the remuneration committee should stand for re-election if the remuneration report fails to secure 75% of votes cast.

- There should be disclosure of the remuneration committee's powers to enhance the termination benefits of "high end" employees and when any termination benefits are enhanced, the particulars should be disclosed.

- There should be a code of conduct for remuneration consultants and all remuneration committees should use the code as the basis for drawing up a contract to appoint a remuneration consultant.

The Walker Review sets out the expected mode of implementation of the recommendations which includes a review by the Financial Reporting Council of the Combined Code on Corporate Governance, now known as the UK Corporate Governance Code. Some of the recommendations have already been implemented through revisions to the Code. The FRC also accepted responsibility for the UK Stewardship Code for institutional investors, which was published in July 2010 and requires all authorised asset managers, such as pension funds, insurance companies, investment trusts and other collective investment schemes to apply the code on a "comply or explain" basis. Furthermore, the Remuneration Consultants Group has also been established as a result of the Walker Review recommendations. The Remuneration Consultants Group has published a voluntary code of conduct for remuneration consultants advising UK listed companies.

Other modes of implementation of the recommendations include the financial regulator and government. With such reviews, it is usually government who ultimately decides which recommendations will be acted upon.

5. Basel II and III

5.1 Basel II (2004)

In 1999, the **Basel Committee on Banking Supervision** issued a proposal for a revised Capital Adequacy Framework to supersede the existing capital measurement and credit risk management system for banks, commonly known as the 1988 Basel Capital Accord or Basel I. The initial framework required banks to maintain capital corresponding with their level of exposure

Basel Committee on Banking Supervision is a committee, established in 1974 by the central-bank Governors of the G10 countries, which formulates supervisory standards and guidelines and recommends statements of best practice which it expects the relevant supervisory authorities in member countries to implement in an appropriate manner.

to credit risk and the 1999 amendment established some additional market risk rules.

After extensive consultation with industry and supervisory authorities, the revised framework, known as Basel II, was issued in June 2004. The framework is documented in the Basel Committee's paper entitled "International Convergence of Capital Measurement and Capital Standards – A Revised Framework" and included an operational risk framework for the first time.

The principal objectives of the Basel II framework were to:

◆ further strengthen the soundness and stability of the international banking system;

◆ maintain sufficient consistency such that capital adequacy regulation would not be a significant cause of competitive inequality among internationally active banks;

◆ closer align regulatory capital requirements with economic capital needs; and

◆ promote the adoption of stronger risk management practices by the banking industry.

Basel II encompasses a "three pillars" concept with the first pillar setting out "minimum capital requirements", the second pillar setting out the "supervisory review process" and the third pillar establishing measures, such as enhanced disclosure requirements, to improve "market discipline".

Pillar 1: Minimum capital requirements

Basel II introduces enhanced regulatory capital requirements that capture risks more fully and cater for the varying complexity of international banks. The minimum regulatory capital requirements for banks are set out in Pillar 1 and are based on the following three types of risk:

◆ credit risk;

◆ market risk; and

◆ operational risk.

Maintaining a minimum capital level serves as a safeguard against such risks and an adequately capitalised bank is, broadly speaking, better placed to survive a market downturn, a financial crisis or the effects of reduced credit lines, for example, than a bank that is undercapitalised. The general principle is that the greater the level of risk to which a bank is exposed, the greater the level of capital the bank should maintain.

As the capital requirements under Basel II are more sensitive to risk than under Basel I, for some banks (e.g. retail lending and mortgage lending banks) this means the level of capital they need to maintain may be lower under Basel II. Banks with lower risk profiles are, therefore, permitted to lend more money for a given amount of capital than they were previously under Basel I. Conversely, banks that are exposed to greater levels of risk need to maintain higher levels of capital than they might have had to previously under Basel I.

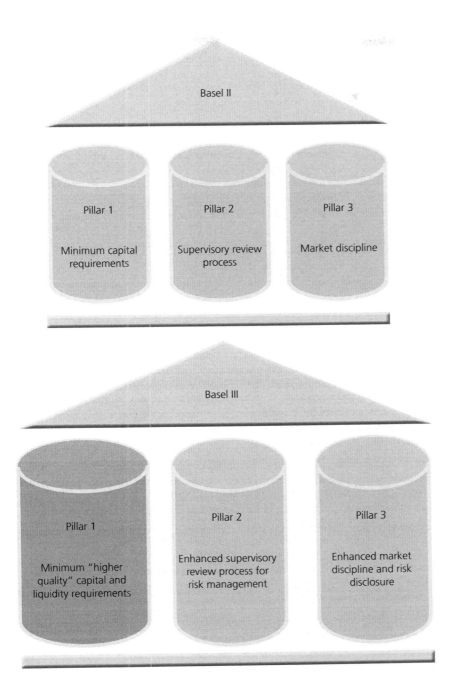

Pillar 2: Supervisory review process

Under the Pillar 2 conceptual framework, a bank must have an internal capital assessment process. The supervisory authority should review it to determine if the self-assessed capital level is sufficient to ensure that capital is maintained above this minimum level.

Pillar 3: Market discipline

Pillar 3 only applies to the top consolidated level of a banking group that reports under Basel II. It aims to enhance market discipline through the use of information disclosures in order to enable market participants to judge capital adequacy. By improving market discipline, Pillar 3 should be a valuable complement of the other two pillars.

Basel II was implemented by the Crown Dependencies of Jersey, Guernsey and the Isle of Man as a result of a pan-island approach with the objective of harmonising the regulatory requirements insofar as possible. The three island supervisory authorities formed a tripartite group, not only to simplify implementation for a number of international banks that operate in all three jurisdictions (or at least two of them), but also to reduce the scope for regulatory arbitrage whereby international banks might choose to locate in the jurisdiction with the least regulatory requirements.

The three regulators issued a joint consultation paper, known as the "Tri-Partite" paper in May 2006 on "National Discretions for the Standardised Approaches to Credit and Operational Risk under the Basel II Capital Framework". In summary, it reflected the agreed positions of the Jersey Financial Services Commission, the Guernsey Financial Services Commission and the Isle of Man Financial Supervision Commission and proposed implementation of Basel II from 1 January 2007 either using Basel standardised approaches or for banks to agree plans with the respective Commissions if using a non-standard advanced approach to Basel II implementation. Basel II was successfully implemented in the Crown Dependencies, with banks in Jersey and the Isle of Man being required to report under Basel II since 2008, and since 2009 in Guernsey.

5.2 Basel III (2010)

In response to the financial crisis which began at the tail end of 2007, resulting in the collapse of a number of international banks, many of which were exposed to complex financial instruments such as credit default swaps and asset back securities, the Basel Committee and its oversight body, the Group of Governors and Heads of Supervision, developed new global banking standards to address both firm-specific and wider systemic risks. The revised requirements are commonly known as Basel III. Basel III introduces stricter limits on leverage, tighter controls on capital and liquidity, an enhanced supervisory review process and increased disclosure and market discipline. Imposing tighter controls, should lead to the improved quality of capital, enhanced liquidity and a stronger coverage of risk.

Tier 1 capital
capital which is considered to be a safer form of capital than Tier 2 and Tier 3 capital and comprises largely equity and retained profits.

Basel III seeks to strengthen the quality of capital by requiring banks to increase common equity and **Tier 1 capital** and by excluding certain financial instruments from Tier 1 capital. Banks will also need to phase out Tier 3 capital.

Basel III also introduces the new capital conservation buffer with effect from 2016. This serves to absorb losses during periods of financial and economic difficulty which must be met exclusively with common equity. Whilst the buffer is not obligatory, banks which fail to maintain the 2.5% buffer will be restricted from making payments from distributable reserves, such as dividend payments.

Under Basel III, banks undertaking complex activities with greater exposures and which are considered systemically important will be required to increase their capital the most.

An additional **countercyclical buffer**, in a range of 0% to 2.5% of common equity, can be imposed at the discretion of regulators. The purpose of the countercyclical buffer is to restrict banks from growing too quickly during boom times by building up a buffer to enable them to survive times of economic or financial stress.

countercyclical buffer is a buffer whose purpose is to restrict banks from growing too quickly during good times in order to limit credit expansion and build up credit reserves to enable them to survive times of economic or financial stress.

With regard to improving liquidity in the banking system, the Basel Committee has introduced the Liquidity Coverage Ratio, to ensure that a bank can cover its total net cash outflows for at least a month, underpinned by a Net Stable Funding Ratio to ensure at least a year's stable funding during times of market stress. These ratios will be implemented in 2015 and 2018 respectively.

It is argued that requiring banks to maintain greater liquidity will increase the cost of short-term funding, will impede economic growth and will reduce the bank's return on equity. Basel III should, however, ensure greater liquidity and stability during times of financial and economic uncertainty and should reduce the problems witnessed in 2008 when banks stopped lending to one another.

The adoption timescale for Basel III varies by jurisdiction. The Basel Committee has proposed a phased approach with implementation commencing 1 January 2013 and full compliance expected within six years of this date.

The US and EU plan to implement most of the Basel III requirements or similar measures. With regard to offshore regulation, the Jersey Financial Services Commission and other international finance centre supervisory authorities are due to publish papers on the implementation of Basel III during the second half of 2012.

6. Sarbanes–Oxley Act (2002)

The Sarbanes-Oxley Act (hereinafter referred to as, the "Act"), commonly referred to as SOX, was introduced in the USA in 2002 following the high-profile corporate scandals of a number of US companies, including WorldCom (MCI Inc.), the energy giant Enron and global auditing firm, Arthur Anderson. In an attempt to restore public confidence in corporate governance, to combat accounting fraud and to protect the interests of investors, the US federal government enacted new and enhanced corporate governance standards with an increased focus on corporate disclosure. The legislation is wide reaching and applies to all US public companies, their management, their boards and their accountants. It also applies to non-US public companies carrying out business in the US. This effectively means that the Sarbanes–Oxley Act affects both UK and offshore public companies dealing with the US or processing transactions in US dollars.

Sarbanes–Oxley Act (2002) is legislation which was passed in the US in 2002 in an attempt to restore public confidence, improve the transparency of financial statements and protect investor interests. The Act introduced new and more stringent measures for public companies in respect of corporate disclosure requirements and corporate governance.

The Act is named after its co-sponsors, US Senator Paul Sarbanes and US Representative Michael Oxley. The Act is referred to in the Senate by its official name, the "Public Company Accounting Reform and Investor Protection Act".

In the House of Representatives it is commonly known as the "Corporate and Auditing Accountability and Responsibility Act". Upon signing it into law, US President George W. Bush, described the Act as "the most far reaching reforms of American business practices since the time of Franklin Delano Roosevelt. The era of low standards and false profits is over; no boardroom in America is above or beyond the law."

The Act introduced a number of significant changes leading to much wider share ownership in the US and tighter regulation. Since the Act was passed in 2002, all US companies and companies dealing with the US have had to ensure compliance with the relevant provisions of the Act which has driven up the costs of the compliance function for these entities. However, the increase in accountability for senior executives has led to enhanced reporting and improved disclosures to shareholders.

Publicly traded companies have been forced to make it a priority of their compliance function to review the provisions of the Act which holds top executives more accountable for their actions. As well as leading to adverse publicity, failure to comply with the requirements or failure to accurately certify documents could lead to the offending officers of the company being extradited to the US to face charges. The Act imposes tough penalties which includes fines of up to US$5 million and/or imprisonment of not more than 20 years for certifying financial statements which do not comport with all the requirements.

The provisions of the Act include:

The **Public Company Accounting Oversight Board (PCAOB)** is charged with the oversight and supervision of public company accounting firms and oversees the audits of public companies in order to protect investor interests and further the public interest in the preparation of informative, accurate and independent audit reports.

- Improved accuracy, transparency and reliability of corporate disclosures.
- Tightening of internal controls.
- Increased corporate board responsibilities and holding of chief executive officers and chief financial officers personally liable for the accuracy and timeliness of financial reporting (CEOs and CFOs to review and certify quarterly and annual accounts).
- Establishment of the **Public Company Accounting Oversight Board (PCAOB)** charged with the oversight and supervision of public company accounting firms providing audit services.
- Auditor independence, auditor rotation and conflicts of interest.
- Increased corporate board responsibilities.
- Pre-certification of non-audit work by a firm's audit committee.
- Ban on loans to directors and officers.
- More timely reporting of insider trading.
- Ban on insider trades during pension fund blackout periods.
- Disgorgement of bonus and compensation payments.
- Criminal and civil penalties for white collar crime, for non-compliance and for securities violations.
- Disclosure of analyst conflicts of interest to restore investor confidence in reporting.
- Protection for whistleblowers.

◆ The powers of the **US Securities and Exchange Commission (SEC)** to censure or ban securities brokers, broker-dealers and advisors from the financial services industry.

The key provisions are covered in more detail in the following key sections of the Act:

◆ Section 302 – Corporate responsibility for financial reports.

◆ Section 401 – Disclosures in periodic reports.

◆ Section 404 – Management assessment of internal controls.

◆ Section 409 – Real time issuer disclosures.

◆ Section 802 – Criminal penalties for altering documents.

◆ Section 806 – Protection for employees of publicly traded companies who provide evidence of fraud.

◆ Section 807 – Criminal penalties for defrauding shareholders of publicly traded companies

◆ Section 906 – Corporate responsibility for financial reports.

US Securities and Exchange Commission (SEC)
is one of the main financial services regulatory authorities in the US whose remit includes the protection of investor interests and the maintenance of fair, orderly, and efficient markets.

6.1 Section 302 – Corporate responsibility for financial reports

A key part of section 302 is that quarterly and annual reports filed or submitted under the Securities Exchange Act 1934 require certification by the Chief Executive Officer (CEO), the Chief Financial Officer (CFO) or officers performing similar functions.

The certifier must confirm that:

◆ the signing officer has reviewed the report;

◆ based on the officer's knowledge, the report is free from material misstatement, does not contain an untrue statement and is not misleading;

◆ based on such officer's knowledge, the financial statements, and other financial information included in the report, fairly present in all material respects the financial condition and results of operations for the periods presented in the report;

◆ the signing officers:
    (a) are responsible for establishing and maintaining internal controls;
    (b) have designed such internal controls to ensure that material information relating to the issuer and its consolidated subsidiaries is made known to such officers by others within those entities, particularly during the period in which the periodic reports are being prepared;
    (c) have evaluated the effectiveness of the issuer's internal controls as of a date within 90 days prior to the report; and
    (d) have presented in the report their conclusions about the effectiveness of their internal controls based on their valuation as of that date;

◆ the signing officers have disclosed to the issuer's auditors and the audit committee of the board of directors (or persons fulfilling the equivalent function):

    (a) all significant deficiencies in the design or operation of internal controls which could adversely affect the issuer's ability to record, process, summarise, and report financial data and have identified for the issuer's auditors any material weaknesses in internal controls; and

    (b) any fraud, whether or not material, that involves management or other employees who have a significant role in the issuer's internal controls; and

◆ the signing officers have indicated in the report whether or not there were significant changes in internal controls or in other factors that could significantly affect internal controls subsequent to the date of their evaluation, including any corrective actions with regard to significant deficiencies and material weaknesses.

There is also an anti-avoidance provision preventing organizations from avoiding or lessening the legal force of the requirements of section 302 by reincorporating their activities, or transferring their domicile, outside the United States.

6.2 Section 401 – Disclosures in periodic reports

This section requires the annual report and audited financial statements to be presented accurately and free from material misstatements. In order to improve the quality and reliability of financial statements, all material transactions that are held off the statement of financial position, arrangements, relationships and obligations, e.g. contingent liabilities, are to be disclosed.

Pursuant to section 401, the SEC is also required to determine whether transactions that are held off the statement of financial position and results of operations reported under generally accepted accounting principles result in transparent and meaningful reporting by issuers. There are specific rules on pro forma figures to ensure any report filed with the SEC does not contain any inaccuracies or omits a material fact which does not make the pro forma statement misleading.

6.3 Section 404 – Management assessment of internal controls

The section covering management assessment of internal controls pertains to enhanced financial disclosures and states that each annual report required by the Securities Exchange Act of 1934 shall contain an internal control report stating the responsibility of management for establishing and maintaining an adequate internal control structure and procedures for financial reporting. The annual report should also contain an assessment of the effectiveness of such internal control procedures for financial reporting.

In addition, the registered accounting firm responsible for the audit report shall, as a function of its engagement, report on and certify the assessment made by the management of the reporting entity.

6.4 Section 409 – Real time issuer disclosures

This section also relates to enhanced financial disclosures, specifically disclosures to the public on a real-time basis and must be easy to understand. The disclosures should cover material changes in respect of a company's financial state. Section 409 amends section 13 of the Securities Exchange Act of 1934 by adding the following wording regarding real time disclosures:

"REAL TIME ISSUER DISCLOSURES – Each issuer reporting under section 13(a) or 15(d) [of the Securities Exchange Act of 1934] shall disclose to the public on a rapid and current basis such additional information concerning material changes in the financial condition or operations of the issuer, in plain English, which may include trend and qualitative information and graphic presentations, as the Commission [the SEC] determines, by rule, is necessary or useful for the protection of investors and in the public interest."

6.5 Section 802 – Criminal penalties for altering documents

Section 802 is found under Title VIII of the Act relating to corporate and criminal fraud accountability. It sets out the criminal penalties for knowingly altering, destroying, concealing or falsifying documents with the intent to obstruct or impede an investigation. The penalties include a fine or not more than 20 years' imprisonment, or both.

This section also stipulates a requirement for auditors to retain all working papers and documents pertaining to the audit for a period of five years from the end of the fiscal period in which the audit was completed. All such records in respect of the audit should be maintained including memoranda, correspondence, electronic records. The penalty for "knowingly and willfully" violating the rules shall be a fine and/or imprisonment of up to 10 years.

6.6 Section 806 – Protection for employees of publicly traded companies who provide evidence of fraud.

Section 806 discusses protection for whistleblowers. It prohibits the discrimination, demotion, suspension and harassment of employees who blow the whistle on their employer by providing information or assisting in an investigation regarding any conduct which the employee believes is unlawful, relates to a fraud against shareholders, or breaches regulations of the SEC in this respect.

Section 806 is governed by the burden of proof as set out in the United States Code; any action by an employee must commence within 90 days of the alleged violation.

The whistle blower provisions provide that an employee prevailing in any such action shall be entitled to all relief necessary to compensate the loss sustained (both economic and non-economic). This includes reinstatement with the same status that the employee would have had but for the discrimination, back pay with interest, compensation for special damages including litigation costs, expert witness fees and reasonable attorney fees.

6.7 Section 807 – Criminal penalties for defrauding shareholders of publicly traded companies

The section on criminal penalties for defrauding shareholders sets out the maximum penalty for securities fraud which is a fine and/or imprisonment of up to 25 years.

6.8 Section 906 – Corporate responsibility for financial reports

Section 906 of the Act states the requirements in respect of the certification of financial reports. The signing officers of the company should confirm that financial statements filed with the SEC are in compliance with sections 13(a) or 15(d) of the Securities Exchange Act of 1934 and that information contained in the financial statements fairly presents, in all material respects, the financial condition and results of the company.

There are criminal penalties of up to US$1million and/or imprisonment of up to 10 years for certifying any statement knowing that financial report does not comport with all the requirements. The penalties for willfully certifying such a statement knowing that it does not comport with the requirements are significantly tougher and can lead to a US$5million fine and/or imprisonment of up to 20 years.

6.9 Public Company Accounting Oversight Board (PCAOB)

In order to monitor compliance with the Act, the SEC worked with the US Congress to establish the PCAOB, which was charged with the oversight and supervision of public company accounting firms providing audit services. Since the introduction the PCAOB there has been greater focus on auditor independence, the provision of non-audit services by audit firms, audit-related and non-audit-related fee disclosures, audit partner rotation and the role and functions of the audit committee. Prior to the Act and the establishment of the PCAOB, auditing firms were predominantly self-regulated. The provision of lucrative non-audit work by audit firms, e.g. consultancy services, threw into question auditor independence and created conflicts of interest. This is addressed in section 201 of the Act, which prohibits auditors from having lucrative consultancy agreements with the very firms they audit.

6.10 Sarbanes–Oxley – global implications

There have been legislative and regulatory reforms, similar to the Sarbanes–Oxley legislation, in other jurisdictions, such as France, Germany, Italy, Turkey, India, Japan, Canada, South Africa and Australia, focusing on enhanced corporate governance and disclosure requirements. The tangible benefits of these reforms may never be known with any degree of accuracy, but the increase in market confidence (resulting from enhanced ethical standards, improved reporting, greater accountability and transparency) probably outweighs the costs of implementation and the ongoing costs of compliance. Furthermore, companies that are able to demonstrate strong risk management and internal control systems can benefit from an increase in share price, due to improved investor confidence and decreased borrowing costs, as lenders of finance have greater confidence that the loans will be repaid.

Following the enactment of the Sarbanes–Oxley legislation, a number of smaller public companies have favoured a listing in London because the compliance requirements for UK public companies are perceived to be less costly than in the US. Furthermore, the UK has a more principles-based approach to regulation, which is often preferred by companies to the predominantly rules-based approach to regulation adopted in countries like the US and Germany.

With regard to the offshore environment, a number of collective investment funds specifically preclude investments or dealings with the US because of the costs of compliance and the tough penalties that may be imposed on officers and senior executives under the Act. Offshore vehicles are still able to install investor confidence by locating themselves in highly regulated and reputable international finance centres such as the Crown Dependencies of Jersey and Guernsey. The directors and officers of these offshore vehicles still need to be aware, however, of the implications of the Act if they are transacting with the US.

Stop and think 11.5

Can you think of at least three benefits and three drawbacks of the increased requirements introduced by the Sarbanes–Oxley Act of 2002?

Stop and think 11.6

According to portfolio theory, if investors have a portfolio of different investments in various industry sectors then their overall exposure to risk falls. Whilst one investment may suffer due to poor performance or corporate governance failings, the other investments might generate gains which collectively negate any losses. Why, then, is there a need to increase the costs of compliance by introducing tough new legislative requirements, such as the provisions of the Sarbanes–Oxley Act, in response to a few high-profile corporate scandals?

Stop and think 11.7

Why do you think a large number of smaller firms and non-US firms delisted from US stock exchanges in 2002? In this respect, how do you think the Sarbanes–Oxley Act has affected the competitive position of the US?

Test yourself 11.5

What are the main provisions of the Sarbanes–Oxley Act (2002) and who is affected by the Act?

7. Dodd–Frank Act (2010)

The Dodd–Frank Wall Street Reform and Consumer Protection Act (the "Dodd–Frank" Act) was passed in the USA in 2010 by President Barack Obama in response to the global financial crisis which began in 2008 with the collapse of large financial institutions, particularly in the US, the bailout of banks by governments across the world, and the downturn in global stock markets. The Act is named after its co-architects, Senator Chris Dodd and Representative Barney Frank. The aim of the Dodd-Frank Act is, as its official name suggests, to reform the US regulatory framework and to protect consumer interests. This has been achieved by addressing a number of issues including the enhanced supervision of banking activities with a view to avoiding another major financial crisis.

The Dodd–Frank reform seeks to reduce dependence on large financial institutions, improve accountability and transparency in the financial system, end government bailouts by keeping the financial system under a closer watch and protect consumers from poor and abusive financial services practices. As well as addressing corporate governance issues and enhanced disclosure requirements, it covers a number of other key areas including:

◆ Financial stability.

◆ Orderly liquidation.

◆ Proprietary trading.

◆ Insurance.

◆ Credit rating agencies.

◆ Financial product regulation and trading restrictions.

◆ Whistleblowers and consumer protection.

Financial Stability Oversight Council (FSOC) is a US government organisation established pursuant to the Dodd–Frank Act. Its role is to promote market discipline and to monitor, identify and address systemic risk in the US financial system to ensure threats to financial stability are dealt with in an effective and timely manner.

7.1 Financial stability

The Dodd–Frank Act has also led to the creation of important new agencies, notably the **Financial Stability Oversight Council (FSOC)**. This is attached to the US Treasury Department and its role is to promote market discipline and to monitor, identify and assess systemic risk in the US financial system to ensure threats to financial stability are dealt with in an effective and timely manner.

The FSOC has a wide range of powers to monitor, identify and assess risk. It has the authority to:

- facilitate regulatory co-ordination among member agencies and other Federal and State agencies in order to bridge regulatory gaps and uphold a more stable financial system;

- access data and information from non-bank financial institutions with over US$50bn in assets and, if necessary, place them under the supervision of the Federal Reserve, the SEC or the Commodities Futures Trading Commission;

- require consolidation supervision of non-bank entities;

- recommend more stringent standards for the largest financial institutions, including rules for leverage, liquidity, capital and risk management;

- break up large "too big to fail" firms that threaten financial stability by requiring large, complex, financial companies to submit credible **funeral plans** and orderly liquidation procedures which clearly set out their plans for rapid and orderly shutdown should they be faced with financial failure; and

- report to Congress and recommend gaps and other areas of regulation to be addressed.

Title I of the Dodd–Frank Act has also led to the creation of the Office of Financial Research (OFR), which is also attached to the US Department of the Treasury. Its aim is "to improve the quality of financial data available to policymakers and facilitate more robust and sophisticated analysis of the financial system". The OFR effectively supports the FSOC by helping it to collect relevant information on non-bank financial institutions and bank holding companies.

7.2 Orderly liquidation

Title II of the Dodd–Frank Act covers the orderly liquidation of financial institutions and the creation of an orderly liquidation fund to provide funds to be used in case of a non-bank or non-security financial company's liquidation. Financial supervisory authorities are able to take control and arrange the liquidation of failing financial institutions if their collapse threatens the financial stability of the US.

7.3 Proprietary trading

The **Volcker rule**, named after former Federal Reserve chairman Paul Volcker, is a section of the Dodd–Frank Act restricting US banks from entering into certain kinds of speculative transactions, known as **proprietary trading**, whereby banks speculate with their own capital by using deposits to trade in shares, bonds, commodities, private equity funds, hedge funds, derivatives and other types of financial instruments for direct gain rather than trading on its customers' accounts for commission. The Volcker rule limits banks to investing a maximum of 3% of their Tier 1 capital in proprietary trading and imposes new registration and reporting requirements for hedge and private equity funds.

It is argued that proprietary trading contributed to the current financial crisis by exposing banks to additional risk and volatility with proprietary desk traders

funeral plan
is the term given to a company's plans for rapid and orderly shutdown should it be faced with financial failure. The plan should be credible and act as a roadmap in order to help regulators clearly understand the business so that it may be may be wound up in an orderly fashion if it fails.

Volcker Rule
is a section of the Dodd–Frank Act restricting US banks from entering into certain kinds of speculative transactions, known as proprietary trading.

proprietary trading
describes the activities of banks which use deposits to trade in shares, bonds, commodities, private equity funds, hedge funds, derivatives and other types of financial instruments on a bank's own account for direct gain rather than on its customers' accounts for commission.

leveraging capital up to 15 or even 20 times. Since the introduction of the Volcker rule, major investment banks with operations in the US (e.g. Goldman Sachs, Morgan Stanley, Deutsche Bank, JP Morgan, Barclays) have ceased their proprietary trading operations and their proprietary desk traders have moved into the hedge fund industry where leveraging tends to be significantly less at around 2 to 3 times in the current macro-economic climate.

By enacting the Volcker rule, Dodd-Frank has therefore helped transfer some of the risk from banks to hedge funds. More importantly, it has helped address the overall level of risk taking within the US financial system.

7.4 Regulation of hedge fund advisers

Before the implementation of the Dodd–Frank Act, investment advisers were not required to register with the SEC if they had fewer than 15 clients in the prior year and did not hold themselves out as investment advisers. Title IV of the Dodd–Frank Act deals with the regulation of hedge funds and Section 403 eliminates the private adviser exemption, which means private advisers are now subject to the Private Fund Investment Advisers Registration Act of 2010. The Dodd–Frank Act also introduces, in Section 404, enhanced reporting requirements for investment advisers requiring them, *inter alia*, to inform the SEC of their investment positions. As there is no longer an exemption for hedge fund managers, it means that all investment advisers and sub-advisers of hedge funds are subject to supervisory oversight and the additional administrative burden that comes with it. Venture capital fund advisers do, however, have an exemption under Section 407.

The collapse of the financial markets in 2008 highlighted the need to address excessive exposure to risk, much of which had passed almost unnoticed prior to the crisis. However, the enhanced reporting requirements introduced by the Dodd–Frank Act have driven up the costs of compliance, which critics believe could cancel out the benefits of the legislation.

7.5 Insurance

The bailing out of the US insurance giant, American International Group Inc. (AIG) by the Federal Reserve Bank in September 2008 has resulted in large insurance companies being subject to certain provisions of the Dodd–Frank Act. Insurance companies now fall under the supervisory oversight of the US Treasury's Federal Insurance Office and, if systemically significant, could be designated a non-bank financial company and be subject to prudential oversight by the Federal Reserve. This could mean being subject to liquidity and capital requirements, enhanced financial disclosures, restrictive limits on short-term borrowings, leverage and credit exposure and having to submit a plan to the Federal Reserve setting out a swift and orderly resolution plan in case of financial distress. Insurance industry matters are specifically dealt with in Title V of the Dodd-Frank Act.

7.6 Credit rating agencies

The Dodd–Frank Act imposes new standards and disclosure requirements on credit rating agencies. Credit rating agencies were heavily criticised for failing to apply appropriate credit ratings to the collateralised debt obligations and subprime mortgage-backed securities prior to the collapse of the US housing market in 2007. Credit rating agencies appear not to have fully understood the complex financial instruments which were used as collateral for mortgages and succumbed to pressure from the banks to apply credit ratings which were wholly unsuitable, particularly in respect of collateralised debt obligations (CDOs). This lack of product understanding and failure to carry out proper due diligence on the instruments of issuers contributed to the financial crisis. Many CDOs were not diversified and were simply BBB subprime mortgage bonds packaged with tranches of AAA and AA bonds so as to give the impression they were less risky. In order to sell these financial instruments, the banks ensured the agencies rated these CDOs AAA or AA when in many cases they should have been no more than BBB rated because they were highly exposed to subprime home loans. The rating agencies accepted the banks' explanations and failed to exercise independent judgement. Credit rating agencies were accused of being conflicted because their fees were paid by the very issuers whose financial products they were rating and the banks were passing the business to the agencies prepared to give the highest rating.

Under Title IX of the Dodd-Frank Act, Subtitle C, because of the systemic importance of credit rating agencies and the reliance placed on them by individual and institutional investors, credit rating agencies became more accountable for the quality of their ratings and became subject to enhanced regulation and transparency rules. They lost their exemption from liability and this resulted in them refusing to have their ratings on asset-back securities published in offer documents. In order to rescue the inevitable collapse of the market for asset-back securities, the SEC issued a no action letter in July 2010 confirming that no action would be taken against the agencies for inaccurate credit ratings. The Asset-Backed Market Stabilization Act of 2011 was later passed into law to repeal the liability provision of the Dodd–Frank Act. The SEC does have the authority, however, to deregister a credit rating agency if, over a period of time, there is evidence its ratings have been inaccurate.

In Europe, credit rating agencies have also been held more accountable. Since 2009, they have been subject to regulatory registration and oversight of the European Securities and Markets Authority (ESMA).

7.7 Financial product regulation and trading restrictions

There are new clearing and exchange trading rules for over-the-counter derivatives and swap transactions which aim to reduce systemic risk and improve transparency so that large derivative exposures do not pass unnoticed. Swap transactions have come under scrutiny and Section 716 of the Dodd–Frank Act prohibits the US Federal Government from bailing out swap entities. US regulatory authorities are likely to introduce margin requirements for uncleared derivative transactions and the need to post collateral. Under the provisions of the Dodd–Frank Act, issuers of asset-backed securities are also required to retain a minimum 5% of the credit risk associated with the assets securitisation.

As with the Sarbanes–Oxley legislation, there is concern in the US that the Dodd–Frank Act puts American banks and other financial institutions at a competitive disadvantage to their foreign counterparts. The wide reach of Dodd–Frank stretches to US branches and subsidiaries of non-US banks as well as to non-US transactions of US banks, for example derivative transactions. In other words, the rules apply to US banks wherever they are located, be it in the US or overseas. This extra-territorial application means that the action of a US bank registering as a swap dealer in the US might lead to its overseas branches and subsidiaries also having to register. If a branch or subsidiary manages to avoid the requirements to register then it may still have to be careful that none of its swap obligations are guaranteed by affiliated companies. Due to the global reach of the Dodd–Frank Act, it follows that non-US intermediaries are likely to favour non-US business.

An offshore swap market participant transacting with a branch of a US bank in the Channel Islands, for example, is subject not only to legislation and regulations in the Channel Islands governing derivatives but also to the provisions of the Dodd–Frank Act. It would currently be less onerous, in most cases, for the Channel Island swap counterparty to deal with a local branch of a European or Asian bank in order to keep the transaction outside the scope of Dodd–Frank.

The question of legal jurisdiction is covered in Section 722 of the Dodd–Frank Act (Title VII, Part II – Regulation of swap markets). Section 722(d)(i) covers applicability and states that the provisions should not apply to activities outside the US unless the activities have a direct and significant connection with activities in, or effect on, commerce in the US. However, Section 722(a)(2) refers to exclusive jurisdiction and the facts that there are no limits to the jurisdiction conferred on the SEC by the Dodd–Frank Act with regards to security-based swap agreements.

One of the criticisms of Dodd–Frank is that the rules governing derivatives may result in banks separating out US and non-US derivative transactions by using different legal entities to trade these financial instruments. This could lead to an increase in systemic risk because the banks would lose the ability to net transactions which are no longer carried out by the same legal entity.

7.8 Whistleblowers and consumer protection

The SEC has greater enforcement powers as a result of the new financial crime of whistle-blowing provisions introduced by the Dodd–Frank Act which rewards whistleblowers up to 30% of fines imposed by the SEC where fines exceed US$1m. Greater protection is given to whistleblowers than was provided for under Sarbanes–Oxley and this includes protection for employees of non-US subsidiaries of US banks. A whistleblower's anonymity will be safeguarded under Dodd–Frank and, if a whistleblower is identified, he or she will be subject to a protection programme.

Critics of Dodd–Frank are concerned that, by offering rewards to whistleblowers based on a percentage of the overall fine imposed, a company's problems might be allowed to escalate before an employee blows the whistle. This would increase the likelihood of a larger fine being imposed by the SEC and thereby increase the employee's reward. In the UK and in several offshore jurisdictions, such as Jersey, the financial regulators have set up whistle-blowing hotlines where individuals can leave messages which cannot be traced back to them. There is currently, however, no reward scheme for whistleblowers like there is under the Dodd–Frank Act.

The Dodd–Frank Act has also led to the creation of the **Consumer Financial Protection Bureau (CFPB)** which is funded by the Federal Reserve and whose mission is to "make markets for consumer financial products and services work for Americans – whether they are applying for a mortgage, choosing among credit cards, or using any number of other consumer financial products". By providing consumers with access to unbiased financial information, the CFPB aims to educate consumers so that they understand the nature of the transactions they enter into with financial companies. Its stated core functions are to:

Consumer Financial Protection Bureau (CFPB)
is an consumer protection agency born out of the Dodd–Frank Act which promotes financial education, restricts unfair, deceptive and abusive practices, takes customer complaints and upholds Federal consumer financial protection laws.

◆ conduct rule-making, supervision, and enforcement for Federal consumer financial protection laws;

◆ restrict unfair, deceptive, or abusive acts or practices;

◆ take consumer complaints;

◆ promote financial education;

◆ research consumer behaviour;

◆ monitor financial markets for new risks to consumers; and

◆ enforce laws that outlaw discrimination and other unfair treatment in consumer finance.

In fulfilling its functions, the CFPB has broad powers and is able to restrict the type of financial products provided to certain consumers. Whilst this helps to protect retail investors, the tighter regulation of banks is leading to the emergence of a greater range of **shadow banking** activities globally, many of which are currently outside of the regulatory scope, or subject to lesser regulation than banks, yet are hugely significant to the global financial system.

The Dodd–Frank Act is broken down into 16 titles covering the following subject matters:

shadow banking
is a term that describes the activities of institutions operating outside the regular banking system and which use deposits as an additional source of funding thereby creating a quasi banking operation. These activities include repurchase transactions (REPOs), securitisation and securities lending. The entities considered to carry out shadow banking activities include money market funds, exchange-traded funds (ETFs) and finance and insurance companies offering credit guarantees.

1 Financial stability.

2 Orderly Liquidation Authority.

3 Transfer of Powers to the Comptroller of the Currency, the Corporation and the Board of Governors.

4 Regulation of advisers to hedge funds and others.

5 Insurance.

6 Improvements to regulations of bank and savings association holding companies and depository institutions.

7   Wall Street transparency and accountability.

8   Payment, clearing and settlement supervision.

9   Investor protection and improvements to the regulation of securities.

10   Bureau of Consumer Financial Protection.

11   Federal Reserve system provisions.

12   Improving access to mainstream financial institutions.

13   Pay it back act.

14   Mortgage reform and anti-predatory lending act.

15   Miscellaneous provisions.

16   Section 1256 contracts.

The enactment is 848 pages long and is widely criticised for being too complex, too restrictive and stifling for financial innovation. Entities which have to comply with Dodd–Frank are becoming heavily reliant on legal expertise and some trade groups have already successfully challenged the application of the rules by the regulatory bodies.

Whilst similar measures to Dodd–Frank are likely to be brought out in Europe, namely the European market infrastructure regulation, the European measures are not likely to have such wide-reaching territorial scope as Dodd–Frank. There are, however, concerns that European companies subject to both Dodd–Frank and European regulations will have to manage conflicting rules.

With regard to offshore jurisdictions, due to their size and systems of self-government, they are often able to adapt quickly to changes in the financial and regulatory environment and are able to accommodate the needs of a wide number of market participants without compromising consumer protection. Company secretaries, compliance officers and directors of offshore companies do, however, need to be aware of the implications of transacting with the US and the potential costs of compliance.

Making it work 1.1 – Lehman Brothers

Lehman Brothers began trading cotton in Alabama in the 1850s and the family developed the business into a commodities futures trading venture. The business was instrumental in setting up the New York Cotton Exchange before moving into merchant banking and later into investment banking under the company name Lehman Brothers Holdings, Inc.

Richard Fuld was appointed CEO in 1994 and it was not long before his aggressive risk taking had led to considerable exposure to the commercial real estate market in which Lehman Brothers had built up a significant portfolio. The company held positions in subprime mortgage tranches, was highly leveraged, held insufficient capital and had begun to run into liquidity difficulties. The bank was unable to provide sufficient collateral in respect of its positions in poor quality mortgage back securities and was forced to sell off assets. With no credible and clear capital restoration and remediation plan, the bank was eventually downgraded by the credit rating agencies.

Despite offers to rescue the company, Lehman Brothers failed to agree terms with a merger partner. The Federal Reserve was not prepared to use taxpayers' money to bail out the bank. Lehman Brothers had foregone opportunities to save itself. The bank eventually filed for bankruptcy in September 2008 in what was to become the largest bankruptcy case in US history.

At the time of its collapse, the Lehman Brothers board comprised an ageing board of directors including 62-year-old Chairman and CEO, Richard Fuld, 81-year-old Dr Henry Kaufman, 80-year-old John Macomber, 77-year-old Roger Berlind (a theatrical producer), 73-year-old John Akers (former Chairman and CEO of IBM), 64-year-old Michael Ainslie (formerly of Sotheby's), 61-year-old Marsha Evans (a retired US Navy Rear Admiral), 60-year-old Sir Chris Gent (former CEO of Vodafone), Thomas H. Cruikshank who was an ex-energy company CEO as well as Roland Hernandez who came from a media background.

The board came under criticism for a number of failings, including:

- a dominant CEO, accused of putting his own interests ahead of those of the shareholders and for demoting those who challenged him. His aggressive behaviour led to management information being presented to him in a manner that did not show the true extent of the problems;
- no segregation of the roles of Chairman and CEO;
- an inexperienced board with an average age of nearly 70, with four of the ten members being over 75 and only one with current financial sector knowledge. The board had little knowledge of the banking and securities industry;
- a negligent risk committee which only met twice in both 2006 and 2007;
- excessive leverage which was not clearly presented in the financial statements;
- readiness to accept high risk in order to drive up earnings and increase executive bonuses;
- excessive exposure to the US housing market and commercial real estate;
- failure to fully understand the risks involved and the inherent weaknesses of its business model;
- holding the riskiest subprime mortgage tranches;
- poor risk management and internal control systems with little attention paid to the business as a whole;
- insufficient liquidity and failure to inject capital despite senior executives being made aware of liquidity issues as early as January 2008;

- dependent on its short-term obligations being funded by long-term capital;

- compensation committee that gave rewards for poor performance including payouts totalling US$75m to the CEO, Richard Fuld, in the two years leading up to the company's collapse and compensation payments to other executives even when the company was engaged in discussion with the US government over a rescue package;

- lack of accountability for the failings of the board and its members;

- failure to save the company from bankruptcy because the board overestimated the value of the bank and refused to accept a merger deal that did not reflect its own valuation;

- arrogance which led to analysts being ignored when they called for Lehman to inject more capital into the company;

- failing to address the warning signs and have a clear strategy for recovery; and

- relying on the Federal Reserve to bail out the bank because it was "too big to fail".

Stop and think 11.8

Part of the reason for the global economic crisis which began in 2008 was that banks, insurance companies and major financial institutions were taking on the risk of a position without fully understanding the risk itself. Many were highly leveraged, had toxic assets, liquidity problems and no capital restoration plan. Dodd–Frank aims to prevent financial institutions getting themselves into such precarious positions and if they do, they should expect to face the consequences when it all goes wrong rather than be bailed out by the government. Why do you think the US government help bail out some financial institutions, such as the investment bank Bear Stearns, and yet allowed Lehman Brothers to collapse? What considerations come into play when dealing with a financial institution on the brink of failure?

Test yourself 11.5

Explain briefly the extra-territorial impact of the Dodd–Frank Act in the context of margin requirements for derivative transactions and how this might affect the competitive advantage of US banks and brokers.

Test yourself 11.6

Why did the liability provision for credit rating agencies in the Dodd–Frank Act need to be repealed?

Chapter summary

◆ Agency theory is based on the belief that the managers of a company are appointed to act as agents of the owners of the company and that there is an inherent conflict of interest between the managers (who control the company) and the shareholders (who own the company). A problem arises when the directors, who manage and control the company, make decisions that are not consistent with the objective of maximising owner wealth.

◆ Goal congruence describes the alignment and harmonisation of goals and objectives. In the context of agency theory, this means matching the interests of the directors with the interests of shareholders so that directors are incentivised to act in the best interests of the company.

◆ Management incentive schemes such as share option schemes give participants the right to buy a set number of shares at a set price at a specified time in the future. A share option scheme is designed to help achieve goal congruence between managers and owners by rewarding managers for maximising shareholders' wealth.

◆ Corporate governance is the process by which organisations are directed and controlled. Displaying sound governance is good for companies as it helps with their smooth running, attracts inward investment and helps to raise finance.

◆ The Cadbury Code was based on the principles of openness, integrity and accountability and aimed to achieve high standards of corporate behaviour.

◆ The Cadbury Code's principal recommendations are concerned with the following areas: the board of directors; non-executive directors; executive directors; and financial reporting.

◆ The Greenbury report on directors' remuneration is concerned with the following key themes: the remuneration committee; disclosure and approval provisions; remuneration policy; service contracts and compensation.

- The Hampel committee was established in 1995 charged with reviewing the implementation of the findings of the Cadbury and Greenbury committees.

- The Hampel committee drew up a list of corporate governance principles covering also the role of directors, directors' remuneration, the role of shareholders and accountability and audit, built on the findings of Cadbury and Greenbury.

- The Hampel committee recommended that its principles be combined with the Cadbury and Greenbury recommendations and published in one consolidated code – the Combined Code (now known as the UK Corporate Governance Code).

- The UK Corporate Governance Code combines and consolidates the recommendations of Cadbury, Greenbury and Hampel to establish best practice principles and more detailed requirements in respect of board leadership and effectiveness, accountability, remuneration and shareholder relations. The application of the principles by UK listed companies is on a mandatory "comply or explain" basis.

- In addition to the "comply or explain" approach required by the UK Listing Rules, the Code lays down certain disclosure requirements in respect of information which should be included in the annual report, made available on the company's website or included in shareholder communications.

- The UK Corporate Governance Code is due to be updated again in 2012 to incorporate changes in relation to gender diversity on boards and to make possible changes in respect of audit committees and audit retendering. Any changes made are due to take effect from 1 October 2012.

- The Higgs report on the role and effectiveness of non-executive directors was commissioned following a number of corporate scandals in the US which emerged in 2001 and 2002, including the scandals and accounting frauds of WorldCom, Tyco, Enron and Global Crossing.

- The Higgs report increases the responsibilities of non-executive directors who must be influential members of the board who do not just make up the numbers but constructively challenge the decisions and the development of strategy.

- The main changes brought about by the Higgs recommendations were in relation to board structure and composition with the balance of power shifting towards independent non-executive directors.

- The 2003 Smith report sets out the composition, role and responsibilities of audit committees.

- The Turnbull guidance is about adding value to a company through good risk management and strong internal controls.

- The Myners report explains the reasons why many shareholders, particularly institutional investors, such as pension funds, fail to exercise their votes at general meetings of UK companies.

◆ The UK Stewardship Code was born out of the Walker Review and published in 2010 establishing best practice in stewardship of UK listed companies. By encouraging best practice, it seeks to develop and improve engagement between institutional shareholders and the companies in which they invest.

◆ The 2009 Larosière report of the High-Level Group of Financial Supervision in the EU links an overall lack of effective risk management systems with unwarranted risk-taking and highlights the fact that companies and supervisory authorities did not fully understand the risks (e.g. liquidity risk) leading up to the global financial crisis.

◆ The Larosière report also highlighted insufficient stress testing, the lack of transparency within the financial system and the failure of credit rating agencies to give suitable credit ratings.

◆ The Larosière report recommended that the regulatory framework be enhanced to reduce the risk and impact of future financial crises. It recommended the creation of a European Systemic Risk Council and a European System of Financial Supervisors, made up of three European Supervisory Authorities, one for the banking sector, one for the securities sector and one for the insurance and occupational pensions sector.

◆ The European Commission is currently working on a number of corporate governance initiatives including board composition, diversity and effectiveness; improving shareholder communications; and the application of "comply or explain".

◆ The AIC Code of Corporate Governance provides directors of investment companies with a one-stop approach to corporate governance to ensure they manage the issues pertinent to investment companies and meet the requirements of the UK Corporate Governance Code.

◆ The Guernsey Finance Sector Code of Corporate Governance came into effect 1 January 2012 and establishes eight key principles underpinned by best practice guidelines. The principles cover the following key themes: the board; directors; business conduct and ethics; accountability; risk management; disclosure and reporting; remuneration; and shareholder relations.

◆ Companies subject to the Guernsey Finance Sector Code of Corporate Governance are required to submit an annual assurance statement to the Guernsey Financial Services Commission confirming that its directors have considered the effectiveness of their corporate governance practices and are satisfied that they have applied with the principles of the Code in a manner commensurate with the nature, scale and complexity of their business activities.

◆ A unitary board structure is a form of board structure, common in the UK, in which executive and non-executive directors combine on the same board pooling their skills, knowledge and experience.

◆ In some countries, for example Germany, it is common to have a two tier board structure comprising a separate board for the executive directors (who are involved in day to day management) and non-executive directors (who are independent of management) .

◆ ESMA is the European Securities and Markets Authority which "contributes to safeguarding the stability of the EU financial system by ensuring the integrity, transparency, efficiency and orderly functioning of securities markets, as well as enhancing investor protection".

◆ The parallel banking system is a term that describes the activities of institutions and financial intermediaries operating outside the regular banking system such as the activities of hedge funds, investment banks, finance companies, money market funds, structured investment vehicles, and mortgage brokers (in some jurisdictions) and whose activities could significantly impact the financial system due to inherent risks, e.g. exposure to counterparty risks and interest rate risks.

◆ Proprietary trading describes the activities of banks which use deposits to trade in shares, bonds, commodities, private equity funds, hedge funds, derivatives and other types of financial instruments on a bank's own account for direct gain rather than on its customers' accounts for commission.

◆ Corporate social responsibility (CSR) describes the processes an organisation uses to produce a positive impact on society through its activities. It is about an ongoing commitment of businesses to behave ethically and responsibly towards its employees, its customers, the environment and the community at large. It is about doing business in a responsible and sustainable manner.

◆ Following good CSR can have a positive impact on corporate competitiveness as the public like to see large multi-national companies giving something back to the community.

◆ Recent European policy on CSR has been about encouraging responsible business behaviour and the creation of favourable conditions for sustainable growth to help rebuild consumer confidence and levels of trust in business.

◆ The Walker Review on corporate governance in UK banks makes recommendations on the following five themes: Board size, composition and qualification; functioning of the board and evaluation of performance; the role of institutional shareholders (communication and engagement); governance of risk; and remuneration.

◆ The principal objectives of the Basel II framework were to further strengthen the soundness and stability of the international banking system; maintain sufficient consistency such that capital adequacy regulation would not be a significant cause of competitive inequality among internationally active banks; closer align regulatory capital requirements with economic capital needs; and promote the adoption of stronger risk management practices by the banking industry.

◆ Basel II encompasses a "three pillars" concept with the first pillar setting out "minimum capital requirements", the second pillar setting out the "supervisory review process" and the third pillar establishing measures, such as enhanced disclosure requirements, to improve "market discipline".

- Basel III was introduced in response to the financial crisis which began at the tail end of 2007, resulting in the collapse of a number of international banks.

- Basel III introduces stricter limits on leverage, tighter controls on capital and liquidity, an enhanced supervisory review process as well as increased disclosure and market discipline.

- The adoption timescale for Basel III varies by jurisdiction. The Basel Committee has proposed a phased approach with implementation commencing 1 January 2013 and full compliance expected within six years of this date.

- The Sarbanes–Oxley Act (SOX) was introduced in the USA in 2002 to restore public confidence, tackle accounting fraud and protect the investors following the corporate scandals of a number of US companies, including WorldCom (MCI Inc.), Enron and Arthur Anderson.

- The SOX legislation is wide reaching and applies to all US public companies, their management, their boards and their accountants. It also applies to non-US public companies carrying out business in the US.

- Failure to comply with the requirements of SOX could lead to the offending officers of the company being extradited to the US to face charges. The Act imposes tough penalties which includes fines of up to US$5 million and/or imprisonment of not more than 20 years for certifying financial statements which do not comport with all the requirements.

- The Dodd–Frank Wall Street Reform and Consumer Protection Act was passed in the USA in 2010 by President Barack Obama in response to the global financial crisis.

- The Dodd–Frank reform seeks to reduce dependence on large financial institutions, improve accountability and transparency in the financial system, end government bailouts by keeping the financial system under a closer watch and protect consumers from poor and abusive financial services practices.

- A funeral plan is the term given to a company's plans for rapid and orderly shutdown should it be faced with financial failure. The plan should be credible and act as a roadmap in order to help regulators clearly understand the business so that it may be may be wound up in an orderly fashion if it fails.

Directory of web resources

Accountancy Age
www.accountancyage.com

Appleby
www.applebyglobal.com

Association of Chartered Certified Accountants
www.accaglobal.com

Bank for International Settlements
http://www.bis.org

Basel Committee on Banking Supervision
www.bis.org/bcbs

Bermuda Monetary Authority
www.bma.bm

Companies House
www.companieshouse.gov.uk

Consumer Financial Protection Bureau (CFPB)
www.consumerfinance.gov

Deloitte – International Accounting Standards
www.deloitte.com
http://www.iasplus.com

Department for Business Innovation and Skills
www.bis.gov.uk

Economist
www.economist.com

European Commission
http://ec.europa.eu

Financial Risk Management News
http://www.risk.net

Financial Supervision Commission (of the Isle of Man)
http://www.fsc.gov.im

Financial Times
www.ft.com

The Group of International Finance Centre Supervisors
www.ogbs.net

The Guardian
www.guardian.co.uk

Guernsey Finance
www.guernseyfinance.com

Guernsey Financial Services Commission
www.gfsc.gg

Hedgeweek
www.hedgeweek.com

HM Treasury
www.hm-treasury.gov.uk

IFRS Foundation and the IASB (International Financial Reporting Standards & International Accounting Standards Board)
http://www.ifrs.org

Institute of Chartered Accountants of England and Wales
http://www.icaew.com

Institute of Chartered Secretaries and Administrators
http://www.icsa.org.uk

International Accounting Standards Board
http://www.iasb.org

International Monetary Fund
www.imf.org

Jersey Bankers Association
http://www.jerseybankersassociation.com

Jersey Finance Limited
www.jerseyfinance.je

Jersey Financial Services Commission
www.jerseyfsc.org

Jersey Legal Information Board
www.jerseylaw.je

The Law Pages
www.thelawpages.com

Mourant Ozannes
www.mourantozannes.com

National Audit Office
www.nao.org.uk

Ogier
www.ogier.com

Organisation for Economic Co-operation and Development (OECD)
www.oecd.org

Public Company Accounting Oversight Board
http://pcaobus.org

Securitization.Net
www.securitization.net

UK Parliament
www.parliament.uk

The University of Cincinnati College of Law – The Sarbanes–Oxley Act of 2002
http://taft.law.uc.edu/CCL/SOact/toc.html

US Department of the Treasury
http://www.treasury.gov

US House of Representatives Office of the Law Revision Counsel
http://uscode.house.gov

US Securities and Exchange Commission
www.sec.gov

World GAAP Info
http://www.worldgaapinfo.com

Glossary

Accounting policies are principles, bases, conventions, rules and practices for recognising, selecting measurement bases for, and presenting assets, liabilities, gains, losses and changes to shareholders' funds.

The **Accounting Standards Board (ASB)** forms part of the Financial Reporting Council (FRC) and is the standard-setting body in the UK responsible for issuing Financial Reporting Standards (FRS).

The **Accounting Standards Boards Statement of Principles for Financial Reporting** is the conceptual framework underpinning the accounting standards set by the ASB and reflects the accounting standard setter's views on: the activities that should be reported on in financial statements;
- the aspects of those activities that should be highlighted;
- the attributes that information needs to have if it is to be included in the financial statements; and
- how information should be presented in those financial statements.

The **accruals** concept is that transactions should be accounted for in the reporting period to which they relate rather than the period when payment is made.

Adjusting events are events after the reporting period that provides further evidence of conditions that existed at the end of the reporting period. An event that raises going concern issues for the entity is an adjusting event.

Agency theory is based on the belief that the managers of a company are appointed to act as agents of the owners of the company and that there is an inherent conflict of interest between the managers (who control the company) and the shareholders (who own the company).

Aggregation is a term used in IAS 1 to describe the grouping of immaterial assets and presenting the total as a single line item on the face of financial statements or in the notes. Aggregation is not permitted for material items or material classes of similar items.

AML/CFT means anti-money laundering and countering of financing of terrorism.

Anti-avoidance rules are measures introduced to reduce the number of cases of tax avoidance in relation to offshore schemes that have no other purpose than to avoid tax. For example, in the UK, anti-avoidance legislation has helped prevent UK investors avoiding a higher rate of tax by accumulating income in an investment offshore and only being taxed on capital gains when the investment was eventually realised.

Articles of Association form the main constitutional document of a company and lay out the rules for the running of the company, for example directors powers and responsibilities, decision making of directors, the appointment of directors, the allotment of shares, the payment of dividends, capitalisation of profits, the rules governing meetings, voting powers, the production of financial statements and various administrative functions.

An **asset** is the right or other access to future economic benefits controlled by an entity as a result of past transactions or events.

Asset allocation is an investment activity that relies on the selection of markets in which to invest rather than individual stock selection.

Available-for-sale financial assets (AFS) are all non-derivative financial assets designated on initial recognition as available for sale or any other instruments that do not fall into the following categories: (i) loans and receivables; (ii) held-to-maturity investments; or (iii) financial assets at fair value through profit or loss (IAS 39 "Financial Instruments: Recognition and Measurement"). Examples of AFS financial assets are debt instruments and certain types of listed and unlisted equity instruments.

The **Basel Committee on Banking Supervision** is a committee, established in 1974 by the central-bank Governors of the G10 countries, which formulates supervisory standards and guidelines and recommends statements of best practice which it expects the relevant supervisory authorities in member countries to implement in an appropriate manner.

Biological assets are living animals and plants (IAS 41 "Agriculture").

Boiler room scams are share scams which are so called because the fraudsters use unethical sales tactics to "pressurise" investors into parting with their cash in exchange for shares which either do not exist or are overpriced and illiquid.

A **cap** is an option contract which gives the holder of the cap an upper predetermined limit (strike rate) on a floating exchange rate. The holder of the cap pays an option fee to the cap writer and in return has the certainty that the applicable interest rate cannot go above the predetermined strike limit.

A **cash flow hedge** is a hedge of the exposure to variability in cash flows that is (i) attributable to a particular risk associated with a recognised asset or liability (such as all or some future interest payments on variable rate debt) or a highly probable forecast transaction and (ii) could affect profit or loss.

A **cash flow statement** is a primary financial statement found in the annual report and accounts and is concerned with cash flows from operating activities, investing activities and external sources of finance. The statement shows changes in cash and cash equivalents over a financial period and therefore serves as an analytical tool to enable users of accounts to review the past year's cash movements and year-end cash position assess the viability of a business in terms of liquidity, solvency and financial adaptability.

A **cell company** is a private or public company which is able to segregate its assets and liabilities between different cells. Each cell may be used to carry out distinct and independent businesses and the assets of each cell can be ring-fenced.

CESR was the Committee of European Securities Regulators which became the **EMSA** on 1 January 2011.

A **collar** is a hedging instrument that sets the range of both upper and lower interest rate movements. To hedge against interest rate fluctuations, an entity simultaneously purchases an interest rate cap and sells an interest rate floor. The collar determines the range of interest rates which the holder is exposed to. The cap element of a collar can be used to protect against increases in floating rates of interest, but the floor element limits the benefits if there is a fall in the floating rate.

A **collateralised debt obligation (CDO)** is a security backed by bonds, mortgage loans and other assets. A CDO is typically packaged into different tranches each with varying maturity dates and risks associated with them. During the economic downturn of 2008, many mortgage-backed CDOs defaulted. These were typically the tranches backed entirely by poor quality subprime loans. Some CDOs comprised layers of other repackaged CDOs with credit risks hidden within the complexity of the structures. Accordingly, the credit rating agencies were either unable or insufficiently experienced in the products to give an accurate credit rating. As home owners were unable to meet their mortgage repayments, so the subprime bonds, which acted as collateral for CDO investors, defaulted.

Commercial substance is concerned with economic rights and control rather than the exact legal form of a transaction.

Consignment stock is the term given to inventory which is in possession of a party who is not the legal owner. The inventory has neither been sold, nor does it form part of the legal owner's inventory. The risks and rewards of ownership may effectively have been passed on to the other party.

The concept of **consistency** is that reporting entities should be consistent with their accounting policies and methods, from one reporting period to the next, and treat similar transactions in a like manner.

Constructive obligation – an obligation to a third party which has been construed due to an entity having either:
- set a precedent through past practice;
- published policies; or
- undertaken to accept certain responsibilities
- and, in so doing, has created a valid expectation on the part of a third party.

Examples of a constructive obligation:
- A company has previously made generous redundancy payments in excess of the statutory requirement;
- Land contamination by a chemical company if the company's policy is to clean up even if it is not legally obliged to do so;

- A retailer has a returns policy for unused and undamaged goods returned within, say, four weeks;
- A marketing company has undertaken to give out cash prizes and laptops to 10% of participants of a recent survey and the undertaking was communicated to all participants before they undertook the survey;
- A company has a restructuring plan in place and has created a valid expectation by those affected that the restructuring will be carried out.

Consumer Financial Protection Bureau (CFPB) is an consumer protection agency born out of the Dodd–Frank Act which promotes financial education, restricts unfair, deceptive and abusive practices, takes customer complaints and upholds Federal consumer financial protection laws.

A **contingent asset** is a possible asset that arises from past events and whose existence will be confirmed only by the occurrence or non-occurrence of uncertain future events not wholly within the entity's control.

A **contingent liability** is a possible obligation to transfer economic benefit as a result of a past transaction or event and whose existence will be confirmed only by the occurrence or non-occurrence of uncertain future events not wholly within the entity's control. A contingent liability may also be a present obligation which is not recognised either because it is unlikely payment of the liability will materialise or because the amount cannot be measured reliably.

Corporate citizenship is another term used to describe the responsibilities of a business towards society and its role in the community. It is about sustainable strategy, promoting good governance and focus on social responsibilities and not just the statutory responsibilities. It is a term that is often associated with CSR.

Corporate governance is a set of policies and procedures, laws, frameworks and practices under which companies are administered, governed and controlled in order to ensure accountability and the protection of the interests of shareholders.

Corporate social responsibility (CSR) is a term used to describe the processes an organisation uses to produce a positive impact on society through its activities. It is about the ongoing commitment of businesses to behave ethically and responsibly towards its employees, its customers, the environment and the community at large. It is about doing business in a responsible and sustainable manner.

A **countercyclical buffer** is a buffer whose purpose is to restrict banks from growing too quickly during good times in order to limit credit expansion and build up credit reserves to enable them to survive times of economic or financial stress.

Current assets are assets that are readily realisable and likely to be held for less than 12 months (e.g. inventory, trade receivables, investments traded on a stock exchange, cash at bank and in hand).

Current ratio is a measure of short-term liquidity which shows a company's ability to meet short-term obligations from short-term assets.

Debt factoring is where a number of debts are sold to a finance company (at a fixed percentage in order to help the business improve its cash flow) and replaced with one receivable, the factor (i.e. the finance company).

Debt financing occurs when a company raises finance by issuing bonds, bills or notes and, in exchange, promises to repay the lender the interest and capital on the loan.

A **derivative** is a financial instrument that derives its value from something else such as an underlying asset or assets, for example an interest rate, commodity price or index. Derivative contracts are, typically, settled at a future date and are entered into at no, or minimal, initial investment. Examples of derivatives contracts include interest rate swaps, currency swaps, futures contracts, forward contracts, options, collars, caps, floors and commodity contracts.

A **discovery examination** describes the type of examination which may be wide in scope and might include a review of a wide range of activities as well as a bank's risk management systems and internal controls, policies and procedures, processes, conduct of business, financial standing and corporate governance.

A **double tax treaty** is an agreement between two jurisdictions, under which individuals who find themselves subject to tax in the two jurisdictions are able to claim under the relevant agreement to avoid a double taxation charge.

Equity is capital raised by selling shares in the company, typically by public offering. Investors buy the shares and become shareholders or owners of the company's equity.

Equity financing is capital raised by selling shares in the company, typically by public offering. Investors buy the shares and become shareholders or owners of the company's equity.

EPS (or earnings per share) is a frequently used indicator of a company's profitability and is often used by shareholders for comparing a company's financial health with a company with similar earnings.

ESMA is the European Securities and Markets Authority which "contributes to safeguarding the stability of the EU financial system by ensuring the integrity, transparency, efficiency and orderly functioning of securities markets, as well as enhancing investor protection".

Estimation techniques are the methods used by an entity to implement accounting policies and arrive at estimated values, corresponding to the measurement bases selected for assets, liabilities, gains, losses and changes to shareholders' funds, e.g. measuring depreciation of non-current assets, measuring obsolescence of inventory, measuring work-in-progress, measuring the fair value of financial assets and liabilities.

The **EU white list** is a list of jurisdictions considered to have the equivalent anti-money laundering controls as EU member states.

The **European Savings Directive (ESD)** is an agreement between EU member states to automatically exchange information with one another about clients who earn savings income in one EU member state but reside in another.

Events after the reporting period are those events, whether favourable or unfavourable, that have occurred between the date of the statement of financial position and the date when the financial statements were authorised for issue.

Exchange differences are gains and losses arising from settlement or from converting monetary items back to one currency from another, using different exchange rates to those used for the initial recognition.

Fair presentation in the context of financial statements means that an entity should adopt appropriate accounting policies and practices to ensure information presented in the financial statements is relevant, reliable, comparable and understandable. Where the adoption of IFRS is insufficient to enable users to understand a specific transaction, additional disclosures should be given to ensure that the financial statements give a fair representation of the results, financial position and cash flow.

Fair value is the amount for which an asset could be exchanged, or a liability settled, between a buyer and a seller in a free transaction.

A **fair value hedge** is a hedge of the exposure to changes in fair value of a recognised asset or liability or an unrecognised firm commitment or an identified portion of such an asset, liability or firm commitment that is attributable to a particular risk and could affect profit or loss.

Faithful representation means complete, free from bias and error.

A **fiduciary** is a legal person, such as an individual or body corporate, entrusted to look after the affairs and assets of another.

Fiduciary duty is the legal obligation of a fiduciary to act in the best interests of another party.

Financing activities describe the raising of finance in the form of debt or equity and includes short- and long-term borrowings as well as proceeds from the issuance of ordinary shares.

The **Financial Reporting Council (FRC)** is the UK's independent regulator responsible for promoting high quality corporate governance and reporting to foster investment.

The **Financial Stability Oversight Council (FSOC)** is a US government organisation established pursuant to the Dodd–Frank Act. Its role is to promote market discipline and to monitor, identify and address systemic risk in the US financial system to ensure threats to financial stability are dealt with in an effective and timely manner.

A **floor** is an option contract which gives the holder of the floor a lower predetermined limit (strike rate) on a floating exchange rate. The holder of the floor pays an option fee to the floor writer and in return has the certainty that the applicable interest rate cannot go below the predetermined strike limit.

A **focused examination** is targeted at specific matters related to the regulated entity, be it to do with risk management, internal systems and controls, conduct of business, financial standing, corporate governance or any other matter, and includes monitoring corrective action taken following an earlier examination of that bank.

Forced heirship is essentially a feature of civil law jurisdictions and Islamic countries which do not recognise the full freedom of testation. This means, for example, that an individual making his will may not be able to leave an equal proportion of his assets to his surviving children and spouse. In order to prevent all the assets going to the eldest child, the individual may use a foundation or trust and thereby avoid the forced heirship rules.

A **forward contract** is an agreement that obliges the holder to purchase or sell a specified amount of a financial product (e.g. commodity) or foreign currency at a specified price at a specified date in the future. Unlike futures contracts, forwards are usually tailor-made contracts rather than exchange-traded contracts.

The **FRSSE** is the Financial Reporting Standard for Smaller Entities which enables smaller entities to apply accounting standards which have reduced reporting and disclosure requirements compared with UK GAAP. Where the FRSSE does not cover a particular issue, the entity can fall back on UK GAAP and apply the relevant principles to ensure appropriate accounting treatment.

Functional currency means the currency of the primary economic environment in which an entity operates.

A **fundamental error** is a significant material error which jeopardises the true and fair view statement in the accounts.

Funeral plan is the term given to a company's plans for rapid and orderly shutdown should it be faced with financial failure. The plan should be credible and act as a roadmap in order to help regulators clearly understand the business so that it may be may be wound up in an orderly fashion if it fails.

A **futures contract** is a contract that obliges the holder to purchase or sell a specified amount of a financial product (e.g. commodity) at a specified price at a specified date in the future. Futures are typically exchange-traded contracts.

GAAP (or Generally Accepted Accounting Principles/Practice) are a common set of principles-based accounting standards used for the preparation and presentation of an entity's financial statements.

Gearing is a measurement of long-term debt to equity and measures the extent to which a company is leveraged by comparing borrowed funds to shareholder funds.

The **general partner (GP)** is the person who assumes the management responsibility for the limited partnership. The general partner has unlimited liability for the debts and obligations of the partnership and, therefore, is typically a limited company.

Goal congruence describes the alignment and harmonisation of goals and objectives. In the context of agency theory, this means matching the interests of the directors with the interests of shareholders so that directors are incentivised to act in the best interests of the company.

Going concern refers to an entity that has the ability to continue to operate in the foreseeable future.

Golden handshake is term used to describe a severance payment, typically of significant value, which is given to senior executives as compensation for termination of employment, for example due to layoff, firing or retirement.

Goodwill is a term used to refer to the value of an intangible asset such a brand or the value of the workforce, a client list, the value of having good customer relations and so on. Goodwill often arises when a company makes an acquisition insomuch as the purchase price reflects the book value plus a premium (which is the goodwill) for the company name, client list and other intangible attributes.

Green-washing describes the practice of misleading markets concerning a company's products and their environmental impact in order to give the perception that the products are green.

The **guardian** is the person who empowered to oversee the foundation's council and performs a similar function to the protector of a trust. The founder might choose to appoint a guardian to a foundation, which may be himself, to ensure the foundation is run in an appropriate manner and in accordance with the foundations charter.

Hedging is a risk-management strategy in which an investment is undertaken to offset a position and reduce exposure to price, currency or other fluctuations, e.g. a forward contract is used to hedge against changes in foreign currency exchange rates.

The **hurdle rate** of a company is the minimum rate of return which the company will accept on a particular project or investment. If the project goes according to plan, the rate of return will exceed the hurdle rate. The hurdle rate is also used as a benchmark for determining when investment managers are entitled to incentive fees.

A **hyperinflationary economy** is an economy where inflation is extremely high, resulting in rapid price rise increases and depreciation of the currency.

Intangible non-current assets are assets that you cannot touch or see and which have no physical substance. Examples include goodwill, patents, copyrights, licenses, marketing rights, customer lists and customer relations.

The **internal auditor** is an employee of the company whose role it is to provide independent confirmation that the company's systems of corporate governance, internal control and risk management are operating effectively.

The **International Monetary Fund (IMF)** is an organisation of nearly 200 countries, "working to foster global monetary cooperation, secure financial stability, facilitate international trade, promote high employment and sustainable economic growth, and reduce poverty around the world." (Source: www.imf.org)

Accounting **interpretations** are statements issued by standard setters (e.g. the IASB) to clarify how standards should be applied. Interpretations are typically published to address issues arising that were not foreseen when the standards were first set.

Investing activities refers to acquisitions and disposals of investments which are not classified as cash equivalents.

Just in time procurement (JIT) is a term used to describe a procurement policy whereby inventory is ordered just before it is needed. It relies on close customer and supplier relations to ensure the inventory arrives "just in time". JIT production methods are commonly used in the motor industry and other manufacturing industries enabling flexible manufacturing processes which keep inventory levels to a minimum.

Legal obligation – an obligation that derives from a contract, law or other form of enactment.

Leverage describes the use of debt and borrowed funds by a business with a view to increasing the return on an investment. A business that is highly leveraged will have a high debt to equity (or gearing) ratio.

A **liability** is the obligation of an entity to transfer economic benefits as a result of past transactions or events.

A **limited partnership agreement (LPA)** is a written document setting out the powers and obligations of the limited partners and of the GP. It will include the name of the LP and GP, will state the purpose for which the LP was formed, will set out how income and capital should be allocated, how distributions should be made, the various rights and obligations of both parties (e.g. the obligation of the GP to contribute to the debts of the LP) and the administrative arrangements.

Linked presentation is a provision under FRS 5 in UK GAAP which allows the finance amount of a securitisation transaction to be deducted from the gross amount of the asset it finances. The items are linked and the net figure is recognised on the face of the statement of financial position. There is no concept of linked presentation under IFRS.

Loan covenant is a restrictive measure placed on the borrower by the lender as a means of safeguarding the loan. Measures might include restricting the level of gearing of the borrower by insisting more equity is put into the company. If a company breaches its loan covenant then it may be forced to repay the loan or find an alternative lender who is likely to insist on a high rate of return on the loan to reflect the high level of gearing.

Liabilities due in more than one year are those liabilities falling due in more than one year such as bank loans and other financing arrangements.

Materiality describes the effect of an item (or event) on the financial statements of an entity, such that its inclusion or omission (occurrence or non-occurrence) would significantly alter the position. For example, an investor might not have subscribed for shares in a company had certain adverse and relevant information in relation to pending legal action been published in the annual report. Such information is material because it can influence an investor's decision.

Measurement bases are defined in FRS 18 as the monetary attributes of the elements of financial statements – including assets, liabilities, gains, losses and changes to shareholders' funds – that are reflected in the financial statements. The attributes are the different qualities of an item which may have a value attributed to it. For example, one attribute may be an asset's historic cost and another might be its current market value.

The **Memorandum of Association** is a document evidencing the subscribers' intention to incorporate a company and become members of that company on incorporation. For a company that is to be limited by shares, the memorandum also confirms the agreement of the members to take at least one share each in the company. Once the company has been incorporated, the Memorandum cannot be amended;

Many companies rely on **model articles** which are set out in Schedules 1–3 of The Companies (Model Articles) Regulations 2008. Although the members of the company can determine their own Articles, the Model Articles provide a good standard set of rules often used by members as a guide or framework around which they develop their own specific Articles. For example, where a company only has two directors, the directors may decide to remove the Chairman's casting vote clause which is provided for in the Model Articles.

Non-adjusting events are events after the reporting period that is indicative of a condition that arose after the end of the reporting period.

Non-current assets are assets that are likely to be held for more than 12 months.

Non-executive directors (NEDs) are directors, who are not employees of the company, and who are not involved in the day-to-day management responsibilities. They, therefore, have no executive responsibilities.

Offsite supervision describes the desk based supervisory activities undertaken by the regulator at its own offices such as the review of financial statements and prudential returns.

Onerous contract – this is a present obligation where the unavoidable costs of fulfilling the contract are higher than the economic benefits that are expected to be received. Onerous contracts can arise where a firm undertakes a contract to supply a product or service and the cost of the raw materials or human resource costs more than originally anticipated.

Onsite supervision is the term given to examinations undertaken by the regulator at the licensee's place of business in order to monitor compliance with relevant legislation and regulations and to determine whether the bank has the necessary processes, procedures, systems and controls in place to mitigate risks.

Operating activities are the main income-producing activities of a business and include other activities that are neither investing nor financing activities.

An entity's **operating cycle** is the period of time from the acquisition of assets (materials or services) to their realisation in cash receipts. For a retailer this is the length of time inventory is held before receiving proceeds from its sale.

An **option** is contract that gives the option holder the right, but not the obligation, to buy (call option) or sell (put option) a specified amount of a financial product at a specified price (the strike price), during a specified period of time.

Overcapitalisation is an over-investment in working capital which can lead to excessive inventory, high receivable/low payable level and an unnecessarily large amount of cash. Overcapitalisation can result in a lower return on investment and unnecessary use of long-term funds to meet short-term obligations.

The **parallel banking system** is a term that describes the activities of institutions and financial intermediaries operating outside the regular banking system such as the activities of hedge funds, investment banks, finance companies, money market funds, structured investment vehicles, and mortgage brokers (in some jurisdictions) and whose activities could significantly impact the financial system due to inherent risks, e.g. exposure to counterparty risks and interest rate risks.

Presentation currency is the currency in which the financial statements are presented.

The **primary financial statements** are the statement of financial position, income statement (also known as the income statement) and cash flow statement. These three primary statements provide the key information to users of accounts in order for them to assess financial performance and the financial position of the organisation.

Principal describes the capital element of the loan which is the amount outstanding less the interest.

Probable obligation – an obligation is probable if it is more likely than not to occur.

Proprietary trading describes the activities of banks which use deposits to trade in shares, bonds, commodities, private equity funds, hedge funds, derivatives and other types of financial instruments on a bank's own account for direct gain rather than on its customers' accounts for commission.

A **provision** is a liability of uncertain timing or amount.

Prudence is an accounting concept which aims to ensure that income and assets are not overstated and that expenses and liabilities are not understated.

Prudential regulation is the term given to the regulatory framework surrounding capital adequacy and liquidity requirements of financial institutions such as banks and deposit takers.

The **Public Company Accounting Oversight Board (PCAOB)** is charged with the oversight and supervision of public company accounting firms and oversees the audits of public companies in order to protect investor interests and further the public interest in the preparation of informative, accurate and independent audit reports.

A **public offering** is an offer to the public for subscriptions for sale of shares in a company in accordance with the terms of the offering document.

Qualitative characteristics are the attributes that make the information in financial statements useful and meaningful for users.

Quick ratio is a measurement of short-term liquidity which focuses on those items that can be turned into cash easily and quickly; therefore does not include inventory which may not be easily realisable at full net book value.

Reconciliation of operating profit to net cash flow from operating activities is a note in the financial statements which shows non-cash item adjustments made to operating profit in order to determine the net cash flow from operating activities. The non-cash reconciling items include depreciation, movement in inventory and movement in receivables and payables. The reconciliation does not form part of the primary cash flow statement but may be presented alongside to the cash flow statement or as a separate note in the financial statements.

Remaindermen is the term given to beneficiaries who receive the remaining capital upon termination of a life interest trust, e.g. after the death of the life tenant.

Required rate of return is the minimum percentage return that investors expect to receive on an investment. Investors should consider all investments whose rate of return meets or exceeds the required rate of return.

Return on capital employed (ROCE) is a measure of a company's success at achieving a return on capital invested. It is calculated by multiplying operating profit margin by net asset turnover.

Revenue is the gross inflow of economic benefits such as cash and other receivables during the period arising from the ordinary operating activities of an entity when those inflows result in increases in equity, other than increases relating to contributions from equity participants.

Ring-fencing is a protective measure to prevent the assets of a ring-fenced cell from being used to pay off the debts of another cell.

The Sarbanes–Oxley Act (2002) is legislation which was passed in the USA in 2002 in an attempt to restore public confidence, improve the transparency of financial statements and protect investor interests. The Act introduced new and more stringent measures for public companies in respect of corporate disclosure requirements and corporate governance.

Satisficing describes the behaviour of managers to do just enough to satisfy shareholders and achieve an adequate return on their investment rather than maximising the return for shareholders.

Secondary legislation is subordinate legislation which supplements primary law. It is enacted by a person or body, other than the legislature, who has been granted the relevant authority. This enables secondary legislation to be enacted in a more timely manner. For example, in Jersey, primary legislation must be put before the UK's Privy Council whilst secondary legislation, such as an Order, may be approved locally by the relevant Minister, for financial services secondary legislation e.g. The Minister for Economic Development.

Securitisation is a method of raising finance by creating and issuing asset backed securities, such as mortgage bonds.

Shadow banking is a term that describes the activities of institutions operating outside the regular banking system and which use deposits as an additional source of funding thereby creating a quasi banking operation. These activities include repurchase transactions (REPOs), securitisation and securities lending. The entities considered to carry out shadow banking activities include money market funds, exchange traded funds (ETFs) and finance and insurance companies offering credit guarantees.

A **share option scheme** is a management incentive scheme which gives participants the right to buy a set number of shares at a set price at a specified time in the future. A share option scheme is designed to help achieve goal congruence between managers and owners by rewarding managers for maximising shareholders' wealth.

Shareholders' funds are all the assets of a company less all the liabilities. It is the equity amount in a company that is due to the owners (the shareholders).

Shelf company is a term given to a company which is inactive and has been put 'on the shelf'. As a shelf company is already formed, financial service providers keep them until they have a client wishing to have immediate use for the company. The service provider can simply transact in the company's name on behalf of the client and transfer the beneficial ownership of the company without having to go back through the incorporation process. Shelf companies are less common nowadays as the Companies Registry in many offshore jurisdictions offer a fast-track incorporation service enabling companies to form in a matter of hours.

A foreign exchange **spot rate** is the market fx rate used in transactions with immediate delivery.

A **swap** is where two parties agree at a specified date, or series of specified dates, to exchange cash flows (such as liabilities on outstanding debts). For example, one party swaps his fixed interest rate payments in exchange for the counterparty's floating (or variable) rate interest payments.

Tail risk is a term used to describe the risk of an investment moving more than three standard deviations from the mean price, i.e. the distribution of returns does not follow the normal expected pattern.

Tangible non-current assets means assets which are capable of being physically touched (e.g. property; plant and machinery, fixtures and fittings, motor vehicles).

Tax nomads are high net worth individuals who keep on the move to avoid spending 91 days or more in the UK on average over a four-year rolling cycle, thereby ensuring they are neither resident nor deemed ordinarily resident in the UK.

A **themed examination** is an examination on a specific theme, e.g. wire transfers, corporate governance, anti-money laundering/countering of financing of terrorism. The theme is derived from an analysis of recent data or significant changes to legislation such as the implementation of the Dodd-Frank Act. A number of regulated entities will be subject to the same themed examination to enable the supervisory body to analyse trends and draw comparisons between regulated entities.

Tier 1 capital is capital which is considered to be a safer and more stable form of capital than Tier 2 capital (supplementary capital such as undisclosed reserves, revaluation reserves and subordinated debt) and Tier 3 capital (such as short term subordinated debt) and comprises largely equity and retained profits.

Treasury shares are shares in a company held in the company's own name.

A **trust** is a legal arrangement whereby one or more persons, known as the trustee(s), are entrusted with the legal ownership of the assets of another party, the settlor, and to hold those assets (which might include property, investments and cash) "on trust" for the benefit of one or more beneficiaries.

A **trust deed** is a legal document setting out the terms of the trust and includes details of the interested parties, such as the settlor, trustees and beneficiaries as well as details of the trustee's powers – such as powers to invest and powers to distribute capital and income.

Two-tier board system: In some countries, for example Germany, it is common to have a two-tier board structure comprising a separate board for the executive directors (who are involved in day-to-day management) and non-executive directors (who are independent of management) .

The **unitary board structure** is a form of board structure, common in the UK, in which executive and non-executive directors combine on the same board pooling their skills, knowledge and experience.

The **Urgent Issues Task Force (UITF)** is a body made up of senior industry representatives and accountants which handles pressing accounting issues that require urgent attention. The UITF issues Abstracts to address such issues and these abstracts take immediate effect.

The **US Securities and Exchange Commission (SEC)** is one of the main financial services regulatory authorities in the US whose remit includes the protection of investor interests and the maintenance of fair, orderly, and efficient markets.

A **UTIF abstract** is an immediately binding abstract, reflecting a consensus arrived at by the Urgent Issues Task Force, which sets out the accounting treatment that should be adopted where unsatisfactory or conflicting interpretations have developed in respect of accounting standards or the Companies Act.

The **Volcker Rule** is a section of the Dodd–Frank Act restricting US banks from entering into certain kinds of speculative transactions, known as proprietary trading.

Window dressing describes the use of deceptive accounting practice in order to present the reporting entity in a better light. For example, the misuse of provisions to smooth profits might mislead stakeholders into believing a company is financially stable and does not suffer from volatility.

Working capital is a measure of how a company meets its short-term obligations (i.e. current liabilities) with its current assets and is calculated by deducting current liabilities from current assets.

Index